THE BRAIN, COGNITION, AND EDUCATION

Edited by

SARAH L. FRIEDMAN
National Institutes of Health
Bethesda, Maryland

KENNETH A. KLIVINGTON
Scientific Planning
The Salk Institute
San Diego, California

RITA W. PETERSON
Teacher Education
University of California, Irvine
Irvine, California

1986

ACADEMIC PRESS, INC.
Harcourt Brace Jovanovich, Publishers
Orlando   San Diego   New York   Austin
London   Montreal   Sydney   Tokyo   Toronto

ACADEMIC PRESS, INC.
Orlando, Florida 32887

United Kingdom Edition published by
ACADEMIC PRESS INC. (LONDON) LTD.
24–28 Oval Road, London NW1 7DX

LIBRARY OF CONGRESS CATALOGING-IN-PUBLICATION DATA

Main entry under title:

The Brain, cognition, and education.

    Includes index.
    1. Cognition.   2. Cognition in children.
3. Brain—Psychophysiology.   4. Learning, Psychology of.
5. Learning—Physiological aspects.   6. Educational
psychology.   I. Friedman, Sarah L.   II. Klivington,
Kenneth, A.   III. Peterson, Rita.
BF311.B68   1986   153.1   85-18606
ISBN 0-12-268330-7 (alk. paper)

PRINTED IN THE UNITED STATES OF AMERICA

86 87 88 89   9 8 7 6 5 4 3 2 1

Contents

PART I INTRODUCTION

1. Building Bridges among Neuroscience, Cognitive Psychology, and Education
KENNETH A. KLIVINGTON

PART II ATTENTION

2. Attention and the Brain
TERENCE W. PICTON, DONALD T. STUSS, and KENNETH C. MARSHALL

3. Attention and the Control of Cognition
MICHAEL I. POSNER and FRANCES J. FRIEDRICH

4. The Role of Attention in Cognition
HERBERT A. SIMON

PART III   KNOWLEDGE ACQUISITION, REPRESENTATION, AND USE

5. Biological Preprogramming for Language Learning?
LILA R. GLEITMAN

6. Education and Recent Research on Attention and Knowledge Acquisition
MERLIN C. WITTROCK

7. Memory and the Brain
LARRY R. SQUIRE

8. Integrating Three Perspectives on Learning
SUSAN F. CHIPMAN

PART IV   COGNITIVE AND NEURAL DEVELOPMENT

9. Setting the Stage: Neural Development before Birth
PATRICIA S. GOLDMAN-RAKIC

10. Notes on Cognitive Development: Recent Trends, New Directions
HOWARD GARDNER

11. The Influence of Neuroscience upon Educational Practice
JEANNE S. CHALL and RITA W. PETERSON

12. Instructional Influences on Cognition and on the Brain
SARAH L. FRIEDMAN and RODNEY R. COCKING

PART V   DISCUSSION

13. Multiple Models of Memory
MARK R. ROSENZWEIG

Index

Contributors

Numbers in parentheses indicate the pages on which the authors' contributions begin.

Jeanne S. Chall (287), Graduate School of Education, Harvard University, Cambridge, Massachusetts 02138

Susan F. Chipman (203), Personnel and Training Research, Office of Naval Research, Arlington, Virginia 22217

Rodney R. Cocking (319), University of Delaware, Newark, Delaware 19716

Sarah L. Friedman (319), National Institutes of Health, Bethesda, Maryland 20894

Frances J. Friedrich (81), Department of Psychology, University of Utah, Salt Lake City, Utah 84112

Howard Gardner (259), Harvard Project Zero, Graduate School of Education, Cambridge, Massachusetts 02138, and Veterans Administration Medical Center, Boston, Massachusetts 02130

Lila R. Gleitman (119), Department of Psychology, University of Pennsylvania, Philadelphia, Pennsylvania 19104

Patricia S. Goldman-Rakic (233), Section of Neuroanatomy, Yale University School of Medicine, New Haven, Connecticut 06510

Kenneth A. Klivington (3), Scientific Planning, The Salk Institute, San Diego, California 92138

Kenneth C. Marshall (19), Department of Physiology, University of Ottawa, Ottawa, Canada K1H 8L6

Rita W. Peterson (287), Teacher Education, University of California, Irvine, Irvine, California 92717

Terence W. Picton (19), Department of Medicine, University of Ottawa, and Ottawa General Hospital, Ottawa, Canada K1H 8L6

Michael I. Posner (81), Department of Psychology, University of Oregon, Eugene, Oregon 97403

Mark. R. Rosenzweig (347), Department of Psychology, University of California, Berkeley, Berkeley, California 94720

Herbert A. Simon (105), Department of Psychology, Carnegie-Mellon University, Pittsburgh, Pennsylvania 15213 mate the difficulty of this enterprise. Perhaps the most difficult question is, is there a single mental language into which all of cognitive knowledge is translated? Another question of primary importance concerns the generality of cognitive processes. For example, is it the case that knowledge of language makes use of principles that serve vision as well, or is each cognitive subsystem characterized by its own special-purpose mechanisms? My own feeling is that the latter must be the case. Thus, I am prompted to believe, along with Jerry Fodor, that the mind is nature's own evolved automobile engine, a conglomeration of subsystems under one roof to achieve a common set of purposes. There is no general theory underlying each of these subsystems, however, any more than there is a single theory underlying the magnetic coil and the radiator core.

However, the field is much too young for anything but an open mind on these and other subjects. So, at this stage of the game the best strategy is to welcome enterprises such as the present volume and encourage others, enterprises that bring all of us together for a time in discussion of the questions central to our emerging discipline.

SAMUEL J. KEYSER

Massachusetts Institute of Technology
Cambridge, Massachusetts

PART I

INTRODUCTI

Preface

This volume is an experiment in cross-disciplinary communication. Its authors represent the fields of neuroscience, cognitive science, and education research. Each of these fields has an interest in how people acquire and use knowledge. But do they, in fact, share anything more than this interest? Are concepts, methodologies, and research results from one field useful in guiding research and yielding new knowledge in the others? These are the questions addressed by the experiment conducted here.

As should be expected, the experiment yielded few clear-cut answers to any of its target questions. The results, however, are on the whole encouraging. They are easily examined by a wide audience without advanced training in any of the fields since the authors prepared their ideas in a format intended to be accessible to readers in each of the other fields. There is thus a minimum of technical jargon and no assumption that the reader has had previous exposure to the subject. This does not mean that the discussions are devoid of content. On the contrary, there is much material of profound importance here, and the volume provides suitable discussion material for advanced seminars in many fields of inquiry beyond the three represented in the text.

Three subjects were chosen as foci for the authors' examination: attention; knowledge acquisition, representation, and use; and cognitive and neural development. These are not necessarily obvious choices, nor are they the only possibilities. Nevertheless, they clearly provide the contributors with a great deal of material, both experimental and experiential, to explore and to dispute.

Following an introductory chapter by Klivington, Picton examines the brain processes that participate in the selective activity of paying attention. Posner and Friedrich follow with an examination of the cognitive machinery of attention using the analytic tools of mental chronometry. An overview by Simon emphasizes the subtlety of the phenomena of attention and brings computer models into the discussion.

One of the forms of knowledge central to human learning is the ability to use language. On this theme, Gleitman begins the discussion of or, less optimistically, the cognitive sciences (Gazzaniga, 1984; Malcup & Mansfield, 1983). Its practioners attempt to understand cognitive functions at several different levels, contending that no single level contains the whole story. The idea that there are different levels of understanding in cognitive science is often conveyed in the form of an analogy to understanding computers. Here the topmost level is the software, and understanding how a computer works at this level means knowing how to program. (Of course there are also several levels of programming, from "user-friendly" languages like PASCAL on down to machine language.) An intermediate level of understanding lies in knowing how to design logic circuitry, the hardware of information processing. A very basic level of understanding is at the level of knowledge of the solid state physics of semiconductors in the component transistors. What this analogy makes obvious is the fact that a computer programmer, an electrical engineering circuit designer, and a solid state physicist can each truly say he or she knows how a computer works without knowing anything about what the other two specialists know.

To switch from computers to people, the analogy brings up language as an example. At the most abstract level, an analogy to understanding programming is to understand how children acquire language by means of an experiential program—what inputs are necessary at each stage of learning in order to progress to the next level of complexity of grammar and vocabulary. The circuit designer in cognitive science might be interested in determining what kind of logic system is required to acquire a natural language, given the resources of normally developing children—the kinds of inputs they have, the kinds of correction available, and their surprising creativity. Finally, the cognitive scientist who wants to know how language works at a very basic level examines the brain mechanisms that underlie the perception, processing, and production of language. Today, this often means the study of the effects of brain damage on use of language—written, spoken, or signed by deaf.

This sort of analogy holds up, of course, only so far. It does convey the notion that the understanding of so complex a set of natural phenomena as cognitive processes can involve many levels and that no one of these levels is complete and self-contained. Furthermore, different levels of understanding can inform and enlighten one another. The programmer, the circuit designer, and the physicist can each do a better job if they know one another's needs and capabilities. The last drop is drawn from this particular analogy by asserting that cognitive scientists will do a better job of understanding cognition at any one level if they actively exchange information with their counterparts at other levels.

Simon later explores in more detail just how far we might take this analogy.

II. INTERRELATIONSHIPS AMONG NEUROSCIENCE, COGNITIVE SCIENCE, AND EDUCATION

In this volume, the editors and authors focus on some very limited areas of neuroscience, cognitive science, and education research in order to determine whether investigators in the three fields might genuinely help one another solve the very difficult problems they pose to themselves. There are reasons for both optimism and pessimism in answering this question; the authors make clear that an affirmative consensus would be fallacious. It is true, however, that all of these fields concern themselves with the acquisition and processing of information in one way or another. Is there enough intellectual content in this rather obvious assertion to warrant practitioners of each of the participating disciplines to spend time talking with one another?

In addition to the belief that the answer to the last question is "yes," there are two other premises behind this volume:

1. The removal of disciplinary barriers can open new scientific frontiers.
2. Research at these new frontiers can help to solve practical problems.

In and of themselves, these assertions are not particularly controversial. Molecular biology is an obvious demonstration of their validity. In the 1930s, certain physicists and biologists were bold enough to venture into one another's territory. Who could have foreseen that X-ray crystallography would lead the way to the cracking of the genetic code (Judson, 1979)? While it took many years to mature, the resulting field is clearly at the forefront of science today. And the medical, agricultural, and environmental problems now near solution with the help of molecular biologists are front-page news. The molecular design of plants that resist diseases and pests and can tolerate hostile environments is just one example of this field's enormous promise (Board on Agriculture, National Research Council, 1984).

What is controversial in the assertions here is both the set of disciplines that claim to offer a whole greater than the sum of its parts and the practical problems they join to address. The contributors to this volume are neuroscientists, cognitive scientists, and educational researchers. Their chapters speak to scientific issues such as the brain changes that occur during learning and how brain processes underlie thought and language. Together they examine the possibility that new insights into neural operations and cognitive processes will help solve the seemingly intractable problems of education.

The editors have identified three central foci that they have asked the authors to address, each with an emphasis on his or her own special approach, but also with consideration to questions of special interest to educators. These foci are attention; knowledge acquisition, representation, and use; cognitive and neural development. These are not necessarily the areas in which the most intense research activity is taking place or where the most burning questions are under attack. Rather, they are areas that appear to evoke considerable common interest among neuroscientists, cognitive scientists, and educators. Here, the research findings are solid, dispute is to the point, and measurement is generally as prevalent as observation. And, most relevant of all, there is at least the suggestion that practical application of research findings is near to hand.

The editors have purposely looked beyond many research areas currently in the limelight. There is, for example, significant and exciting neuroscientific research now directed toward understanding the role of opiate receptors in the brain. Important though this research may be, its relevance to education is problematic. Cognitive scientists, for their part, keenly pursue computer understanding of stories, but the implications of their findings are not likely to reach education for some time yet. And many educators now agonize over the problems of technical illiteracy, which cognitive science may someday help alleviate, but just how is not yet clear.

One major difficulty in designing a volume such as this is that there are too many important research problems from which to choose. The editors have tried to compromise between simplicity and importance, choosing problems that are at once tractable and yet of sufficient significance to draw serious intellectual attention. The authors have risen to the challenge. Their responses will help to show the way toward addressing even more difficult problems in the future. Each has provided special insights into the kinds of barriers to and opportunities for building future research programs. Such programs promise paradigm shifts that will advance knowledge in ways we have not been able to achieve in the past. A practice of education that has a strong scientific foundation, like today's practice of medicine may remain a distant goal, but it no longer seems quite so unattainable.

All areas of human inquiry have a certain degree of commonality. Most superficially, it is in their language. The futility of pursuing these apparent commonalities is easy to see. The use of the word *group* in mathematical group theory, for example, may seem similar to its common English use to refer to a collection of people. A classic mathematics text on the subject (Smirnov, 1961) tells us, however, "the set of all unitary transformations forms a group." On the other hand, a mathematically oriented social scientist (Arrow, 1968) tells us, "We may therefore be led to generalize and form a theory whose subject is the total behavior of a group. So long as it is understood that such a theory is really a resultant of certain as yet unanalyzed laws of individual behavior, no harm will be done, and the greater convenience of empirical analysis on groups may be highly beneficial." Despite the superficial similarity of language, there would be no point whatever in trying to apply the first author's tools to the second author's problems.

At a more significant level, commonality appears in methodology. The problem-solving tools of one discipline may on occasion help unravel the puzzles of another. The x-ray spectroscopy of physics, for example, enabled biologists to visualize proteins, DNA, and other macromolecules essential to life. But at the most profound level are the advances gained when the concepts developed to explain the phenomena of concern to one discipline prove useful in resolving problems in another. It is precisely in this way that theories developed in subatomic particle physics have revolutionized the way in which cosmologists now envision the origins of the universe. Indeed, the study of the forces that hold together the quarks and leptons inside the atom now makes it possible to peer back nearly to the smallest fraction of a second after the "big bang" (Davies, 1984).

These illustrations only suggest the many levels at which the authors of this volume have attempted to explore the commonalities among their disciplines. Many other potential channels for cross-fertilization are explored in the chapters to come. Taken together, they suggest a wealth of opportunities to overcome problems that today appear insoluble.

III. ATTENTION

The volume begins (Part II) with the most primitive of the subjects chosen: attention. It is most primitive in the sense that it is a universal property of organisms possessing a nervous system. All such creatures must limit the amount of sensory input they can process at any one time. They must focus their attention. This can be done in humans both consciously and subconsciously. How we do this and the role the process plays in learning are the subject of Part II. Here it becomes apparent that cognition and attention are strongly related but at least partly independent processes.

Picton opens with a review of what is known about the brain mechanisms that operate in the processes underlying the phenomena of attention. As he notes, data prevail over theories. From his discussions of the neurology of attention defects, which in a way provide a caricature of variations in the normal processes, it becomes clear that attention involves a number of interactive brain systems. Animal studies further reveal that certain brain centers modulate the activity of others in a way that may control the attention of the system as a whole.

When it comes to attempts to monitor the brain processes involved in attention in normal intact humans, the tool that is at the same time most promising and most frustrating is electroencephalography, the recording from the scalp of electrical potentials that are generated by the brain. We can break the code for certain of these signals and have found evidence that they reflect such attributes of attention as selectivity, resource allocation, and attended sensory channels. Picton points, however, to the frustration that has so far rewarded attempts to relate these messages from the brain to intelligence, a poorly defined property of the individual which is nonetheless considered a sine qua non in education.

In the ensuing chapter, Posner applies the precisely machined tools of mental chronometry to the processes of attention in the visual field. His demonstration of the process of covert selection—the shifting of attention without eye movement—provides new insights into not only the basic processes that control attention but also the individual differences in these processes. His preliminary findings on the correlation between certain of these processes and some measures of intelligence provide hope that the electrophysiological correlates suggested by Picton may some day be identified.

The discussion of attention concludes with an overview by Simon. He proposes that the attentional bottleneck exists in order to identify those stimuli that are relevant to the organism. And of course he addresses the issue of how educators can break through this bottleneck by motivating students. Finally, Simon reveals his computational bias in a consideration of computer models for human performance as a contribution to improved education.

IV. KNOWLEDGE ACQUISITION, REPRESENTATION, AND USE

Part III, Knowledge Acquisition, Representation and Use, deals with learning and memory in the broadest sense. Discussions in this section deal largely with language acquisition, school learning, and the brain functions involved in these processes. They provide insights into some of the many different kinds of learning processes that take place in the course of a lifetime, which are potentially helpful in the improvement of the educational process. Of the many possible approaches to the concerns of this section, one notable omission here is the potentially important insights computer science is beginning to provide into representation and manipulation of information (Sleeman & Brown, 1980).

The problem of internal representation is one that is central to cognitive science. How are patterns of light, sound, and other sensory information identified as people, things and events and represented as such in the brain? Once again, the question may be addressed at several different levels. In the computer analogy, information at a fundamental level is represented by the presence or absence of a voltage, or, to the machine language programmer, as a "1" or a "0." In a high-level computer program, however, it may be in the form of a complex network of logical functions. Similarly, in the brain we may consider information as electrical impulses passing from nerve cell to nerve cell. In another sense it may be in the form of diffuse activity patterns in various parts of the cortex. At yet a higher level, the information may be in the form of the visual image of a complex geometric shape that can be mentally rotated in space.

Gleitman first addresses the complex subject of language acquisition. How do young learners master the complex cognitive tools of language? Her assertion is that they do so by means of a biological program that is modulated by experience. It is a challenge to project the generalities of a grammar from samples that the learner must somehow represent mentally.

That the mental machinery specifically designed for this task is built in is evidenced by the relative uniformity of the language learned despite the diversity of inputs to each learner. Furthermore what the learners learn is clearly not related in any simple way to the input the learner receives. And finally, Gleitman notes that the learners are capable of making linguistic generalizations that extend beyond their experience.

Gleitman provides support for her view of the biological substrates of language with evidence from her own research. Her program involves the search for changes in language learning when there are differences in any of the components of the learning process. Surprisingly, she finds that major variations in the type of input (e.g., "motherese" vs. adult language), deafness (learning sign language), blindness, mental retardation, and so on result in relatively minor changes in the pattern of language acquisition.

Not everyone, of course, shares Gleitman's view that there is a bioprogram for language acquisition. Others lean more toward the idea that many mental processes, including language processing, are carried out by a sort of general-purpose problem-solving system. In this view, many of the features of language acquisition are seen as consequences of the structure of language itself (Papert, 1980). Nevertheless, her arguments are highly compelling and more readily account for many phenomena such as the creation of creole languages than alternative views are capable of doing. Her analysis suggests important tools for analysis of brain function, and we would do well to heed her assertion that both cognitive scientists and teachers can learn a great deal from the knowledge of language a child brings to school.

Wittrock brings an education researcher's point of view to the analysis of the detrimental effects of deficient attention mechanisms on several aspects of the learning process. He proposes that emerging neural and cognitive models of the attention process are useful in the design of effective learning techniques.

The discussion of knowledge acquisition in Wittrock's chapter underlines the importance of an active role for the acquirer. He cites numerous studies that seem to suggest a direct ratio of acquisition to involvement, whether in the form of creating imagery or underlining text. Again he invokes the role of neural and cognitive models in the design of studies on verbal and spatial processes and in analytic or holistic modalities.

While he is enthusiastic about the use of models to understand how people acquire knowledge, Wittrock raises a cautionary note against confusing the several levels of analysis of neural, cognitive, and educational research. His prescription for the future of a collaborative effort among the three fields clearly delineates the hierarchical interaction of neural, cognitive, and educational models of the learning process.

Hierarchical analysis comes into play once again, but in a somewhat different way in Squire's discussion of the neural mechanisms of learning. Neuroscientists know many details of simple learning processes in the primitive brain of the sea snail. What they have discovered about the changes in connections between nerve cells that underlie learning at this level provide important insights into the process of learning in more-complex brains.

Squire's own extensive work on various forms of amnesia constitutes a still-higher-level neuropsychological analysis of the very complex processes of human memory. Amnesia itself is not just simply a general inability to recall memories; it has a variety of subtle forms. Brain damage of different sorts makes it possible to tease apart the many components of the memory acquisition and retrieval process. Squire's work further reinforces the emerging concept that humans have more than one kind of memory, a possibility which he notes has clear implications for both teaching and testing.

Part III concludes with Chipman's assessment of the existing links among neuroscience, psychology, and education and her specific recommendations for overcoming present shortcomings. Her warnings to educators not to swallow sugar-coated neuroscience pills are especially timely. She finds neural and cognitive science to be mutually supportive to a degree, feeding one another with hypotheses and experimental results. She also finds cognitive research and education to be supplying one another with facts and ideas. It is the interplay between neuroscience and education that she finds seriously wanting.

Chipman notes the rarity of suggestions that neuroscientists might learn something from education research, limited almost solely to the notion that experience can affect brain structure. In the other direction, she finds neuroscience research results being adopted uncritically and often inappropriately by educators.

This last pessimistic assessment is followed by Chipman's five-part program intended not just to rectify the misconnections between neuroscience and education, but also to strengthen the threads of the neural-cognitive-education fabric. Her recommendations include interdisciplinary tool development, applications of well-understood concepts to poorly understood phenomena and development of models with parameters that are meaningful across disciplines. Most important, however, is her caution, "First, do no harm." It casts the burden of responsibility for the successful sale of not only worthless, but sometimes downright dangerous educational "snake-oil" on overly reclusive neuroscientists.

V. COGNITIVE AND NEURAL DEVELOPMENT

In Part IV, Cognitive and Neural Development, the nature-versus-nurture controversy is reexamined in the context of the problems shared by the three fields represented here. Both environmental and innate biological processes clearly play critical roles in cognitive development. The work discussed in this section indicates how far we have come in understanding the subtleties of the interplay between these factors in determining adult capabilities. All too evident, too, is the frustration of realizing how far we have yet to go in gaining from this knowledge the ability to optimize the learning process.

The prospects of providing more effective use of neuroscience results in educational practice is examined from another perspective by Chall and Peterson. They share Chipman's view that previous application of neuroscience results to educational practice has had less than notable success. They suggest, however, that the area of reading disabilities promises new opportunities for neuroscientists both to help overcome the handicap of reading disabilities and to improve educational practice in general.

This chapter's opening discussion makes painfully clear the lack of knowledge that has impeded the teaching of the reading disabled. The pendulum of theoretical fashion has swung back and forth among constructs of varying plausibility, each coupled with its own particular form of treatment. Sometimes neurological disorders were invoked, sometimes not. And all along no one really produced any evidence that would permit comparison of efficacy among methods.

What Chall and Peterson recommend to remedy this situation is a new conceptual framework based on four principles currently prominent in neuroscience: (1) genetically determined brain circuitry, (2) critical periods in development, (3) neural plasticity, and (4) the modularity of neural systems. Taken together, these provide a decidedly dualistic view of the influence of biological and environmental factors on the normal or disrupted acquisition of reading skills. The resulting prescription, while somewhat wanting for cognitive guidelines, is on target in specifying clinical-level involvement of neuroscientists and provision for long-term evaluation of the results of new practices.

Central to the process of cognitive development is, of course, the development of the brain as the instrument of cognitive capability. Goldman-Rakic provides a clear analysis of the exquisitely subtle orchestration of neocortical development, as it is this part of the brain that is particularly relevant to cognition. The brain arises from a single layer of cells lining the wall of the embryonic neural tube. From this layer must arise the precisely patterned network of adult neurons that carry out the functions of sensory perception, motor control, and cognitive processing. For the brain to function properly, cells must not only migrate to appropriate locations but also make specific chemical and electrical connections with other cells in their same functional system, cells that are often physically far removed.

In the course of her narrative, Goldman-Rakic notes certain developmental abnormalities such as the abnormal neurons and reduced synaptic density that occurs in Down's syndrome. As Gleitman finds the acquisition of language in children a useful tool in her analysis of that cognitive development, it should be clear that abnormal as well as normal brain development can illuminate the neural substrates of cognition. Indeed, Goldman-Rakic points out in her conclusion that even armed with all the powerful neuroanatomical tools at our command, an understanding of cognitive function will certainly require the conjunction of morphological, biochemical, and behavioral knowledge.

The scope of Gardner's chapter is especially broad and perhaps touches on more of the varied issues raised in this volume than any of the others. Gardner recognizes well the many authoritative voices in developmental theory that have so often been in conflict, and only on occasion in synergy. He has studied closely the evolution of the study of cognitive development. Now that the excesses of the mechanistic and the mentalistic schools have dissipated, he finds the field particularly fragmented. In his view, the fragmentation into separate schools of information processing only recasts old disagreements into different and equally unresolvable form.

Gardner is firmly and unabashedly opposed to studies of cognitive development that ignore the social and cultural context in which the development is taking place. This position amplifies his opposition to the information-processing approach to cognition and leads him to appeal more to neurobiology to explain some of the complexities of such phenomena as critical periods, individual differences, and language acquisition, for which he feels there are no other reasonable sources of explanation.

In the end, Gardner declares himself to be a multinationalist. He proposes that there are many natural kinds of intelligence, such as spatial, musical, and linguistic, which various strengths and weaknesses contribute to any one individual's cognitive profile. Once again raising the issue of levels of analysis, he proposes that for cognitive science these are biological, computational, psychological, and cultural. But he, like many of his colleagues, also insists that the levels of analysis must be consistent with one another and, moreover, inform one another.

The final chapter of this section on cognitive development proposes to help provide some missing links noted in several earlier contributions— that is, the stimulation of neuroscience and cognitive science research by scholarly work in education. Friedman and Cocking argue that the present concepts and techniques of neuro- and cognitive science are sufficiently powerful to understand how environmental influences can alter certain aspects of brain function and behavior, focusing specifically on the effects of instruction and guided learning.

Earlier chapters have made clear that we lack any sort of useful theory concerning widely recognized effects of environmental conditions on brain and behavior. Friedman and Cocking discuss the evidence concerning the effects of socioeconomic status on intellectual performance and note that not only genetic factors but also critical period factors bedevil the analysis of such effects. The effects of instruction and environmental enrichment are somewhat easier to document. There are indeed many fragments of information to support the notion that instruction changes brain organization, as in deaf individuals taught to use sign language. It is clearly a challenge to the investigators of brain activity and cognitive skills to assemble these fragments into a theory that will help educational researchers explain the rich diversity of their observations.

VI. DISCUSSION

The final chapter of this volume (Part V) is set apart from the others. It is a discussion piece reflecting Rosenzweig's personal view of what message or messages the preceding chapters delivered. He is in a special position to assess what they accomplished because, for one thing, his own research was among the first to demonstrate that differences in environmental richness can affect brain structure. In addition, he played a principal role in organizing a symposium about in the mid-1970s, which brought together neural and behavioral scientists to consider the possible implications of their work for education (Rosenzweig & Bennett, 1976). That event provides a benchmark against which he measures the results of the current effort.

Rosenzweig points out many exceptions to the role of attention in learning posited by some of the authors of this volume. He then recasts some of the concepts of memory formation presented in Part IV of this volume and illuminates them with some observations of his own. He notes too the absence here of any discussion of postnatal development and plasticity of the nervous system, which he suggests may be more relevant to teaching than prenatal development.

For a stimulating finale, Rosenzweig proposes a challenging model of memory which incorporates many of the concepts contained in this volume. His notion of both direct and modulatory processes in the formation and maintenance of memories is again a hierarchical scheme. It integrates neurochemical, cellular, and system concepts in a behavioral framework that has direct implications for education.

VII. CONCLUSION

What does this volume accomplish? Will it enhance cross-disciplinary communication and foster the opening of a new era in education? Or is it simply a collection of essays rehearsing the disciplinary problems and praising the accomplishments of each author's own field?

The editors believe that this volume represents the most forceful effort to date at communication among the participating disciplines, with the aim of exploring mutually beneficial cooperation. The authors did air complaints and rightly emphasized the importance of many significant discoveries in their own fields. Both, however, have been done in a spirit of cooperation. It is the same with the many challenges the authors have posed for future research. The real success of this volume will be judged by the extent to which it stimulates the opening of previously inaccessible research frontiers. That is a measure only its readers can provide.

REFERENCES

Arrow, K. J. (1968). Mathematical models in the social sciences. In M. Brodbeck, *Readings in the philosophy of the social sciences*. New York: Macmillan.

Board on Agriculture, National Research Council. (1984). *Genetic engineering of plants: Agricultural research opportunities and policy concerns*. Washington, D.C.: National Academy Press.

Davies, P. (1984). *Superforce: The search for a grand unified theory of nature*. New York: Simon and Schuster/Heinemann.

Gazzaniga, M. S. (Ed.) (1984). *Handbook of cognitive neuroscience*. New York: Plenum Press.

Judson, H. F. (1979). *The eighth day of creation: Makers of the revolution in biology*. New York: Simon and Schuster.

Malcup, F., & Mansfield, V. (Eds.) (1983). *The study of information: Interdisciplinary messages*. New York: Wiley.

Papert, S. (1980). *Mindstorms: Children, computers and powerful ideas*. New York: Basic Books.

Rosenzweig, M. R., & Bennett, E. L. (Eds.). (1976). *Neural mechanisms of learning and memory*. Cambridge, MA: MIT Press.

Sleeman, D., & Brown, J. S. (Eds.) (1980). *Intelligent tutoring systems*. New York: Academic Press.

Smirnov, V. I. (1961). *Linear algebra and group theory* (p. 267). New York: McGraw Hill.

PART II

ATTENTION

the concatenation of association into insight. The measurement of attention must demonstrate these effects for particular aspects of the environment and not for others. This involves assessing how much better some processing is performed when it is attended to than when it is ignored.

The selectivity of attention requires that there be some controlling process to direct and maintain the state of attention, to allocate attentional resources, or to organize attentional selectivity. Because attention is thus goal-directed, it cannot be measured without evaluating the motivational goals of the attentive individual and the strategy being used to attain these goals. Attention that is controlled from within is called "active," whereas attention that is elicited by significant external stimuli is called "passive." The process of passive attention involves the orienting response, a set of reflexes invoked whenever something unexpected happens. The orienting response is often considered in terms of a world model that is maintained within the brain and updated (by the orienting response) after the detection of something significantly different from what the model predicts.

This chapter considers attention from the point of view of neuroscience. Its basic assumption is that our understanding of attention and its disorders can be helped by studying the brain (Figure 2.1). Theories of attention are generally proposed and evaluated at the level of psychology. Information from neuroscience, however, can provide limits for such theories and suggest processes that may be involved in attention. Furthermore, some neuroscientific understanding is essential in dealing with the disorders of attention that are caused by cerebral dysfunction or treated by neuropharmacology.

There are two main approaches to studying attention in terms of the brain. The first is to evaluate the effects of lesions. The effects of lesions are difficult to interpret. Attention depends on the functional integrity of many interconnected areas of the brain. Lesions are therefore much more likely to point to a particular organization of the brain than to localize some defined function to a single area. The process of attention can only break down in certain ways. By studying the particular patterns of breakdown one may be able to infer the organization of normal attention.

The second approach to the cerebral mechanisms of attention is to record electrical signals from the brain during attention. Such recordings may provide information about the structure of attentional processes that is not available to behavioral examination. Recordings from animals are precise in that they can assess the activity of single neurons, but only one or several out of many million neurons are evaluated. Furthermore, it is extremely difficult to train an animal to attend to certain stimuli and

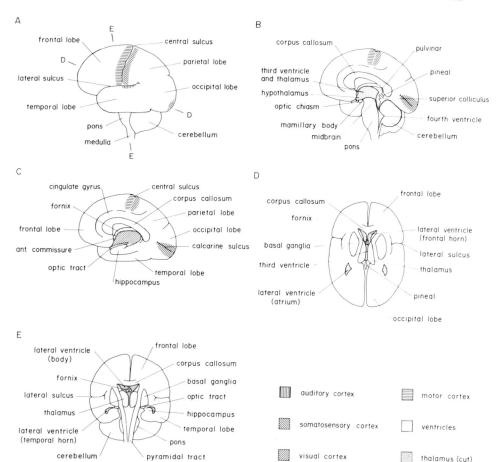

Figure 2.1 Diagrammatic views of the human brain. (A) A left lateral view of the brain showing the major lobes of the cerebral cortex, the primary sensory receiving areas and the motor cortex. (B) Medial view of the brain cut midsaggitally to show the corpus callosum and brainstem structures. (C) This represents the same view as in B but with the brainstem removed by cutting through the thalamus in order to show the hippocampus on the medial aspect of the temporal lobe. (D) Cross-section of the brain taken through the plane labelled D in part A of this figure and showing the structures that are visible on a computerized tomography. (E) Coronal section of the brain taken through the plane marked E in part A of this figure.

to ignore others, and it is impossible to ask an animal whether it is using the strategy assumed by the experimental design. It is far easier to instruct and evaluate human subjects. Neurophysiological recordings from human subjects are, however, made at some distance from the brain using electrodes attached to the scalp. Such recordings assess only those cerebral processes that create fields at a distance, but they can allow clear correlation of these processes to attention.

This chapter reviews some neuroscience research on attention. There are three main sections: neurological disorders, animal studies, and human neurophysiology. Neuroscience is a new discipline with a somewhat greater data-to-theory ratio than more-established disciplines. At present, experimental findings are more numerous than explanatory principles, and models derive from data rather than determine experiments.

II. NEUROLOGICAL DISORDERS

This section initially reviews the neuropsychological tests that can be used to assess attentional disorders. It then discusses two disorders of attention that are clearly related to lesions of the brain: the lack of attentional control observed in patients with lesions of the frontal lobe, and the syndrome of inattention typically seen in lesions of the parietal lobe. We then discuss two attentional disorders that, although undoubtedly caused by brain damage, have as yet no definite pathophysiology: the cognitive problems that occur after head injury and the confusional states that are associated with many different cerebral disorders. Finally, we comment on the functional disorders of attention in schizophrenia and hyperactivity where there is no clearly understood pathology.

II.A. CLINICAL MEASURES OF ATTENTION

The clinician initially assesses the patient's ability to concentrate on a task without giving up or becoming distracted (Lezak, 1976). Tests of digit span (recall a series of numbers in forward or backward sequence), counting (e.g., forward by threes—1,4,7 . . .) or serial subtraction (e.g., of sevens—100,93,86 . . .) are commonly used. Forward digit-span evaluates the capacity of immediate memory; backward digit-span, counting, and serial subtraction evaluate the ability of the patient to operate on the contents of immediate memory prior to their deterioration. Although not commonly used, other kinds of tests are available to evaluate more extensively the temporal stability of attention (Rosvold, Mirsky, Sarason, Bransome, & Beck, 1956) and its resistance to distraction (Stroop, 1935). These clinical tests presume that attention enlarges the capacity of immediate memory, facilitates operations in immediate memory, and limits immediate memory to task-relevant data.

In addition to these general tests, the clinician also evaluates how information from each of the sensory systems is incorporated into the patient's behavior. When questioned, the patient may not report defects such as hemiplegia or blindness that are obvious to the examiner. There may be different levels to this abnormal awareness (Benson & Geschwind, 1975). A patient may show a lack of concern for his or her defects (anosodiaphoria) or the patient may be unaware of or even frankly deny the defects (anosognosia). A patient may not display any awareness of or responsiveness to certain aspects of her or his environment unless they are pointed out or emphasized. This is considered inattention or neglect. Although the patient may respond to stimuli in the neglected field of perception, he or she will not report the stimulus in the neglected field when tested with simultaneous stimuli in both the intact and the neglected fields. This "extinction to double simultaneous stimulation" is the simplest behavioral demonstration of inattention.

Unfortunately, some important characteristics of attention are not examined during the usual neurological or neuropsychological evaluation (Geschwind, 1982). Optimal attentive behavior requires monitoring the environment and shifting attention when necessary. The Wisconsin Card Sorting Test (Grant & Berg, 1948), although not often interpreted as a test of attention, assesses these processes. The patient is given a deck of cards that must be sorted according to one of three criteria. The only instructions provided are to sort the cards and to use the feedback given after each card to sort them as correctly as possible. The sorting criterion is changed without warning after 10 consecutive correct responses. This test demands the discovery of the correct criterion by trial-and-error, the maintenance of a consistent response pattern once the criterion has been discovered, and the monitoring of both the cards and the feedback in order to shift performance once the criterion changes.

II.B.   ATTENTIONAL DISORDERS DUE TO FOCAL BRAIN LESIONS

II.B.1.   FRONTAL LOBE SYNDROMES

Disturbances of attention are frequent in patients with frontal-lobe damage. Patients with large lesions of the frontal lobes, however, often do not show abnormalities on such simple tasks as digit span and serial subtraction (Stuss, Alexander, Lieberman, & Levine, 1978; Stuss, Benson, Kaplan, Weir, & Della Malva, 1981). Intellectual functioning as measured by standard intelligence tests and the ability to make abstractions may be unimpaired (Milner, 1964; Stuss & Benson, 1984).

The disorder is more one of attentional control. The patient is not able to adopt or adapt appropriate cognitive strategies in response to changing task demands (Stuss, Benson, Kaplan, Weir, Naeser, Lieberman, & Ferrill, 1983). Performance on tests of selectivity, coherence of thought and action, monitoring of performance and adapting behavior to task demands—such as required in the Wisconsin Card Sorting Test—is usually severely impaired (Milner, 1964).

This can be difficult to evaluate, because the examiner tends to assist the patient in the performance of the clinical tests, in effect taking over the functions of the defective frontal lobe. Both the spontaneous behavior of the frontally damaged patient and his or her behavior on tests may be characterized at times by inflexibility and perseveration and at other times by impulsivity or the inability to sustain directed attention. Their perceptions lack unity, and at times two completely contradictory interpretations of reality can coexist (Alexander, Stuss, & Benson, 1979).

These apparently diverse findings can be understood by viewing the frontal lobes as responsible for selecting and monitoring behavior for the attainment of the individual's goals. The damaged frontal granular cortex cannot adequately integrate the incoming sensorimotor information of the neocortex with the motivational drives of the limbic system (Nauta, 1971). The result is the disturbed behavior described in Harlow's report (1868) of the famous case of Phineas Gage: "The equilibrium or balance, so to speak, between his intellectual facilities and animal propensities seems to have been destroyed".

> **Case Study of Frontal Damage:** This 53-year-old man suffered bilateral frontal infarcts. Clinical examination revealed a mild left hemiparesis. There was bilateral frontal slowing on the electroencephalogram and a deep left frontal infarct on computerized tomography (Figure 2.2A). Neuropsychological testing occurred several months after admission. He performed well on digit span (8 forward, 4 backward) and could concentrate sufficiently to count by 3s with only occasional errors. On subtracting serial 7s, which was completed after counting by 3s, he was unable to stop himself from subtracting (correctly) by 3s. He verbalized that he should subtract by 7s, and yet said, "Here I go with 3s again." Similarly, in a visuomotor tracking task that required alteration between numbers and letters (Figure 2.2B), this patient was unable to perform the alteration. He verbalized that he was forgetting to insert the numbers in between but continued to join the letters. His copy of the Rey-Osterreith figure was totally disorganized although all of the details were present (Figure 2.2C). His performance on the Wechsler Adult Intelligence Scale (WAIS) showed a verbal IQ in the low normal range, although his performance IQ was significantly infe-

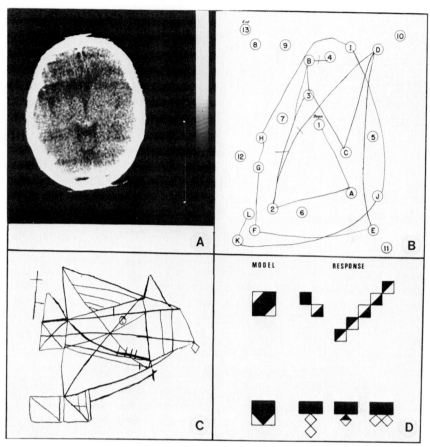

Figure 2.2 Case study of a patient with a frontal lobe lesion. (A) Computerized tomography showing the deep infarct (dark area) in the left frontal lobe. (B) Results of the patient's attempt to alternately connect the numbers and the letters on this page from a trail-making test. The crossed-out lines represent ones that the patient was told were incorrect and asked to redraw. (C) Patient's copy of the Rey-Osterreith figure (original in Figure 3E). (D) Results of the patient's attempt to do the block design subtest of the Wechsler Adult Intelligence Scale.

rior. On the Block Design subtest he frequently reconstructed the design by focusing on salient figural features such as the angle (Goodglass & Kaplan, 1979) (Figure 2.2D). Other deficits were present including confabulation (see Stuss et al., 1978).

This patient illustrates a disorder in the control of attention. He had no difficulty completing a limited and defined task such as the digit span. However, he failed when a task required inhibiting one program of action (counting by 3s) in order to replace it with another (subtracting serial 7s). Both tasks independently were within his capabilities but he could not choose the appropriate behavior. Neither his knowledge of the required behavior nor the overt verbalization of this knowledge was effective in directing his behavior, indicating a dissociation between knowledge and action, and a loss of the verbal regulation of behavior (Luria, 1980). His performance on copying and block design suggested that his perception of the world lacked any overall organization. He was unable to concentrate on general patterns without little details capturing his attention. His tendency to confabulate can be interpreted as an inability to screen the information provided by his memory for its appropriateness to objective reality.

II.B.2. INATTENTION

The syndrome of inattention is a fairly common clinical condition. It is most frequently associated with lesions of sudden onset involving the inferior parietal area of the right hemisphere. It is defined as a failure to report, respond, or orient to the stimuli presented on the side contralateral to the cerebral lesion in the absence of elemental sensory or motor defects (Heilman, 1979). The demonstration of intact sensation and responsiveness requires that the inattention be either incomplete or inconstant. It is best demonstrated when a patient makes some automatic response to sensory input on the neglected side. For example, when given a pair of gloves the patient may use his left hand to put the right glove on but will leave his left hand ungloved (Friedland & Weinstein, 1977).

The lesions of the human brain that lead to inattention are predominantly right-sided. Three possible explanations for this can be considered. The first would be a right hemispheric dominance for attentional processes akin to the left hemispheric dominance for language (Mesulam & Geschwind, 1978). It is possible that the right hemisphere becomes specialized by default "because the synaptic space for analogous functions in the contralateral hemisphere became devoted to language functions" (Mesulam, 1981).

The second explanation would depend on hemispheric rivalry (Kinsbourne, 1977). During the clinical examination the patient is forced to adopt a verbal set in order to understand and answer the questions of the examiner. Because the hemispheres normally inhibit each other, verbal activation of the left hemisphere would inhibit right hemispheric functions. If the right hemisphere were already defective this would exaggerate the neglect of the left side of the body. If the pathology were in the left hemisphere the verbal set would attenuate the defect.

The third explanation involves the length and complexity of the pathways leading to the speech centers from different sensory areas. Schwartz, Marchok, Kreinick, and Flynn (1979) have suggested that the more complex pathway from the right somatosensory cortex to the speech centers of the left hemisphere is more vulnerable to damage than the direct connections between the left somatosensory cortex and the speech centers.

Case Study of Inattention: A 51-year-old architect and amateur artist was admitted with a right frontal headache, weakness and numbness of the left upper extremity, and an absence of response to visual stimuli in the left visual field. Computerized tomography revealed a right frontoparietal lesion (Figure 2.3A). He was referred for neuropsychological examination 3 weeks after his admission. At that time he was alert and cooperative. Bedside examination showed an intact comprehension, normal digit span, normal right–left discrimination, and normal naming of objects and pictures of objects. He was aware of his deficits but appeared quite unconcerned about them. He reported occasional vivid visual hallucinations of a woman lying in his bed or on his left side. He did not respond to stimuli in his left visual field and all stimuli used in the examination were therefore presented on his right. Nevertheless, when asked to bisect lines oriented in various directions on a page of paper he missed many of the lines on the left side of the page and tended to shift to the right on the lines that he actually bisected (Figure 2.3B). In a portrait of the examiner (Figure 2.3C) he overemphasized the right side and the few details produced on the left side were only lightly sketched and detached from the main part of the drawing. He also displayed a striking neglect of the left-sided details in copied pictures (Figure 2.3D). A copy of the complex Rey-Osterreith figure (Figure 2.3E) revealed an incomplete left side although specific left-sided details were incorporated into the right side (Figure 2.3F).

This patient shows many of the characteristic findings of the inattention syndrome. There is not only a defect of processing stimuli in the left visual field but also a difficulty in conceptualizing the left side of things. He was unable to copy the left side of simple or complex objects even though the visual information was presented in his intact visual field. He disregarded the left side of the portrait. These observations suggest that there is a defective representational system disrupting left-sided details during both perception and remembering. Bisiach and Luzzatti

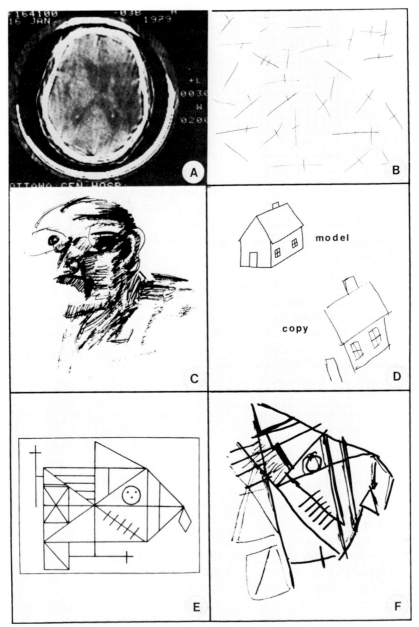

Figure 2.3 Case study of a patient with inattention. (A) Computerized tomography showing the large right frontoparietal infarct as an area of reduced density (darker). (B) Results of the patient's attempt to bisect lines on a page. (C) The patient's portrait of the examiner. (D) Results of the patient's attempt to copy a picture of a house. (E) The complex Rey-Osterreith figure. (F) Patient's copy of this figure.

(1978) have studied this defect of the representational schema in patients with inattention due to right-sided cortical lesions. They asked patients to remember what they could see from a certain vantage point in the main square in Milan. The patients reported many details from their right side but few if any details from their left. When then asked to imagine themselves on the opposite side of the square they could re-member many more details of the side of the square previously poorly remembered on their left but now remembered on their right.

Although inattention is most characteristically seen with lesions of the right parietal lobe, it can also be seen with other lesions. For example, lesions of the frontal lobe can cause very definite inattention (Heilman & Valenstein, 1972; Stein & Volpe, 1983). The apathy noted in patients with frontal lobe damage may represent a mild bilateral inattention. Bilateral damage to the cingulate and septal regions or bilateral mesio-frontal damage may lead to akinetic mutism, a state wherein the patient is awake but unresponsive. This may represent severe bilateral inatten-tion. Other lesions reported to produce inattention in human patients involve the thalamus, the basal ganglia, the superior colliculus and the pulvinar (Damasio, Damasio, & Chang Chui, 1980; Heywood & Ratcliff, 1975; Watson, Valenstein, & Heilman, 1981; Zihl & von Cramon, 1979). The widespread locations of lesions leading to inattention suggest that there is a distributed brain system subserving attention and that this system acts independently of the pathways that process specific sensory information.

II.C.   ATTENTIONAL DISORDERS DUE TO BRAIN DAMAGE WITHOUT CLEAR PATHOPHYSIOLOGY

II.C.1.   HEAD INJURY

Disordered attention is a common observation in patients with closed-head injury. Even when apparently fully recovered, complex tasks in-volving multiple choices show a severe impairment in reaction time (Normann & Svahn, 1961). Even mildly concussed patients were defi-cient in performing a paced serial addition task (Gronwall, 1977). In this test, numbers are presented at one of four different rates. The subject adds two numbers, verbalizes the response, then adds the third number to the second, verbalizes the response, et cetera. The subject must re-member the second of two numbers for addition to the next number despite the interference of adding it to the preceding number.

Van Zomeren (1981) suggests that slowness of processing is the only deficit present in head-injured patients. Others, however, have found particularly poor performance on tests requiring inhibition of interfering stimuli (Stroop phenomenon), rapid alternation between two simultaneous sets of stimuli in tracking tasks (Trail Making Test—Army Individual Test Battery, 1944), or conceptual sorting in the Wisconsin Card Sorting Test (Eson, Yen, & Bourke, 1978; Stuss & Richard, 1982).

The anatomical bases for the deficits in head injury are unknown. Although there is diffuse brain damage secondary to closed-head injury, the brainstem and orbitofrontal and temporal cortex appear to be most affected (Alexander, 1982; Ommaya & Gennarelli, 1976). It is possible that the decreased speed of information processing may be related to brainstem dysfunction and the abnormalities of attentional control may be caused by the orbitofrontal damage. Head injuries are an example of how devastating disorders of attention can be. Even after apparent recovery, these subtle but crippling deficiencies may cause failure in school, work, or social interactions.

II.C.2. Stupor, Delirium, and Confusion

Patients with altered levels of arousal always display abnormalities of attention. Stuporous patients respond briefly to intense stimuli and rapidly return to their somnolent state. Stimuli are responded to on the basis of their intensity and not their significance. This has been described as "drifting attention" (Benson & Geschwind, 1975). These symptoms are due to either diffuse dysfunction of the cerebral hemispheres or to focal abnormalities of the reticular activating system. Delirious patients are alert but unable to maintain attention on the immediate task. They are easily distracted by any external stimulus and have therefore been described as having "wandering attention" (Benson & Geschwind, 1975). Delirium is most commonly found in patients with acute metabolic or toxic brain dysfunction. It is probable that stupor and delirium both represent a generalized cognitive disorder, combined respectively with either reduced or heightened levels of arousal. Attention is abnormal in both: It cannot be sustained in one and cannot be directed in the other.

The definition of *confusional state* varies with different authors. Geschwind (1982), has suggested that confusional states can be differentiated from stupor or delirium by the loss of the normal coherence of thought or action, so that confusion is "not simply a lowering or raising of the arousal level but rather a more profound disruption of the normal hierarchy of rules." In the confusional state, there is a loss of coherence, an inability to maintain selective attention over time, a distortion of memory whereby patients may duplicate facts, a propagation of error, a tendency to occupational jargon, an inattention to environmental stimuli, a prominent disturbance of writing, an unconcern for or denial of illness, and a facetious and playful behavior. Mesulam, Waxman, Geschwind, and Sabin (1976) reported acute confusional states occurring in patients with right hemispheric lesions. Geschwind (1982) has therefore suggested that when this disorder is caused by a focal brain disorder there is a lesion of either the parietal or frontal region of the right hemisphere. Geschwind points out that, although confusional states may be seen in generalized brain disorders such as fever or intoxication, it is possible that these generalized abnormalities may cause their effects by disrupting function in focal areas of the right hemisphere. The major clinical features of the confusional state are similar to those described for frontal lobe damage. We therefore feel that the confusional state may be caused by frontal lobe dysfunction. This can be related to a direct lesion to the frontal lobes or a functional disconnection of the frontal lobes from the other regions of the brain.

II.D. FUNCTIONAL DISORDERS OF ATTENTION

II.D.1. SCHIZOPHRENIA

Disordered attention has been considered as a prominent, if not primary, psychological deficit in schizophrenia. It has been observed not only in patients with active schizophrenic symptoms but also in children who are vulnerable to the disease (Asarnow, MacCrimmon, Cleghorn, & Steffry, 1978; McGhie & Chapman, 1961; Zubin, 1975). The most striking abnormalities are seen in tasks that require planning, maintaining performance during distraction, or changing strategies of behavior. These findings are similar to those in patients with lesions of the frontal lobe. The current treatment of schizophrenia is based on the major tranquilizers that block the function of dopamine in the brain (Carlsson, 1978). Abnormal cerebral blood flow to the frontal regions of the brain has been reported in schizophrenia (Ingvar & Franzen, 1974). A disorder of dopamine regulation in the frontal cortex may perhaps underlie the schizophrenic disorder (Joseph, Frith, & Waddington, 1979). The possible relation between the schizophrenic disorder of attention and a frontal lobe abnormality could explain why leucotomy of the frontal lobes improves the performance of the schizophrenic patient on the commonly used clinical tests of attention (Stuss et al., 1981).

II.D.2.   HYPERACTIVITY

Attentional difficulties are also prominent in the childhood disorders that are grouped under such labels as "hyperactivity," "minimal brain dysfunction," and "attention deficit disorder." Two main subtypes have been suggested. One is characterized by a combination of inattention, impulsivity, and hyperactivity. These children are easily distracted, act without thinking, and cannot stay still. The second subtype has a disorder of attention but no hyperactivity. Behavioral similarities between hyperactive children and patients with frontal lobe pathology have been reported (Stamm & Kreder, 1979). Difficulties with tasks requiring sustained attention or planning are common to both groups. It is possible that delayed maturation of the frontal lobes may contribute to the disorder of attention in at least some of the children with minimal brain dysfunction. Such a hypothesis has also been presented as a theoretical explanation for delinquent children who act impulsively and cannot learn from their mistakes (Pontius & Yudowitz, 1980). Patients with frontal lobe damage frequently have dissociation between what they say and what they do—a loss of the verbal regulation of behavior (Luria, 1980). In order to overcome similar problems in patients with functional disorders of attention, self-instruction and self-talk has been used in the treatment of hyperactive school children (Meichenbaum & Goodman, 1971). Hyperactive children are often treated with stimulant medications (Barkley, 1977; Margolin, 1978). These drugs facilitate the actions of brain catecholamines, and it is therefore possible that the attentional disorder in hyperactive children is related to some deficit in one or more of the cerebral catecholamine systems.

II.E.   CONCLUSION

No single brain system is responsible for all aspects of selective attention. Nevertheless, although attention involves the interaction of several different brain systems, it is possible that each system may play a specific role in the overall process. The frontal lobes appear to play an important role in controlling attention; the right parietal lobe appears to provide a spatial organization whereby attention can be allocated. Mesulam (1981) has suggested that five different cerebral regions compose an integrated functional system subserving attention. The limbic region provides the motivational salience; the reticular formation is necessary for optimal arousal; the parietal lobe gives an internal sensory map; the sensory association areas provide the raw information to be attended to; and the frontal lobe explores, monitors, fixates, and shifts the direction of attention. Watson and his colleagues (1981) have provided a more detailed mapping of the different brain regions involved in sensory attention (Figure 2.4). This model stresses the role of the nucleus reticularis thalami (NR) in the gating of incoming sensory information. This gating is under the control of the frontal and parietal cortices (Arrow 7 in the figure).

III. ANIMAL STUDIES

This section evaluates some animal studies relevant to understanding the normal processes of attention and the treatment of attentional disorders. We initially review work on two kinds of neurotransmitters—the catecholamines and the peptides. After that we discuss some of the physiological theories that postulate that selective attention is mediated by a gating of incoming sensory information prior to its arrival at the cerebral cortex. Finally, we consider the role of three different cortical regions—the hippocampus, the frontal lobe, and the parietal lobe—in the processes of attention.

III.A. NEUROTRANSMITTER SYSTEMS

III.A.1. BRAIN CATECHOLAMINES

Two lines of evidence point to some involvement of the catecholamines in attention: the treatment of some human attentional disorders with drugs that affect the activity of cerebral catecholamines, and the alteration of animal attention that can be caused by disrupting catecholamine metabolism. Three catecholamines have been identified as neurotransmitters in the central nervous system: dopamine, noradrenaline, and adrenaline (Figure 2.5). There are extensive dopaminergic and noradrenergic neuronal connections in the brain (Moore, 1982). The main cell bodies of the dopamine system are located in the substantia nigra and in the ventral tegmental area of the mesencephalon. These cells project to the striatum (part of the basal ganglia) and to the limbic cortex (hippocampus and cingulate gyrus), respectively. The major noradrenergic system has its cell bodies in the locus coeruleus, a small bluish area in the pons. The neurons of the locus coeruleus project via the dorsal noradrenergic bundle to widespread areas of the brainstem, diencephalon, neocortex, and hippocampus. There are also descending connections to the gray matter of the spinal cord. The widespread projections from the locus coeruleus are apparently consistent with the notion that noradrenaline is ubiquitously distributed in the brain and that it

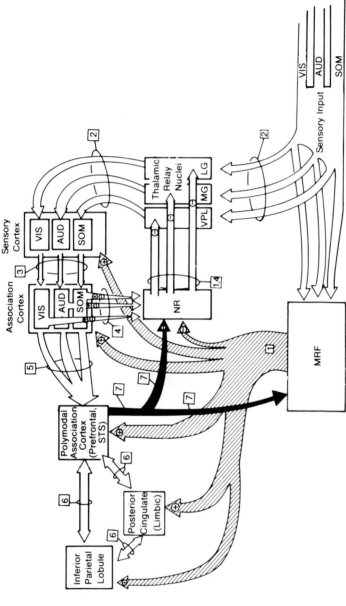

Figure 2.4 Diagrammatic view of the pathways involved in sensory attention. (1) The various areas of the cerebral cortex and the nucleus reticularis thalami (NR) are all affected by tonic arousal from the mesencephalic reticular formation (MRF). (2) Visual (VIS), auditory (AUD), and somatosensory (SOM) sensory information is transmitted along the sensory pathways through the thalamic relay nuclei where it is subject to gating from the nucleus reticularis thalami. (3) The primary sensory cortices project to association areas of cortex. (4) The association areas of cortex and the mesencephalic reticular formation both control the activity of the NR. (5) The association areas of cortex project to polymodal association cortices in the frontal and temporal lobes (STS—superior temporal sulcus). (6) These polymodal association areas and the limbic regions of the brain interact with the inferior parietal lobule. (7) Cortical structures can feedback to the thalamic and mesencephalic reticular formation. This figure is taken from Watson et al. (1981), *Archives of Neurology, 38*, 501–506. Copyright 1981, American Medical Association.

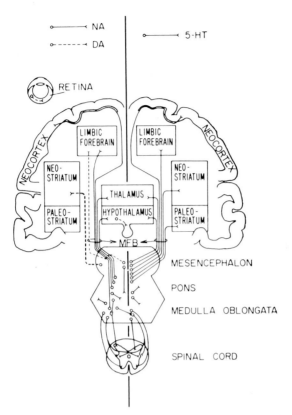

Figure 2.5 Schematic drawing showing, in highly simplified form, the main mo-noamine neuron systems in the central nervous system. The three main systems involve noradrenaline (NA), dopamine (DA) and 5-hydroxytryptamine (5-HT). Noradrenaline is also known as norepinephrine and 5-HT as serotonin. The neostriatium and paleos-triatium are divisions of the basal ganglia. Many of the aminergic neurons have fibers that travel in the medial forebrain bundle (MFB). This figure is taken from Anden et al. (1966), *Acta Physiological Scandinavia, 67,* 313–326.

may subserve rather nonspecific regulatory functions. However, this idea must be qualified by the observation that there are intracerebral differences in noradrenergic distribution (Morrison, Foote, O'Connor, & Bloom, 1982).

Catecholamines are capable of exerting different cellular actions at different sites in the nervous system. Inhibition of electrical activity is produced by noradrenaline on some nerve cells, while excitation or biphasic inhibition and excitation is seen in others (Marshall, 1983). An observation of great interest is that noradrenaline can have a *neuromodu-latory* action—that is, it can alter the responsiveness of a neuron to other neurotransmitter substances, without apparently changing the overall excitability of the cell (Moore, 1982; Woodward, Moises, Waterhouse, Hoffer, & Freedman, 1979).

Bloom (1978) has therefore suggested that the catecholamine systems may function to enable or to adjust the bias of the regions that they innervate. The application of noradrenaline (or noradrenaline-like drugs) to the cerebral cortex can improve the signal-to-noise ratio or clarity of the neuronal responses to auditory (Foote, Freedman, & Oliver, 1975) or somatosensory (Waterhouse, Moises, & Woodward, 1981) stimuli. Microelectrode studies of neurons within the locus coeruleus (Aston-Jones & Bloom, 1981a; Aston-Jones & Bloom, 1981b) have shown phasic increases in activity when there is spontaneous or sensory-induced interruptions of tonic vegetative functions such as sleeping, grooming, or eating. These results suggest that the nucleus is involved in arousal or orientation.

Mason (1981) has proposed that the locus coeruleus controls the ability to ignore irrelevant stimuli. This proposal is based on behavioral experiments with rats subjected to 6-hydroxydopamine lesions of the dorsal bundle, the major ascending pathway of the locus coeruleus. The toxin 6-hydroxydopamine is relatively selective for neurons using noradrenaline and dopamine. Lesions of the noradrenergic dorsal bundle that have been accomplished using localized injections of 6-hydroxydopamine into the pathway can almost completely deplete noradrenaline from its target areas. Rats lesioned in this way showed a delayed extinction of operant responses (such as lever-pressing or alley-running) that were learned after the lesion. This resistance to extinction was not seen if the lesions were made subsequent to training, or if the reinforcement was partial rather than continuous. The lesioned rats showed no impairment during the learning of the response, and could be readily switched from one learned response to another, provided it was not the exact reverse. It is possible therefore that the locus coeruleus is somehow involved in filtering out irrelevant stimuli that occur together with the actual discriminant stimuli during the learning situation. Lesioned animals would be unable to prevent such stimuli from becoming associated with the response and the reward. This increased breadth of association would be more resistant to extinction. A lesion of the locus coeruleus would therefore result in a "failure to ignore irrelevant stimuli" (Mason, 1981).

Several experiments have suggested that catecholamine-depleted animals are more distractible than normal ones. Roberts, Price, and Fibiger (1976) demonstrated that noradrenaline-depleted rats were more distracted than normal by irrelevant visual stimuli during the performance of a runway response. Oke and Adams (1978) showed that catechol-amine-depleted rats performed poorly on a black–white discrimination task when irrelevant visual stimuli were added to the visual cues. Crow, Deakin, File, Longden, and Wendlandt (1978) have, however, found no evidence for increased distractibility in 6-hydroxydopamine-lesioned an-imals subjected to loud distracting auditory stimuli during drinking. Mason (1981) has suggested that the locus coeruleus cannot prevent the behavioral effects of excessively salient stimuli that will disrupt perfor-mance in both lesioned and normal animals.

Two reports (Pisa & Fibiger, 1983; Tombaugh, Pappas, Roberts, Vick-ers, & Szostek, 1983) have been unable to replicate the resistance to extinction observed by Mason in 6-hydroxydopamine-lesioned animals, although another report (Dragunow & Laverty, 1983) does demonstrate this effect. These discrepancies might be due to subtle differences in the training situations. The animals' attention might have been more or less focussed by the environmental stimuli independently of any activity in the locus coeruleus. The concept of attention in animal discrimination learning does not allow for easy measurements. It is used to explain rather than control results—an animal associated a particular stimulus to a reward while not so associating another stimulus because the one was attended and the other was ignored. These explanations can be unconvincing unless there is some measure or control of attention dur-ing the learning process.

A conceptual difficulty with the Mason hypothesis involves the mech-anism by which the noradrenergic system could mediate attention that is selective for certain events within a specific modality. The locus coeru-leus has a very widespread pattern of innervation, and a mechanism for selective filtering of signals is not easily compatible with a diffuse projec-tion system. A further argument against the intrinsic selectivity of this system is the observation that large numbers of locus coeruleus neurons appear to discharge synchronously (Aston-Jones & Bloom, 1981b). It is possible that the locus coeruleus may not impose its own selectivity but may facilitate selective processing in the regions that it innervates. The different patterns of noradrenergic innervation in different cortical areas (Morrison et al., 1982), however, suggest some degree of specificity within the noradrenergic system (Foote, Bloom, & Aston-Jones, 1983).

These suggestions from animal experiments that the catecholamine systems may be involved in attention are important to our understand-ing of human attentional disorders. The most effective treatments for these disorders have their primary actions on catecholamines. The neuroleptic drugs used in schizophrenia block the activity of dopamine (Carlsson, 1978). A model for schizophrenia can be found in the psychotic state produced by amphetamines (Ellinwood, 1971). Amphetamines appear to act by elevating the levels of both noradrenaline and dopamine in the brain by increasing their release from neurons and decreasing their reuptake (Holmes & Rutledge, 1976). The concentration of dopamine receptors in schizophrenic brains is abnormally elevated (Lee, Seeman, Tourtellotte, Farley, & Hornykiewicz, 1978).

The attention deficit disorders of childhood (hyperactivity, minimal brain dysfunction) are frequently treated with amphetamines or amphetamine-like drugs such as methylphenidate that increase the release of catecholamines (Margolin, 1978; Shekim, Dekirmenjian, Chapel, Javaid, & Davis, 1979) or with monoamine oxidase inhibitors such as pargyline that decrease the breakdown of catecholamines (Wender, Wood, Reimherr, & Ward, 1983). Shaywitz, Cohen, and Shaywitz (1978) have suggested that dopamine-depleted developing rats may be a model for minimal brain dysfunction, although this model does not show several of the characteristics of the clinical disorder (Pappas, Gallivan, Dugas, Saari, & Ings, 1980).

On superficial examination, it would therefore appear that either increased or decreased levels of the cerebral catecholamines can result in attentional disorder. In schizophrenia, there may an excess of catecholamines, and in hyperactivity a depletion. We could postulate that the processes of attention can only function effectively at some optimal middle concentration of catecholamines. However, the actions of the different drugs may be more complex than initially presumed. The prolonged changes in transmitter concentration brought about by chronic drug administration may alter the sensitivity of the receptors and the metabolism of the transmitter (Chiodo & Bunney, 1983). Exactly how the catecholamines are involved in normal and abnormal attention therefore remains a mystery.

III.A.2. Peptide Hormones

Much recent work has indicated that another family of neurotransmitters (or neurohormones) may be the peptides (Krieger & Martin, 1981). Nerve cells in different parts of the brain have been stained by labelled antisera to peptides, which in some cases are well known for other functions: angiotensin, which is also involved in the regulation of blood pressure; adrenocorticotrophic hormone (ACTH), which also controls the function of the adrenal gland; vasopressin, which is also involved in fluid and electrolyte balance; the enkephalins; and many others. These substances can alter neuronal excitability, and have durations of action that may last for minutes. The enkephalin systems in the brain are closely related to the catecholamine systems. Enkephalin and opiate analgesic drugs such as morphine inhibit the activity of neurons in the locus coeruleus (Korf, Bunney, & Aghajanian, 1974; Williams, Egan, & North, 1982). Opiate antagonists such as naloxone have opposite effects.

The antidiuretic hormone, vasopressin, has been found to be related to learning and attention. Vasopressin is synthesized by neurons of the hypothalamus and released from their terminals in the neurohypophysis. Some of this hormone may also be released into the third ventricle. Vasopressin causes a prolongation of extinction in rats (Koob et al., 1981). Conversely, extinction is more rapid in rats in which vasopressin levels are reduced after ablations of the neurohypophysis (de Wied, van Wimersma Greidanus, Bohus, Urban, & Gispen, 1976), or after administration of a vasopressin-antagonist (Koob et al., 1981).

The second group of peptides that have been related to attention includes ACTH and beta-endorphin. These adenohypophyseal hormones may also be synthesized and released by neurons of the brain. An active peptide component of ACTH (ACTH 4-10) and beta-endorphin have also been found to prolong extinction of active avoidance response in rats (de Wied, Bohus, van Ree, & Urban, 1978). Studies have shown that subcutaneous injections of ACTH 4-10 improve performance on several tests of human attention (Ward, Sandman, George, & Shulman, 1979).

III.A.3. IMPLICATIONS

We have reviewed many experiments suggesting relations between attention and the catecholamine and peptide neurotransmitters. Research has demonstrated that in some cases the primary action of a neurotransmitter may be to influence the responsiveness of a neuron to other synaptic signals rather than to change its overall excitability. This neuromodulation is a key concept for attention. By varying the levels of modulation, the brain may be able to attend to certain aspects of the available information and ignore others. Much additional work will be necessary to clarify the relations between animal studies and human attention. Animal studies of these neurotransmitters using behavioral tests that better reflect attention and that better discriminate between attention and learning will be particularly valuable.

III.B. SUBCORTICAL GATING MECHANISMS

Another active area of investigation is based on the theory that attention is achieved by gating or filtering the sensory signals being transmitted to the cerebral cortex. This gating could occur at any level of the sensory pathways—at the peripheral receptor, at the first synapse in the central nervous system, or in the thalamus, which is the final relay structure of the sensory pathways before the cerebral cortex. Inhibitory feedback mechanisms exist that could prevent or attenuate transmission at all of these levels. However, it is not yet known whether any of these mechanisms are under the control of attention.

One of the earliest physiological theories for attention was that selective gating of attended and ignored sensory information occurred at the level of the first synapse in the sensory pathway (Hernandez-Peon, Scherrer, & Jouvet, 1956). The auditory evoked potential in the cochlear nucleus of an unanesthetized cat decreased in amplitude when two mice in a jar distracted the cat's attention away from the auditory stimuli. These studies were criticized because they lacked any control of the sensory input to the nervous system. The auditory response could have been attenuated by movements of the pinnae away from the source of the sound and not by the postulated central inhibitory processes. Experiments wherein the acoustic input to the nervous system was controlled through the use of earphones and the cutting of the middle-ear muscles showed no definite attentional change in the auditory evoked potentials recorded from the brainstem auditory nuclei (Wickelgren, 1968). However, studies by Oatman (1976), using similarly prepared cats, have shown consistent reductions in the responses of the cochlear nerve and nucleus during attention to a visual stimulus. The primary sensory pathways may therefore show some variability with attentional changes, although this is much less than in the multimodality sensory systems of the brainstem reticular formation and association cortex.

An attractive proposal for the neural basis of selective attention is that sensory input to the cerebral cortex is mainly gated at the level of the thalamus (Scheibel, 1980; Skinner & Yingling, 1977; Yingling & Skinner, 1977). Experiments in cats have shown that the transmission of sensory information through thalamic relay nuclei can be suppressed by cells of the nucleus reticularis thalami, a shell-like layer of cells located around the relay nuclei. The activity of these reticular cells is regulated by inhibitory input from the midbrain reticular formation and excitatory input from the frontal cortex and medial thalamus. Stimulation of the midbrain reticular formation or blockade of the mediothalamic–frontocortical system brings about three physiological events that have been associated with attention: a desynchronization of the electrical activity of the cortex, an enhancement of the sensory evoked potentials in the cortex, and a negative slow potential in the frontal cortex. Modality specificity in selective attention can be explained by this model because neurons in the nucleus reticularis thalami project preferentially to proximal thala-

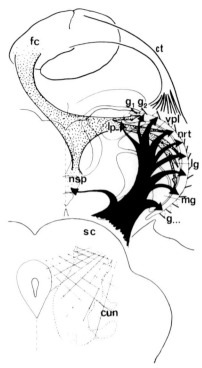

Figure 2.6 Schematic representation of some of the systems operating conjointly upon the gatelets (g1, g2 − g . . .) of the nucleus reticularis thalami (nrt). These gatelets allow or prevent the passage of information from the sensory receptors through the thalamic relay nuclei to the cortex. The ventral posterolateral nucleus (vp1) is the relay nucleus for the somatosensory system. The lateral geniculate (1g) and medial geniculate (mg) nuclei are the relay stations for the visual and auditory systems respectively. The lateroposterior nucleus (1p) is an association nucleus of the thalamus that has extensive connections to the dorsolateral regions of the parietal lobe. The blackened arrow system represents the projection from the deep layers of the superior colliculus (sc) and underlying nucleus cuneiformis (cun) of the mesencephalic tegmentum. Note the shape and the position of the animunculus representing the spatial envelope believed to be coded in this system. The dotted arrow system represents the projections from the frontal granular cortex (fc) and the medial nonspecific thalamus (nsp). The clear arrow system represents the descending corticothalamic projections (ct). The ascending projections from the thalamic relay nuclei to the cortex are not shown. Figure taken from A. B. Scheibel in *The reticular formation revisited* (p. 63) edited by J. A. Hobson and M. A. B. Brazier, 1980, New York: Raven Press. Copyright 1980 by Raven Press. Reprinted by permission.

mic relay nuclei, and there is some evidence that different parts of the reticular nucleus can be selectively activated by the mediothalamic–frontocortical system.

The model is described diagrammatically in Figure 2.6. There are two basic conditions for selective attention: a sufficient degree of alertness (mediated through the midbrain reticular formation) to make it possible to open the thalamic gates, and an intention (mediated through the mediothalamic–frontocortical system) to open one set of gates and close all the others. The model is intuitively appealing but it is difficult to determine whether the effects noted in cats are either necessary for attention or homologous to the attention-related changes recorded in human event-related potentials. Human cortical responses to sensory stimuli are not always altered by attention. Furthermore, the sensory evoked potentials that are most consistently affected by attention in human subjects have much longer latencies than those affected by the thalamic reticular nucleus in cats.

Given the possible activity of subcortical gating mechanisms, the responses of the primary sensory cortices should change with attention. In general, these responses are not very variable. Furthermore, the effects of attention on the responsiveness of the primary sensory cortices differ with the modality of the stimulus. The response of cells in the auditory cortex to tones delivered to an attended ear are larger than their responses to tones in the other ear (Benson & Hienz, 1978). Although there are a few cells in the primary somatosensory area that are affected by attention (Hyrvärinen, Poranen, & Jokinen, 1980), the majority of cells are stable to changes in attentive behavior. Certainly, these cells are much less variable than those of the association cortices (Poranen & Hyrvärinen, 1982). Wurtz and Mohler (1976) found some changes in the responses of striate neurons to visual stimuli in relation to attention. However, these changes were much less than those observed in the parietal cortex or the superior colliculus.

III.C.   Cortical Processes

III.C.1.   Hippocampus

Several experiments indicate that the hippocampus may subserve some aspect of attention. This laminated structure is a phylogenetically old area of cortex that forms an important component of the limbic system of the brain. This structure has a characteristic rhythmic theta activity of 4–7 Hz, the generation of which involves connections from acetylcholine-releasing neurons in the septal area. Three lines of evidence suggest some involvement of the hippocampus in attention: the relations between hippocampal theta activity and the orienting response, the responses of the hippocampus to attended stimuli, and the effects of hippocampal lesions on attention and memory.

There are several reports associating the hippocampus and its characteristic theta activity with the processes involved in orienting and attention. Grastyan, Lissak, Madarasz, and Donhoffer (1959), during studies of conditioned reflexes in cats, noted a strong correlation between theta activity of the hippocampus and the orienting response. They suggested that the hippocampus exerts an inhibitory influence on the orienting response, that theta activity reflects relative inactivity in the hippocampus, and that during theta activity the orienting response is activated by a removal of inhibition. Bennett and his collaborators have extensively studied the relationship of hippocampal theta rhythm to attention (Bennett, 1975). They found the theta rhythm in cats to be strongly correlated with attention to environmental stimuli. When the anticholinergic drug scopolamine was used to block the hippocampal theta activity in cats trained to traverse a runway and make a brightness discrimination, a task normally associated with theta activity, the drug markedly depressed theta activity but had relatively little effect on performance of the task. It must be concluded that although theta activity is strongly correlated with attention, it is not essential for it. In view of the reported associations of attention with both hippocampal theta rhythm and the dorsal noradrenergic bundle, it is interesting to note one report indicating a relationship between them. Gray, McNaughton, James, and Kelly (1975) have found that the septally mediated hippocampal rhythm is facilitated by a noradrenergic input.

The electrical responses of the hippocampus to sensory stimuli depend on their importance to the animal and on how they relate to previous stimuli. Deadwyler, West, and Lynch (1979) reported a large hippocampal negative wave beginning at about 65 ms in response to an auditory tone that was the discriminant stimulus for an operant response. This wave became apparent after the animal had learned the significance of the tone and disappeared during extinction. It seemed to reflect the extraction from the stimulus of information that was important to behavior. Vinogradova (1970) demonstrated that some hippocampal neurons responded to stimulation with an extrapolatory firing pattern that persisted over several seconds. She interpreted her data in terms of the hippocampus comparing the actual sensory input (as coded in the neurons with a transient response) to trace memories of previous input (as coded in the neurons with an extrapolatory response) in order to detect the novelty or the significance of incoming information.

Lesions of the hippocampus can cause disorders of attention and orienting. Rogozea and Ungher (1968) investigated the effect of hippocampal lesions on responses of cats to various types of stimuli. Orienting and investigational responses were generally reduced following the lesions. Hendrickson, Kimble, and Kimble (1969) found that lesions of the dorsal hippocampus in rats resulted in a reduction of orienting responses to a novel auditory stimulus while the animal was involved in other activities, such as drinking after water deprivation or attending to a barrage of noise. The orienting response to the same novel stimulus was not significantly reduced if the animals were not preoccupied with a different activity. In similar experiments, Senba and Iwahara (1974) found that small lesions of the medial septal region abolished hippocampal theta activity and reduced orienting responses to tones during drinking activity. These results suggest that the hippocampus is important for the shifting of attention from one target to another, or for the suppression of ongoing behavioral activity to permit attention to a novel stimulus.

Hippocampal lesions also cause memory problems. Theories have suggested that the hippocampus is involved in cognitive mapping (O'Keefe & Nadel, 1978) or in working memory (Becker, Olton, Anderson, & Breitinger, 1981). It is tempting to speculate that the hippocampus acts in some way to allow attention to incoming information and that this facilitates the imprinting of attended information into long-term memory. Mishkin (1982) has proposed a recognition memory model that involves both the hippocampus and the midline thalamic nuclei in the imprinting of memories in the sensory association areas of the brain. Both circuits may be related to attention, the hippocampus organizing memories on the basis of how they fit with previous knowledge and the midline thalamus (and the frontal cortex) organizing memories on the basis of the individual's needs and goals.

III.C.2. FRONTAL LOBE

Animal experiments on the frontal lobe have indicated that it may function to control attention. Because the role of the frontal lobe in cognition is covered elsewhere in this volume (Goldman-Rakic), this section will only briefly mention some of the basic findings related to attention. Nonhuman primates with bilateral frontal-lobe lesions are unable to perform delayed response or delayed alternation tasks, in which there is a time delay before the required response (Jacobsen, 1936).

Further experiments revealed that the deficit was probably an attentional disorder. Performance could improve if distractions were minimized and if the animal's attention was captured and focused on the task (Malmo, 1942). Furthermore, parsing the events of the task in such a way as to make it easier to remember provided sufficient organization for the lesioned monkeys to overcome their deficit (Pribram & Tubbs, 1967). Cooling of the prefrontal cortex caused a reversible impairment in a delayed matching-to-sample task (Fuster & Bauer, 1974). This deficit was increased when distracting stimuli were presented during the delay interval. Brody and Pribram (1978) showed that monkeys with lesions of the frontal lobe had difficulty in learning a sequence of stimulus–response contingincies when they were presented in a distracting spatial context. These experiments suggest that the frontal lobe acts in some way to prevent distraction.

Several workers (Fuster, 1980; Kojima & Goldman-Rakic, 1982; see also Goldman-Rakic in this volume) have shown that frontal neurons may discharge during the delay period of a delayed-response task. Suzuki and Azuma (1977) found units in the prefrontal cortex that discharged when a monkey gazed at a light spot until it dimmed. These units may have been related to the maintenance of attention on the visual stimulus. In summary, the frontal lobe appears to maintain attention over time and to prevent its distraction.

III.C.3. PARIETAL LOBE

Mountcastle and his colleagues (Lynch, Mountcastle, Talbot, & Yin, 1977; Mountcastle, 1978; Mountcastle, Andersen, & Motter, 1981) have pursued the relationship of single unit activity in the parietal cortex to selective attention. Monkeys were trained to observe a light stimulus and were rewarded for operant responses indicating detection of a slight dimming of intensity of the light. The activity of single neurons of the inferior parietal lobule (area 7) of the cerebral cortex was recorded from chronically implanted recording chambers, permitting the classification of about 70% as having activity changes correlated to behavior. Of these neurons, about 50% could be classified as "visual fixation" neurons, which were active during the fixation of desired objects, or experimental stimuli related to such objects.

Figure 2.7 shows the activity of one of these fixation neurons. The actual function of these cells is not known. They may function in some way to maintain gaze, or they may facilitate sensory processing during the attentive gaze, or they may be related to the preparation for behavioral response to the expected visual stimulus. Other cells fired in relation to saccadic movements that initiated fixation on these stimuli. The increases in neuronal activity were specific in that they did not occur in response to light stimuli or eye movements unrelated to the object of attention; nor did the changes seem simply related to differences in the

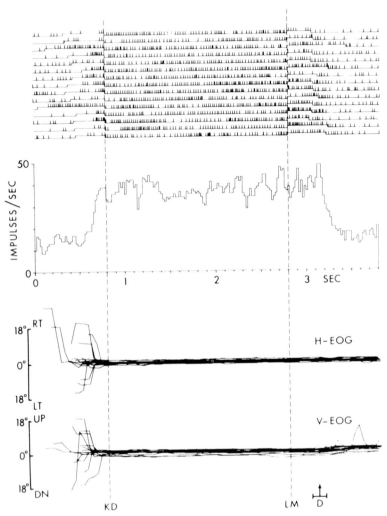

Figure 2.7 A visual fixation neuron. The top of the figure shows the unit discharges recorded during several fixations. In the center is the average neural activity plotted as a histogram in relationship to the time at which the monkey depressed a signal key (KD) in order to detect the dimming of a light (LM) and release the key (D) for reward. At the bottom of the figure are horizontal and vertical oculograms. These show the absence of any eye movement during the period of fixation. Figure taken from Lynch et al. (1977), *Journal of Neurophysiology, 40*, 362–389.

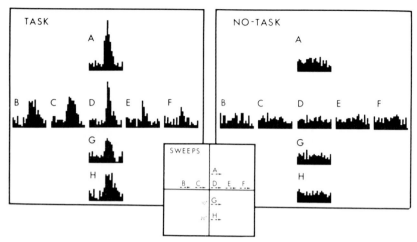

Figure 2.8 The effects of attention upon the responses of a parietal light-sensitive neuron. Histograms are plotted for the neuron's response to a moving visual stimulus. Each histogram represents the average frequency of neuronal discharge over 1.1 seconds. The stimulus begins 400 ms after the initiation of the sweep. The histograms labelled D represent the responses to stimuli moving in the foveal region; histograms B and F represent the responses to stimuli moving in the left and right visual field; histograms A and H represent the responses to stimuli moving above and below the fixation point. During the TASK condition, the monkey fixated a small target light in order to detect a dimming of this light and earn a reward. In the NO-TASK condition, the alert monkey sat facing the visual screen but did not have to attend to any stimuli. Responses were recorded to stimuli presented to the same retinotopic location as in the Task condition. This neuron could be activated in the task state by a stimulus moving toward the right only when the monkey was attending to visual information. When the stimuli were presented to an alert monkey who was not performing any task the same neuron showed no response to the stimuli. Figure from Mountcastle et al. (1981), *Journal of Neuroscience, 1,* 1218–1235. Copyright 1981, the Society for Neuroscience.

state of arousal of the animal. These results have led to the suggestion that the parietal cortex may command eye movements toward a stimulus of interest and visual fixation upon that stimulus.

An important characteristic of one testing paradigm (Mountcastle et al., 1981) was the use of a behaviorally irrelevant stimulus for assessing the excitability of the test neurons. In this case, the test stimulus was not the light that determined the response of the animal but was very similar in character and presented in a different location within the visual field. The enhancement of responses to this passive probe during visual fixation (Figure 2.8) provides both an elegant demonstration that the effect is independent of the behavioral response and an interesting indication of nonspecificity. The attention mechanism appears to have been induced to facilitate responses to many stimuli within a large attended

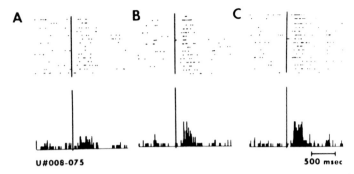

Figure 2.9 Demonstration of both presaccadic and eye-movement-independent enhancement of activity in a parietal neuron. The upper portion of the figure shows the individual trials, with each dot representing a neuronal discharge. The vertical line indicates the onset of the visual stimulus. The lower portion of the figure represents the histogram obtained by averaging these activities together over 15 or 16 trials. (A) This shows the response of a cell to the onset of a visual stimulus while the monkey fixated a small central light and did not attend to the visual stimulus presented lateral to the fixation point. (B) This illustrates the enhanced response to the onset of the same stimulus when the monkey is required to make an eye movement to it from the central fixation point. (C) This shows that the same cell has an enhanced response when the animal must attend to the lateral visual stimulus (in order to detect when it dims) but must do this while maintaining fixation on the central light and not making any eye movement toward the attended stimulus. Figure taken from Bushnell et al. (1981), *Journal of Neurophysiology, 46,* 755–772.

field. If the altered responsiveness truly reflects activity of an attention mechanism, there would appear to be a limit to its selectivity. The task, however, did not require much selectivity since the monkey did not necessarily have to ignore the "irrelevant" stimuli. Paradigms requiring greater attentional tuning may have given a more precise definition of selective facilitation.

Wurtz, Goldberg, and Robinson (1980) have studied cells in the superior colliculus, the visual cortex, the frontal eye fields and the parietal cortex in relation to attention and eye-movements. Monkeys were trained to fixate and to respond to the dimming of a light stimulus. In some cases, the fixated point dimmed, while a separate light stimulus in the receptive field of the recorded cell was used to probe the responsiveness of the cell. In other cases, the fixated light was extinguished and the animal would make a saccadic movement to the second light, which would be dimmed. In other tasks, the animal would be required to detect a lateral stimulus or to reach for it with the hand without moving the eyes from the fixation point (Bushnell, Goldberg, & Robinson, 1981).

Certain cells showed enhanced responses to stimuli that required detection but not any eye movement. Figure 2.9 shows the responses of one such cell. Other cells were activated during saccadic movements to irrelevant stimuli before the operant response, and were thus related to eye movements in a nonselective manner. In their overview of these results, Wurtz and his colleagues have distinguished several kinds of visual neurons. Cells in the primary visual sensory areas may show enhanced responsiveness during attentive behavior but this is spatially nonselective and probably reflects a general arousal process. Cells in the superior colliculus and frontal eye fields can select particular areas of space but only in relation to a required eye-movement. Neurons in the parietal lobe can show an enhanced response to significant stimuli regardless of the type of response that they require. These cells probably function in selective sensory attention.

III.D. Neuronal Models

Attention is a process that involves neurons from many different regions of the brain. The complex relationships among these neurons are very difficult to assess. Two basic principles of neuronal interaction may be important in modelling the processes of attention: lateral inhibition and feedback.

One of the characteristics of neural tissue is the lateral inhibition that results from inhibition between adjacent neurons. An active area of neural tissue will inhibit the responses of less-active adjacent neurons. During sensory processing, this process results in a sharpening of the sensory pattern and an accentuation of selected stimulus characteristics, such as the edges between light and dark visual areas. At higher levels of processing, one can imagine lateral inhibition occurring between the different perceptual templates that are activated by the sensory input in order to select the most appropriate representation for the incoming information. Walley and Weiden (1973) have suggested that lateral inhibition in the association areas of cortex could be the cerebral basis for the attentional selection of one particular set of stimulus–response associations from all of those available. The concept of *contention scheduling* proposed by Shallice (1982) to describe the competition between different stimulus–response action systems for behavioral dominance could be mediated by lateral inhibition, although where this occurs in the brain is unknown. Grossberg (1980) has postulated that the degree and extent of lateral inhibition may be modulated by some general arousal system. Such a system would act to facilitate discrimination and restrict the focus of attention. The catecholamine and peptide systems could possibly function in this way.

Feedback is the process wherein, on the basis of some examination of

potential were small compared to the changes in the later N1 component of the response. Nevertheless, the results do suggest some early selective processes in the analysis of auditory information. Desmedt, Huy, and Bourguet (1983) have reported changes in the somatosensory evoked potential beginning at about 25 ms when subjects discriminated improbable signals. However, in their paradigm, the effects of attention are difficult to distinguish from the effects of probability. Eason, Oakley, and Flowers (1983) have reported changes in the electroretinogram (the electrical response of the retina) when attention is paid to different locations in visual space. These changes were very sensitive to subtle changes in the visual stimuli and were difficult to replicate. Although these ERP studies of human attention have shown some conflicting results, there are some reasonable working conclusions. First, there is no peripheral gating in any all-or-none sense. The brain does not simply turn off unattended sensory receptors. Second, although there may be some attention-mediated alterations in the early analysis of sensory information, these alterations are small.

IV.B.2. PROCESSING NEGATIVITIES

One striking effect of attention on the human ERP is the increase in amplitude of the vertex-negative wave at 100 ms (N100 or N1). Hillyard, Hink, Schwent, and Picton (1973) set up an experiment to evaluate the neurophysiological concomitants of listening to one conversation at a cocktail party and ignoring others. They demonstrated that when a subject attends to auditory stimuli in one ear, the N100 following the attended stimuli is larger than when attention is allocated to the other ear. Some of the results from this experiment are illustrated in Figure 2.10. The N100 effect was best observed at rapid rates of stimulation, perhaps because at slower rates the subject, having nothing better to do, could attend to both ears without decrement in performance (Schwent, Hillyard, & Galambos, 1976a). Furthermore, the N100 effect was less at higher intensities, perhaps because intense stimuli cannot easily be rejected from attentional consideration (Schwent, Hillyard, & Galambos, 1976b). When irrelevant probe stimuli, having similar characteristics to the task-relevant stimuli, were presented in the attended and ignored ears, the evoked potentials to these probes showed the same attentional difference in the N100 as the relevant stimuli (Hink & Hillyard, 1976). This experiment indicates that the N100 effect reflects a selection based not on the significance of the stimuli but on relatively simple physical characteristics—a selection based on stimulus set (Broadbent, 1970; Hillyard & Picton, 1979).

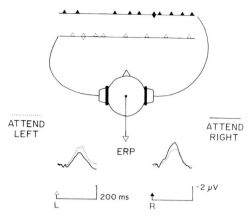

Figure 2.10 Effects of selective attention on the N1 component of the auditory evoked potential. Two concurrent trains of auditory stimuli were presented to the subject, one to each ear. The stimuli were presented fairly rapidly—the diagram shows approximately 4 seconds worth of stimuli. Under one condition, the subject was asked to attend to the stimuli in the left ear (ATTEND LEFT) in order to detect an occasional change in its frequency (indicated by the diamond). In the other condition of the experiment, the subject was requested to attend to the stimuli in the right ear (ATTEND RIGHT) in order to detect an occasional frequency change in the stimuli in that ear. ERPs were recorded from the vertex. The evoked potentials to the stimuli in the left ear (L) are presented on the left and the evoked potentials to the stimuli in the right ear (R) are presented on the right. The evoked potentials recorded when the subject was attending to the stimuli in the left ear are shown by the dotted lines and those recorded when he or she was attending to the stimuli in the right ear are shown by the continuous lines. As can be seen, there is an increase in the amplitude of a negative (upgoing) wave with its peak latency at approximately 100 milliseconds (the N1-component) when the stimuli are attended.

The selective processing that underlies the change in the amplitude of the N100 can occur in the absence of overt response to the attended stimuli. This is useful in several ways. First, the processing of an attentional channel can be evaluated by probe stimuli that elicit an N100 without requiring motor responses that might alter the subject's attentional strategy. Schafer (1978) has shown that the visual evoked potentials to probe stimuli inserted into television programs may demonstrate how interested a viewer is in the program: the smaller the responses to the probes, the more focussed the viewer's attention on the program. Second, the division of attention between channels can be monitored using ERPs. When attention is divided between the ears the amplitude of the N100 wave is between that for the ignored and that for the attended stimuli when attention is focussed on one ear (Hink, Van Voorhis, Hillyard, & Smith, 1977). Finally, the time-course of the N100 effect can delineate how quickly and effectively attention is allocated to a particular channel of sensory information (Donald & Young, 1982).

The change in the amplitude of the N100 with attention is probably best considered in the difference negativity or "Nd" obtained by subtracting the evoked potential to the ignored stimuli from the evoked potential to the same stimuli when they are attended (Hansen & Hillyard, 1980; Hillyard & Kutas, 1983). The exact nature of the Nd wave is unknown. It might represent either the direct facilitation of whatever cerebral processes are responsible for the N100 or an independent cerebral process associated with the attentional selection. In the latter case, it could represent a controlling process directing the selection of stimuli according to certain characteristics, or the accumulation of evidence necessary to decide whether a particular stimulus is to be further evaluated, or the actual processes invoked after a stimulus has been considered appropriate for further analysis. Differences in the scalp distribution of the Nd wave over time raise the possibility that it reflects more than one process—perhaps both the specific attentional processing of sensory association areas and the controlling mechanisms of the frontal cortex. Näätänen and Michie (1979) suggested that the change in N100 amplitude with attention was one example of a processing negativity that is added to the evoked potential when stimuli are selectively attended. They postulated that such a processing negativity might begin earlier and last for a shorter time under conditions of perceptual urgency caused by rapid rates of stimulus-presentation. Then it would appear as an enhancement of the N100 amplitude. Under less-urgent conditions, the processing negativity could begin later and last much longer. In keeping with this concept, Parasuraman (1980) has found the onset of processing negativity to be earlier when attended auditory stimuli are presented more rapidly. Näätänen (1982) has suggested that the processing negativity represents the comparison of incoming information to a sensory template of the stimuli that are to be attended to, and the further processing of those stimuli that fit the template. He postulates two components of the processing negativity: a sensory-specific component that indicates the identification and processing of stimuli within an attended channel, and a frontal component that may reflect the maintenance of the attentional template.

The time-course of the processing negativity varies with the attentional requirements. Hansen and Hillyard (1980) have demonstrated that when the frequencies of the attended and ignored channels are brought closer together, the processing negativity has a later onset. This is illustrated in Figure 2.11. As well, Hansen and Hillyard (1983) have shown that when attention is directed to a stimulus channel characterized by two attributes, one easy to discriminate and one difficult, an early processing negativity occurs in association with the easy discrimi-

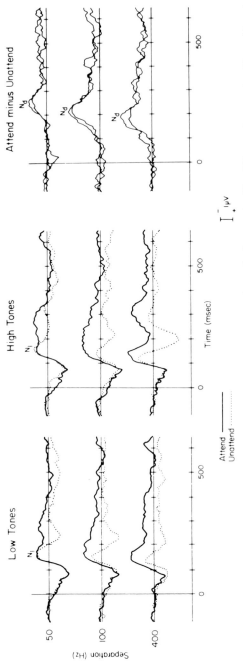

Figure 2.11 The processing negativity or difference wave during attention to channels characterized by different frequencies: The subjects' task was to attend either to a sequence of 300 Hz (low frequency) tones or to a sequence of higher frequency tones in order to detect an occasional tone of longer duration. These waveforms represent the grand average ERPs to the shorter duration tones for 12 subjects at three different interchannel frequency separations. The tracings on the right show the difference waves between the attended and the unattended ERPs for the high tones and the low tones that are plotted on the left and center of the figure. Recordings were taken from the vertex with negativity being represented by an upward deflection. In the difference recordings, there is an Nd wave that has a longer latency when the channels become closer together in frequency. This figure is taken from Hansen and Hillyard (1980), *Electroencephalography and Clinical Neurophysiology, 49,* 277–290.

nation and a second processing negativity is added on if the second attribute is discriminated in a stimulus already recognized as having the first. These findings indicate a hierarchy of processing negativities that may be invoked in the analysis of attended auditory information. Harter and his colleagues (Harter, Aine, & Schroeder, 1982) have suggested a similar series of negative waves in the processing of attended visual stimuli. These negativities are initiated in sequence as different aspects of the visual stimulus are analyzed and continue in parallel until some perceptual decision is made. Ritter, Simson, Vaughan, and Macht (1982) have reported an N_A wave recorded from the occipital region when visual stimuli are being analyzed for selective response. The duration of this wave varies with the complexity of the task and the difficulty experienced in discriminating the stimuli.

It would therefore appear that there are multiple processing negativities. Each would have its own scalp distribution, depending on the different types of analysis required for the attended stimuli. They could represent stimulus-processing that has been facilitated according to the pattern or bias of attentional expectancy. At the same time, there are probably cortical negative waves that reflect the neuronal activity controlling this attentional bias. These ERP studies are complemented by experiments measuring the regional blood flow in human subjects. Roland (1981) has shown that, when attention is directed to the index finger in expectation of a near threshold stimulus, there is an increased blood flow to both the cortical somatosensory area for the finger and the frontal lobe. It is tempting to speculate that these two effects represent the increased processing of attended sensory stimuli in the sensory area and the control of this attentional selectivity by the frontal cortex.

IV.B.3. Signal Detection

The detection of an occasional signal stimulus in a train of standard stimuli is associated with a large negative-positive complex in the evoked potential. The negative wave is called N2 or N200 and the positive wave P3 or P300. Because the latencies of these waves vary, the N2–P3 nomenclature is perhaps more appropriate. Associated with the N2–P3 complex are a late frontal negative wave and a late parietal positive wave, these two components often considered together as the "Slow Wave" (Squires, Squires, & Hillyard, 1975). Figure 2.12 shows the evoked potentials to detected targets in a train of standard auditory stimuli. The N2–P3 components vary more with the psychological sig-

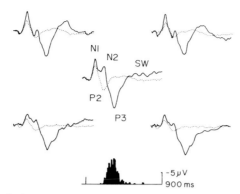

Figure 2.12 Evoked potentials to a detected improbable stimulus. In this experiment, brief tones of moderate intensity were presented every 1.1 seconds to both ears. Most of the stimuli (standards) had a frequency of 1000 Hz, but 10% of the stimuli (targets) had a frequency of 2000 Hz. The subjects were requested to attend to the stimuli and to press a button in their right hand when they detected the occasional targets. Evoked potentials were recorded from left and right frontal (upper line) vertex (second line) and left and right parietal (third line) electrodes using a linked mastoid reference. Negativity at the scalp is represented by an upward deflection. The responses to the standard stimuli are shown with dotted lines and the responses to the occasional targets are shown with continuous lines. In addition to the N1 and P2 components, the evoked potential to the target contains a complex of waves called N2, P3, and slow wave (SW). The N2 of the target-evoked potential overlaps the P2-wave. The slow wave is recorded as a negative wave at the frontal electrodes and as a small positivity in the parietal electrodes (the right parietal). At the bottom of the figure is shown the time scale. The stimulus occurred 50 ms after the beginning of the sweep. Superimposed on the time scale is the reaction time histogram of the button press response. The peak latency of the P3 component is approximately the same as the modal reaction time. The data in this figure represent the average waveforms across four different subjects whose ages were each in the 30s.

nificance of the stimulus to the subject than with the physical characteristics of the stimulus. Indeed, they can be elicited in the absence of any external stimulus when a subject is asked to detect the omission of a stimulus. They are therefore called "endogenous" rather than "exogenous" potentials (Sutton, Braren, Zubin, & John, 1965).

The major determinant of the endogenous components of the evoked potential is the relevance of the signal to the task being performed by the subject. Large endogenous waves are evoked by signals that occur in an attended channel and that the subject perceives as belonging to an improbable category that is relevant to the task being performed (Friedman, Ritter, & Simson, 1978). When signals occur in an unattended

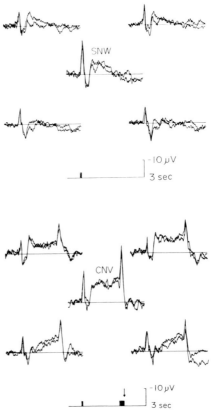

Figure 2.13 Contingent negative variation (CNV): In this experiment, brief tones of either 1000 Hz or 2000 Hz were presented at a rate of once every 6–10 seconds. In the first half of the experiment, the 1000 Hz tones indicated that a buzzer would occur 1.5 seconds later and the 2000 Hz tones indicated that there would not be a buzzer. The subject was requested to turn off the buzzer as quickly as possible by pressing a button. In the second half of the experiment the contingencies were reversed: the 1000 Hz tones indicated that there would be no buzzer and the 2000 Hz tones indicated that there would be an upcoming buzzer to turn off. In the top half of the figure are the ERPs recorded from left and right frontal, vertex, and left and right parietal electrode in association with the stimuli that indicated there would be no buzzer. A slow negative wave (SNW) follows the stimulus. In the bottom half of the figure are shown the ERPs recorded in association with the stimuli that indicated an upcoming buzzer. Now there is a larger negative wave that persists until the buzzer occurs and is turned off (at the time of the arrow). This negative wave is called the contingent negative variation (CNV). The subject was left-handed and was responding with his left index finger. The later part of the contingent negative variation is greater in amplitude over the right frontal region than over the left.

IV.C.   ERPs in Education

IV.C.1.   Evoked Potentials and Intelligence

Intelligence is intimately related to attention. An intelligent individual adopts the most efficient attentive strategy for completing an assigned task. Intelligence is most commonly measured by assessing an individual's performance on problem-solving tests, and expressed as an intelligence quotient or IQ. There has been a long controversy about the relative contributions of genetic and cultural factors to intelligence. If there were large genetically determined individual differences in cognitive ability, a culture-free measurement of these differences could help in determining individual educational requirements. The ERPs have been extensively investigated as possible culture-free indices of intelligence. Five basic kinds of measurement have been assessed: latency, amplitude, scalp-distribution, complexity, and variability.

The basic assumption underlying the latency measurement is that a brain that processes information more quickly will, other abilities being equal, be more capable of solving problems. This argument requires that there be time-limits for the problem-solution (faster processing solving more problems) and/or that there be a time-dependent susceptibility of cerebral processes to noise or decay (faster processing arriving at solutions with less risk of error). Chalke and Ertl (1965) reported a correlation of about -0.3 between peak-latencies in the visual evoked potential and several measures of IQ. These results led to the development and marketing of a "Neural Efficiency Analyzer." Later studies of the relations between ERP latencies and IQ have shown that the correlations vary with the modality and the intensity of the stimulus, with the age, gender, and race of the subject, and with the particular peaks of the ERP being measured (Callaway, 1975). One particular problem with all of the correlations is the variability in alertness that can affect the peak-latencies of the ERP quite independently of intelligence (Shucard & Horn, 1972).

The amplitude of the ERP has not been as extensively related to IQ as the latency, perhaps because the reason for such a relation is not intuitively obvious. Nevertheless, significant correlations between measures of IQ and the amplitudes of certain ERP components have been reported (Eysenck & Barrett, 1985; Shagass, Roemer, Straumanis, & Josiassen, 1981). Robinson (1982) has evaluated the amplitude of the visual steady-state response at different frequencies of stimulation and has derived measures that are purportedly related to activity in a diffuse thalamocortical system. One of these measures, called "V," shows a correlation of about 0.35 to scores on the attention–concentration subtests of the WAIS. Unfortunately, the physiological model on which the measurements are based is too simplistic to allow any meaningful understanding of this correlation.

Scalp-distribution studies may relate the relative activities of different brain areas to intelligent behavior. Rhodes, Dustman, and Beck (1969) reported that visual evoked potentials in more-intelligent children had larger amplitudes over the right hemisphere than over the left. Later studies of this relationship have produced conflicting results. In particular, the correlation of asymmetry to intelligence varies with attention—when subjects attend to the stimuli, the asymmetry decreases. Callaway (1975) hypothesized that the asymmetry recorded in high-IQ subjects merely reflects their tendency to be in a verbal cognitive mode when not attending to the stimuli. This would result in a "busy" left hemisphere unable to respond fully to incoming stimuli.

Hendrickson and Hendrickson (1980) have proposed a complex theory of neural function that relates ERP measures to intelligence. Although the details of the theory are somewhat fanciful, the basic concept is that sensory information is coded in complex neuronal pulse trains. The greater stability of such pulse trains when stimuli conveying the same information are repeated would indicate more intelligent or noise-free cerebral processing. In an intelligent individual, the average evoked potential to an identically repeated stimulus would contain multiple deflections delineating the stable pulse-train coding of the stimulus information. In a less-intelligent individual, noise-induced variations in the pulse train from trial to trial would reduce both the number and the amplitude of the deflections in the average ERP.

The complexity of the average ERP can be assessed using a *string measure*—the waveform is treated like a piece of string and its straightened length is measured. For auditory stimuli, this measure showed a correlation of about 0.5 with measures of IQ. Other researchers have failed to replicate this correlation (Shagass et al., 1981). One difficulty with the string measure of the ERP is that it can be increased by increasing the amount of scalp-muscle noise during the recording. Gritting one's teeth may help one's concentration but it probable does not change one's innate intelligence.

Several experiments have pointed to possible relations between ERP variability and intelligence. These experiments derive from the concept that an intelligent brain is more adaptable and more able to consider the world in different ways. This represents the opposite theoretical position from that underlying the string measure: one person's noise is another's adaptibility. Several measures of trial-to-trial ERP variability may correlate with intelligence (Callaway, 1975) but these relations are far from consistent from one experiment to another. Furthermore, it is extremely difficult to distinguish variability in the actual ERP from variability in the background EEG noise.

Schafer (1982) has assessed the variability of the evoked potential that is related to whether an auditory stimulus can be expected or predicted. The basic hypothesis was that a "brain that efficiently inhibits its response to insignificant stimuli and orients vigorously to potentially dangerous inputs should also be the brain which shows high behavioral intelligence" (Schafer, 1982). In one condition, "self stimulation," the auditory stimulus occurred only when the subject pressed a button; in a second condition, "random stimulation," the stimulus occurred unpredictably at intervals determined by the previous self-stimulation condition. The evoked potentials were smaller during self-stimulation and larger during random stimulation, this difference being larger for more intelligent subjects.

A "neural adaptibility" score derived from ratios between the ERP amplitudes in the different conditions correlated 0.66 with measures of IQ. Although the paradigm is intriguing, there are many confounding variables. Different subjects will find the different conditions more or less interesting and will therefore vary in the amount of attention paid to the stimuli. The act of pressing the button will itself evoke potentials that will add to and distort those evoked by the auditory stimulus. The theory is not totally compatible with the data because a very intelligent individual should have found all of the stimuli equally meaningless.

In this section, we have briefly reviewed several attempts to determine an ERP measure of innate intelligence. The field is characterized by a wealth of disparate and sometimes contradictory theory. No one knows what is required of a brain to be intelligent, let alone how to measure it with ERPs. Many of the studies correlating ERP components to IQ have involved presenting simple stimuli to passive subjects. It is difficult to determine how ERP measures can index intelligence when the brain that is generating the ERPs is not required to act intelligently.

ERPs are affected by the attentive strategy of the subject and because this depends on the subject's educational background, ERP measures are not culture-free. It is probable, however, that certain ERP components, reflecting particular cerebral processes, might correlate with performance on behavioral tests that require these processes. A direct approach to relating ERPs to intelligence would be to record ERPs during the performance of tasks similar to those that are used in intelligence tests. In this way ERPs could be used to provide a physiological task-analysis of intelligent behavior.

IV.C.2.   HUMAN COGNITIVE DEVELOPMENT

There have been many studies evaluating the development of the human brain through changes in the ERPs. Many of these have been mainly concerned with the maturation of sensory pathways, as revealed in the exogenous potentials. Some of the most exciting studies have assessed the development of the endogenous components of the human ERP (Courchesne, 1983). The ERPs can show that the processes of cognition in children are quite different from those in adults. Courchesne and his colleagues have been using a paradigm wherein, while a subject is looking at a sequence of simple visual stimuli (for example "A") in order to detect an improbable "target" stimulus (for example "B"), some equally improbable but "novel" stimuli occur. Each of the novel stimuli is unique and has not been previously seen by the subject. In adults the ERP to the novel stimuli contained a frontal late positive wave. In children, there was a very different response characterized by a large frontal negative wave (Nc) followed by a positive wave (Pc). The Nc wave may be associated with the evaluation of events that are considered interesting but for which there is no immediately available interpretation. The adults would be likely to interpret the novel stimuli as irrelevant nonsense. It is possible that some of the late negative waves reported in adults following semantically incongruous words or pictures represent a similar brain process.

IV.D.   ERPs IN DISORDERS OF ATTENTION

The neurophysiology of human attention has been studied in three groups of patients with attention deficits. Knight and his colleagues (1984) have shown that during a selective attention task, patients with lesions of the frontal lobe have a processing negativity that is smaller than in normal subjects. This suggests that the frontal cortex plays a definite role in the control of stimulus-set attention. Loiselle, Stamm, Maitinsky, and Whipple (1980) have shown both a reduced processing negativity and a reduced P3 amplitude in children with hyperactivity. This suggests a rather general disorder of attention in these subjects. Baribeau-Braun, Picton, and Gosselin (1983) have shown a definite processing negativity in schizophrenic patients during some attention tasks but not in others. The amplitude of the P3 was decreased in all tasks. These results suggest that schizophrenic subjects are able to attend selectively to different channels of information but are unable to process information from those channels in a manner appropriate to the goals of the task. The results of these initial evaluations are promising. Further studies should increase our understanding both of these attentional deficits and of the processes of normal attention.

The effects of different drugs on the ERP may be able to shed some light on the pathophysiology of the disorders that they are used to treat. Although there have been many pharmacological studies of the exogenous potentials there have only been a few concerning the endogenous components. Klorman, Salzman, Bauer, Coons, Borgstedt, and Halpern (1983) have shown that methylphenidate, an aminergic agonist, increases the amplitude of the P3 component of the ERP in children with hyperactivity. Arnsten et al. (1983) have shown that the narcotic antagonist naloxone increases the amplitude of the Nd wave during selective auditory attention. These results suggest that the endogenous opioid peptides (or the catecholamines with which they interact) may be involved in the regulation of selective attention.

Two major systems have used multivariate analysis to evaluate the EEGs and ERPs of children with learning problems: neurometrics (John, 1977) and brain electrical activity mapping (BEAM) (Duffy, Burchfiel, & Lombroso, 1979). The basic idea behind these approaches is that there is much more information in the EEG and ERP than can be assessed by a few simple measures of amplitude, latency, and frequency. Two kinds of data analysis can be performed. The first analysis, which has been used by both systems, is to determine what patterns in the data discriminate different groups of patients that have been diagnosed by other means. This discrimination has a twofold purpose: The measures that best discriminate the groups may portray the characteristic pathophysiology of the disorders; and the resultant discriminant function could be used in undiagnosed groups of patients. The second analysis, which has been used in the neurometric approach, determines whether the data can cluster the patients into different groups, each characterized by a different pattern of physiological measures. This neurophysiological taxonomy could then be used to identify groups of patients that could not be distinguished by other means.

Although these techniques provide intriguing new data, the results should be interpreted cautiously. First, there are many different EEG and ERP patterns that are not clearly correlated to any brain function or dysfunction. Electroencephalographers often recognize unusual or anomalous patterns that have no clinical significance. When the multivariate analysis recognizes similar patterns, the groups of patients that it differentiates may not be meaningful. Some other source of evaluation must be used to validate the physiological taxonomy. Second, the techniques of multivariate analysis are extremely efficient. They can order the data to produce significant distinctions or clusters on the basis of any

Army Individual Test Battery. (1944). *Manual of directions and scoring, U.S. Army.* Washington, DC: War Department, Adjutant General's Office.

Arnsten, A. F. T., Segal, D. S., Neville, H. J., Hillyard, S. A., Janowsky, D. S., Judd, L. L., & Bloom, F. E. (1983). Naloxone augments electrophysiological signs of selective attention in man. *Nature, 304,* 725–727.

Asarnow, R. F., MacCrimmon, D. J., Cleghorn, J. M. & Steffry, R. A. (1978). The McMaster–Waterloo Project: An attentional and clinical assessment of foster children at risk for schizophrenia. In L. C. Wynne, R. L. Cromwell, & S. Matthysee (Eds.), *The nature of schizophrenia.* New York: Wiley.

Aston-Jones, G., & Bloom, F. E. (1981a). Activity of norepinephrine containing locus coeruleus neurons in behaving rats anticipates fluctuations in the sleep-waking cycle. *Journal of Neuroscience, 1,* 876–886.

Aston-Jones, G., & Bloom, F. E. (1981b). Norepinephrine-containing locus coeruleus neurons in behaving rats exhibit pronounced responses to non-noxious environmental stimuli. *Journal of Neuroscience, 1,* 887–900.

Baird, H. W., John, E. R., Ahn, H., & Maisel, E. (1980). Neurometric evaluation of epileptic children who do well and poorly in school. *Electroencephalography and Clinical Neurophysiology, 48,* 683–693.

Baribeau-Braun, J., Picton, T. W., & Gosselin, J.-Y. (1983). Schizophrenia: A neurophysiological evaluation of abnormal information processing. *Science, 219,* 874–876.

Barkley, R. A. (1977). A review of stimulant drug research with hyperactive children. *Journal of Child Psychology and Psychiatry and Allied Disciplines, 18,* 137–165.

Becker, J. T., Olton, D. S., Anderson, C. A., & Breitinger, E. R. P. (1981). Cognitive mapping in rats: The role of the hippocampal and frontal systems in retention and reversal. *Behavioural Brain Research, 3,* 1–22.

Bennett, T. L. (1975). The electrical activity of the hippocampus and processes of attention. In R. L. Isaacson & K. H. Pribram (Eds.), *The hippocampus: Vol. 2. Neurophysiology and behavior* (pp. 71–99). New York: Plenum.

Benson, D. A., & Hienz, R. D. (1978). Single-unit activity in the auditory cortex of monkeys selectively attending left vs. right ear stimuli. *Brain Research, 159,* 307–320.

Benson, D. F., & Geschwind, N. (1975). Psychiatric conditions associated with focal lesions of the central nervous system. In S. Arieti & M. Reiser (Eds.), *American handbook of psychiatry: Vol. 4. Organic disorders and psychosomatic medicine* (pp. 208–243). New York: Basic Books.

Bisiach, E., & Luzzatti, C. (1978). Unilateral neglect of representational space. *Cortex, 14,* 129–133.

Bloom, F. E. (1978). Central noradrenergic systems: Physiology and pharmacology. In M. A. Lipton, A. DiMassio, & K. F. Killam, *Psychopharmacology: A generation of progress* (pp. 131–141). New York: Raven.

Broadbent, D. E. (1970). Stimulus set and response set: Two kinds of selective attention. In D. I. Mostofsky (Ed.), *Attention: Contemporary theory and analysis* (pp. 51–60). New York: Appleton-Century-Crofts.

Brody, B. A., & Pribram, K. H. (1978). The role of the frontal and parietal cortex in cognitive processing. *Brain, 101,* 607–633.

Bushnell, M. C., Goldberg, M. E., & Robinson, D. L. (1981). Behavioral enhancement of visual responses in monkey cerebral cortex. I. Modulation in posterior parietal cortex related to selective visual attention. *Journal of Neurophysiology, 46,* 755–772.

Callaway, E. (1975). *Brain electrical potentials and individual psychological differences.* New York: Grune & Stratton.

Campbell, K. B., Courchesne, E., Picton, T. W., & Squires, K. C. (1979). Evoked potential correlates of human information processing. *Biological Psychology, 8,* 45–68.

Carlsson, A. (1978). Antipsychotic drugs, neurotransmitters, and schizophrenia. *American Journal of Psychiatry, 135*(2), 164–173.

Chalke, F. C. R., & Ertl, J. (1965). Evoked potentials and intelligence. *Life Sciences, 4,* 1319–1322.

Chiodo, L. A., & Bunney, B. S. (1983). Typical and atypical neuroleptics: Differential effects of chronic administration on the activity of A9 and A10 midbrain dopaminergic neurons. *Journal of Neuroscience, 3*(8), 1607–1619.

Courchesne, E. (1983). Cognitive components of the event-related brain potential: Changes associated with development. In A. W. K. Gaillard & W. Ritter *Tutorials in ERP research: Endogenous components* (pp. 329–344). Amsterdam: North-Holland.

Crow, T. J., Deakin, J. F. W., File, S. E., Longden, A., & Wendlandt, S. (1978). The locus coeruleus noradrenergic system—evidence against a role in attention, habituation, anxiety and motor activity. *Brain Research, 155,* 249–261.

Damasio, A. R., Damasio, H., & Chang Chui, H. (1980). Neglect following damage to frontal lobe or basal ganglia. *Neuropsychologia, 18,* 123–132.

Deadwyler, S. A., West, M., & Lynch, G. (1979). Synaptically identified hippocampal slow potentials during behaviour. *Brain Research, 161,* 211–225.

Desmedt, J. E., Huy, N. T., & Bourguet, M. (1983). The cognitive P40, N60 and P100 components of somatosensory evoked potentials and the earliest electrical signs of sensory processing in man. *Electroencephalography and Clinical Neurophysiology, 56,* 272–282.

de Wied, D., Bohus, B., van Ree, J. M., & Urban, I. (1978). Behavioral and electrophysiological effects of peptides related to lipotropin (B-LPH). *Journal of Pharmacology and Experimental Therapeutics, 204,* 570–580.

de Wied, D., van Wimersma Greidanus, Tj. B., Bohus, B., Urban, I., & Gispen, W. H. (1976). Vasopressin and memory consolidation. In M. A. Corner & D. F. Swaab (Eds.) *Progress in brain research: Vol. 45. Perspectives in brain research.* Amsterdam: Elsevier (pp. 181–194).

Donald, M. W. (1979). Limits on current theories of transient evoked potentials. In J. E. Desmedt (Ed.) *Progress in clinical neurophysiology: Vol. 6. Cognitive components in cerebral event-related potentials and selective attention* (pp. 187–199). Basel: Karger.

Donald, M. W. (1983). Neural selectivity in auditory attention: Sketch of a theory. In A. Gaillard & W. Ritter (Eds.), *Tutorials in ERP research: Endogenous components* (pp. 37–77). Amsterdam: North Holland.

Donald, M. W., & Young, M. J. (1982). The time course of selective neural tuning in auditory attention. *Experimental Brain Research, 46,* 357–367.

Donchin, E. (1979). Event-related brain potentials: A tool in the study of human information processing. In H. Begleiter (Ed.), *Evoked brain potentials and behavior* (pp. 13–88). New York: Plenum Press.

Dragunow, M. & Laverty, R. (1983). Failure of dorsal bundle lesions in rats to increase distractability to a low intensity tone. *Pharmacology, Biochemistry & Behaviour, 18,* 673–675.

Duffy, F. H., Burchfiel, J. L., & Lombroso, C. T. (1979). Brain electrical activity mapping (BEAM): A method of extending the clinical utility of EEG and evoked potential data. *Annals of Neurology, 5,* 309–321.

Duffy, F. H., Denckla, M. B., Bartels, P. H., & Sandini, G. (1980a). Dyslexia: Regional differences in brain electrical activity by topographic mapping. *Annals of Neurology, 7,* 412–420.

Duffy, F. H., Denckla, M. B., Bartels, P. H., Sandini, G., & Kiessling, L. S. (1980b). Dyslexia: Automated diagnosis by computerized classification of brain electrical activity. *Annals of Neurology, 7,* 421–428.

Duncan-Johnson, C. C., & Donchin, E. (1977). On quantifying surprise: The variation in event-related potentials with subjective probability. *Psychophysiology, 14,* 456–467.

Eason, R. G., Oakley, M., & Flowers, L. (1983). Central neural influences on the human retina during selective attention. *Physiological Psychology, 11,* 18–28.

Ellinwood, E. H. (1971). Effect of chronic methamphetamine intoxication in rhesus monkeys. *Biological Psychiatry, 3,* 25–32.

Eson, M. E., Yen, J. K., & Bourke, R. S. (1978). Assessment of recovery from serious head injury. *Journal of Neurology, Neurosurgery and Psychiatry, 41,* 1036–1042.

Eysenck, H. J., & Barrett, P. (1985). Psychophysiology and the measurement of intelligence. In C. R. Reynolds & V. Willson (Eds.), *Methodological and statistical advances in the study of individual differences.* New York: Plenum Press.

Fitzgerald, P. G., & Picton, T. W. (1981). Temporal and sequential probability in evoked potential studies. *Canadian Journal of Psychology, 35,* 188–200.

Foote, S. L., Aston-Jones, G., & Bloom, F. E. (1980). Impulse activity of locus coeruleus neurons in awake rats and monkeys is a function of sensory stimulation and arousal. *Proceedings of the National Academy of Sciences of the U.S.A., 77,* 3033–3037.

Foote, S. L., Bloom, F. E., & Aston-Jones, G. (1983). Nucleus locus ceruleus: New evidence of anatomical and physiological specificity. *Physiological Reviews, 63*(3), 844–914.

Foote, S. L., Freedman, A., & Oliver, A. P. (1975). Effects of putative neurotransmitters on neuronal activity in monkey auditory cortex. *Brain Research, 86,* 229–242.

Friedland, R. P., & Weinstein, E. A. (1977). Hemi-inattention and hemisphere specialization: Introduction and historical review. In E. A. Weinstein & R. P. Friedland (Eds.) *Advances in Neurology: Vol. 18. Hemi-inattention and Hemisphere Specialization* (pp. 1–31). New York: Raven.

Friedman, D., Ritter, W., & Simson, R. (1978). Analysis of non-signal evoked cortical potentials in two kinds of vigilance tasks. In D. Otto (Ed.), *Multidisciplinary perspectives in event-related brain potential research,* EPA-600/9-77-043 (pp. 194–197). Washington, DC: Government Printing Office.

Fuster, J. M. (1980). *The prefrontal cortex: Anatomy, physiology and neuropsychology of the frontal lobe.* New York: Raven Press.

Fuster, J. M., & Bauer, R. H. (1974). Visual short-term memory deficit from hypothermia of frontal cortex. *Brain Research, 81,* 393–400.

Geschwind, N. (1982). Disorders of attention: A frontier in neuropsychology. *Philosophical Transactions of the Royal Society of London, series B, 289,* 173–185.

Goodglass, H., & Kaplan, E. (1979). Assessment of cognitive deficit in the brain-injured patient. In M. S. Gazzaniga (Ed.), *Handbook of behavioral neurobiology: Vol. 2. Neuropsychology* (pp. 3–22). New York: Plenum Press.

Grant, D. A. & Berg, E. A. (1948). A behavioral analysis of degree of reinforcement and ease of shifting to new responses in a Weigl-type card-sorting problem. *Journal of Experimental Psychology, 18,* 404–411.

Grastyan, E., Lissak, K., Madarasz, I., & Donhoffer, H. (1959). Hippocampal electrical activity during the development of conditioned reflexes. *Electroencephalography and Clinical Neurophysiology, 11,* 409–430.

Gray, J. A., McNaughton, N., James, D. T. D., & Kelly, P. H. (1975). Effects of minor tranquillisers on hippocampal theta rhythm mimicked by depletion of forebrain noradrenaline. *Nature, 258,* 424–425.

Gronwall, D. M. A. (1977). Paced auditory serial-addition task: A measure of recovery from concussion. *Perceptual and Motor Skills, 44,* 367–373.

Grossberg, S. (1980). How does a brain build a cognitive code? *Psychological Review, 87,* 1–51.

Halgren, E., Squires, N. K., Wilson, C. L., Rohrbaugh, J. W., Babb, T. L., & Crandall, P. H. (1980). Endogenous potentials generated in the human hippocampal formation and amygdala by infrequent events. *Science, 210,* 803–805.

Hansen, J. C., & Hillyard, S. A. (1980). Endogenous brain potentials associated with selective auditory attention. *Electroencephalography and Clinical Neurophysiology, 49,* 277–290.

Hansen, J. C., & Hillyard, S. A. (1983). Selective attention to multidimensional auditory stimuli. *Journal of Experimental Psychology: Human Perception and Performance, 9,* 1–19.

Harlow, J. M. (1868). Recovery after severe injury to the head. *Publications of the Massachusetts Medical Society of Boston, 2,* 327–346.

Harter, M. R., Aine, C., & Schroeder, C. (1982). Hemispheric differences in the neural processing of stimulus location and type: Effects of selective attention on visual evoked potentials. *Neuropsychologia, 20*(4), 421–438.

Heilman, K. M. (1979). Neglect and related disorders. In K. Heilman & E. Valenstein (Eds.), *Clinical neuropsychology* (pp. 268–307). New York: Oxford Press.

Heilman, K. M., & Valenstein, E. (1972). Frontal lobe neglect in men. *Neurology, 2,* 660–664.

Heilman, K. M., & Watson, R. T. (1977). Mechanisms underlying the unilateral neglect syndrome. In E. A. Weinstein & R. P. Friedland (Eds.), *Advances in neurology* (Vol. 18). New York: Raven Press.

Hendrickson, C. W., Kimble, R. J., & Kimble, D. P. (1969). Hippocampal lesions and the orienting response. *Journal of Comparative and Physiological Psychology, 67,* 220–227.

Hendrickson, D. E., & Hendrickson, A. E. (1980). The biological basis of individual differences in intelligence. *Personality and Individual Differences, 1,* 3–33.

Hernandez-Peon, R., Scherrer, H., & Jouvet, M. (1956). Modification of electrical activity in the cochlear nucleus during attention in unanesthetized cats. *Science, 123,* 331–332.

Heywood, S., & Ratcliff, G. (1975). Long-term oculomotor consequences of unilateral collicullectomy in man. In G. Lennerstrand & P. Bach-y-Rita (Eds.) *Symposium on basic mechanisms of ocular motility and their clinical implications* (pp. 561–564). New York: Oxford University Press.

Hillyard, S. A., Hink, R. F., Schwent, V. L., & Picton, T. W. (1973). Electrical signs of selective attention in the human brain. *Science, 182,* 177–180.

Hillyard, S. A., & Kutas, M. (1983). Electrophysiology of cognitive processing. *Annual Review of Psychology, 34,* 33–61.

Hillyard, S. A., & Picton, T. W. (1979). Event-related brain potentials and selective information processing in man. In J. E. Desmedt (Ed.), *Progress in clinical neurophysiology: Vol. 6. Cognitive components in cerebral event-related potentials and selective attention* (pp. 1–50). Basel: Karger.

Hink, R. F., & Hillyard, S. A. (1976). Auditory evoked potentials during selective listening to dichotic speech messages. *Perception and Psychophysics, 20,* 236–242.

Hink, R. F., Van Voorhis, S. T., Hillyard, S. A., & Smith, T. (1977). The division of attention and the human auditory evoked potential. *Neuropsychologia, 15,* 597–605.

Holmes, J. C., & Rutledge, C. O. (1976). Effects of the d- and 1-isomers of amphetamine on uptake, release and catabolism of norepinephrine, dopamine and 5-hydroxytrypt-amine in several regions of rat brain. *Biochemical Pharmacology, 25,* 447–451.

Hyrvärinen, J., Poranen, A., & Jokinen, Y. (1980). Influence of attentive behavior on neuronal responses to vibration in primary somatosensory cortex of the monkey. *Journal of Neurophysiology, 43,* 870–882.

Ingvar, D. H., & Franzen, G. (1974). Distribution of cerebral activity in chronic schizophrenia. *Lancet, 2,* 1084–1086.

Jacobsen, C. F. (1936). Studies of cerebral functions in primates. I. The functions of the frontal association areas in monkeys. *Comparative Psychology Monographs, 13,* 3–60.

James, W. (1950). *The Principles of Psychology.* New York: Dover. (Original work published 1890.)

John, E. R. (1977). *Functional neuroscience: Vol. 2. Neurometrics: Clinical applications of quantitative electrophysiology.* Hillsdale, NJ: Erlbaum.

Joseph, M. H., Frith, C. D., & Waddington, J. L. (1979). Dopaminergic mechanisms and cognitive deficit in schizophrenia. *Psychopharmacology, 63,* 273–280.

Kaye, H., John, E. R., Ahn, H., & Prichep, L. (1981). Neurometric evaluation of learning disabled children. *International Journal of Neuroscience, 13,* 15–25.

Kinsbourne, M. (1977). Hemi-neglect and hemisphere rivalry. In E. A. Weinstein & R. P. Friedland (Eds.), *Advances in neurology: Vol. 18. Hemi-inattention and hemisphere specialization* (pp. 41–49). New York: Raven Press.

Klorman, R., Salzman, L. F., Bauer, L. O., Coons, H. W., Borgstedt, A. D., & Halpern, W. I. (1983). Effects of two doses of methylphenidate on cross-situational and borderline hyperactive children's evoked potentials. *Electroencephalography and Clinical Neurophysiology, 56,* 169–185.

Knight, R. T., Hillyard, S. A., Woods, D. L., & Neville, H. J. (1981). The effects of frontal cortex lesions on event-related potentials during auditory selective attention. *Electroencephalography and Clinical Neurophysiology, 52,* 571–582.

Kojima, S., & Goodman-Rakic, P. S. (1982). Delay-related activity of prefrontal neurons in rhesus monkeys performing delayed response. *Brain Research, 248,* 43–49.

Koob, G. F., Le Moal, M., Gaffori, O., Manning, M., Sawyer, W. H., Rivier, J., & Bloom, F. E. (1981). Arginine vasopressin and a vasopressin antagonist peptide: Opposite effects on extinction of active avoidance in rats. *Regulatory Peptides, 2,* 153–163.

Korf, J., Bunney, B. S., & Aghajanian, G. K. (1974). Noradrenergic neurons: Morphine inhibition of spontaneous activity. *European Journal of Pharmacology, 25,* 165–169.

Krieger, D. T., & Martin, J. B. (1981). Brain peptides. *New England Journal of Medicine, 304,* 876–885, 944–951.

Kutas, M., & Hillyard, S. A. (1980). Reading senseless sentences: Brain potentials reflect semantic incongruity. *Science, 207,* 203–205.

Kutas, M., & Hillyard, S. A. (1984). Brain potentials reflect word expectancy and semantic association during reading. *Nature, 307,* 161–163.

Kutas, M., McCarthy, G., & Donchin, E. (1977). Augmenting mental chronometry: The P300 as a measure of stimulus evaluation time. *Science, 197,* 792–795.

Lee, T., Seeman, P., Tourtellotte, W. W., Farley, I. J., & Hornykiewicz, O. (1978). Binding of 3H-neuroleptics and 3H-apomorphine in schizophrenic brains. *Nature 274,* 897–900.

Lezak, M. D. (1976). *Neuropsychological assessment.* New York: Oxford University.

Loiselle, D. L., Stamm, J. S., Maitinsky, S., & Whipple, S. C. (1980). Evoked potential and behavioral signs of attentive dysfunctions in hyperactive boys. *Psychophysiology, 17,* 193–201.

Loveless, N. E., & Sanford, A. J. (1974). Slow potential correlates of preparatory set. *Biological Psychology, 1,* 303–314.

Lukas, J. (1981). The role of efferent inhibition in human auditory attention: An examination of the auditory brainstem potentials. *International Journal of Neuroscience, 12,* 137–145.

Luria, A. R. (1980). *Higher cortical functions in man* (2nd ed.). (B. Haigh, Trans.), New York: Basic Books.

Lynch, J. C., Mountcastle, V. B., Talbot, W. H., & Yin, T. C. T. (1977). Parietal lobe mechanisms for directed visual attention. *Journal of Neurophysiology, 40,* 361–389.

Malmo, R. B. (1942). Interference factors in delayed response in monkeys after removal of frontal lobes. *Journal of Neurophysiology, 5,* 295–308.

Margolin, D. I. (1978). The hyperkinetic child syndrome and brain monoamines: Pharmacology and therapeutic implications. *Journal of Clinical Psychiatry, 39,* 120–130.

Marshall, K. C. (1983). Catecholamines and their actions in the spinal cord. In Davidoff, R. A. (Ed.), *Handbook of the spinal cord: Vol. 1. Pharmacology* (pp. 275–328). New York: Marcel Dekker.

Mason, S. T. (1981). Noradrenaline in the brain: Progress in theories of behavioral function. *Progress in Neurobiology, 16,* 263–303.

McCallum, W. C., Curry, S. H., Cooper, R., Pocock, P. V., & Papakostopoulos, D. (1983). Brain event-related potentials as indicators of early selective processes in auditory target localization. *Psychophysiology, 20,* 1–17.

McCarthy, G., & Donchin, E. (1981). A metric for thought: A comparison of P300 latency and reaction time. *Science, 211,* 77–79.

McGhie, A., & Chapman, J. (1961). Disorders of attention and perception in early schizophrenia. *British Journal of Medical Psychology, 34,* 103–116.

Meichenbaum, D., & Goodman, J. (1971). Training impulsive children to talk to themselves: A means of developing self-control. *Journal of Abnormal Psychology, 77,* 115–126.

Mesulam, M.-M. (1981). A cortical network for directed attention and unilateral neglect. *Annals of Neurology, 10,* 309–325.

Mesulam, M.-M., & Geschwind, N. (1978). On the possible role of neocortex and its limbic connections in the process of attention and schizophrenia: Clinical cases of inattention in man and experimental anatomy in monkey. *Journal of Psychiatric Research, 14,* 249–259.

Mesulam, M.-M., Waxman, S. G., Geschwind, N., & Sabin, T. D. (1976). Acute confusional states with right middle cerebral artery infarctions. *Journal of Neurology, Neurosurgery and Psychiatry, 39,* 84–89.

Michie, P. T. (1984). Selective attention effects on somatosensory event-related potentials. In R. Karrer, J. Cohen, & P. Teuting (Eds.), *Brain and Information: Event-Related Potentials,* New York: New York Academy of Science. *425,* 250–255.

Milner, B. (1964). Some effects of frontal lobectomy in man. In J. M. Warner & K. Akert (Eds.) *The frontal granular cortex and behaviour* (pp. 313–334). New York: McGraw-Hill.

Mishkin, M. (1982). A memory system in the monkey. *Philosophical Transactions of the Royal Society of London, Series B, 298,* 85–95.

Moore, R. Y. (1982). Catecholamine neuron systems in brain. *Annals of Neurology, 12,* 321–327.

Morrison, J. H., Foote, S. L., O'Connor, D., & Bloom, F. E. (1982). Laminar, tangential and regional organization of the noradrenergic innervation of monkey cortex: Dopamine-B-hydroxylase immunohistochemistry. *Brain Research Bulletin, 9,* 309–319.

Mountcastle, V. B. (1978). Brain mechanisms for directed attention. *Journal of the Royal Society of Medicine, 71,* 14–28.

Mountcastle, V. B., Andersen, R. A., & Motter, B. C. (1981). The influence of attentive fixation upon the excitability of the light-sensitive neurons of the posterior parietal cortex. *Journal of Neuroscience, 1*, 1218–1235.

Näätänen, R. (1982). Processing negativity—evoked potential reflection of selective attention. *Psychological Bulletin, 92*, 605–640.

Näätänen, R., & Michie, P. T. (1979). Early selective-attention effects on the evoked potential: A critical review and reinterpretation. *Biological Psychology, 8*, 81–136.

Nauta, J. H. W. (1971). The problem of the frontal lobe: A reinterpretation. *Journal of Psychiatric Research, 8*, 167–187.

Norrman, B., & Svahn, K. (1961). A follow-up study of severe brain injuries. *Acta Psychiatrica et Neurologica Scandinavica, 37*, 236–264.

Oatman, L. C. (1976). Effects of visual attention on the intensity of auditory evoked potentials. *Experimental Neurology, 51*, 41–53.

Oke, A. F., & Adams, R. N. (1978). Selective attention dysfunctions in adult rats neonatally reated with 6-hydroxydopamine. *Pharmacology, Biochemistry and Behavior, 9*, 429–432.

O'Keefe, J., & Nadel, L. (1978). *The hippocampus as a cognitive map*. London: Oxford University Press.

Ommaya, A. K., & Gennarelli, T. A. (1976). A physiopathological basis for noninvasive diagnosis and prognosis of head injury severity. In R. McLaurin (Ed.). *Head injuries: Second Chicago symposium on neural trauma* (pp. 49–75). New York: Grune & Stratton.

Pappas, B. A., Gallivan, J. V., Dugas, T., Saari, M., & Ings, R. (1980). Intraventricular 6-hydroxydopamine in the newborn rat and locomotor responses to drugs in infancy: No support for the dopamine depletion model of minimal brain dysfunction. *Psychopharmacology, 70*, 41–46.

Parasuraman, R. (1980). Effects of information processing demands on slow negative shift latencies and N100 amplitude in selective and divided attention. *Biological Psychology, 11*, 217–233.

Picton, T. W., Donchin, E., Ford, J., Kahneman, D., & Norman, D. (1984). The ERP and decision and memory processes. In E. Donchin (Ed.), *Cognitive psychophysiology* (pp. 139–177). Hillside, NJ: Erlbaum.

Picton, T. W., & Hillyard, S. A. (1974). Human auditory evoked potentials. II. Effects of attention. *Electroencephalography and Clinical Neurophysiology, 36*, 191–200.

Picton, T. W., Stapells, D. R., & Campbell, K. B. (1981). Auditory evoked potentials from the human cochlea and brainstem. *Journal of Otolaryngology, Suppl. 9*, 1–41.

Pisa, M., & Fibiger, H. C. (1983). Evidence against a role of the rat's dorsal noradrenergic bundle in selective attention and place memory. *Brain Research, 272*, 319–329.

Pontius, A. A., & Yudowitz, B. S. (1980). Frontal lobe system dysfunction in some criminal actions as shown in the Narratives test. *Journal of Nervous and Mental Disease, 168*, 111–117.

Poranen, A., & Hyvärinen, J. (1982). Effects of attention on multiunit responses to vibration in the somatosensory regions of monkey's brain. *Electroencephalography and Clinical Neurophysiology, 53*, 525–537.

Pribam, K. H., & Tubbs, W. E. (1967). Short-term memory, parsing, and the primate frontal cortex. *Science, 156*, 1765–1767.

Rhodes, L. E., Dustman, R. E., & Beck, E. C. (1969). The visual evoked response: A comparison of bright and dull children. *Electroencephalography and Clinical Neurophysiology, 27*, 364–372.

Ritter, W., Simson, R., Vaughan, H. G., & Friedman, D. (1979). A brain event related to the making of a sensory discrimination. *Science, 203*, 1358–1361.

Ritter, W., Simson, R., Vaughan, H. G., & Macht, M. (1982). Manipulation of event-related potential manifestations of information processing stages. *Science, 218,* 909–911.

Roberts, D. C. S., Price, M. T. C., & Fibiger, H. C. (1976). The dorsal tegmental noradrenergic projection: An analysis of its role in maze learning. *Journal of Comparative and Physiological Psychology, 90,* 363–372.

Robinson, D. L. (1982). Properties of the diffuse thalamocortical system, human intelligence and differentiated vs. integrated modes of learning. *Personality and Individual Differences, 3,* 393–405.

Rogozea, R., & Ungher, J. (1968). Changes in orienting activity of cat induced by chronic hippocampal lesions. *Experimental Neurology, 21,* 176–186.

Rohrbaugh, J. W., Syndulko, K., & Lindsley, D. B. (1978). Cortical slow negative waves following non-paired stimuli: Effects of task factors. *Electroencephalography and Clinical Neurophysiology, 45,* 551–567.

Roland, P. E. (1981). Somatotopical tuning of postcentral gyrus during focal attention in man. A regional cerebral blood flow study. *Journal of Neurophysiology, 46,* 744–754.

Rosvold, H. E., Mirsky, A. F., Sarason, I., Bransome, E. D., & Beck, L. H. (1956). A continuous performance test of brain damage. *Journal of Consulting Psychology, 20,* 343–350.

Schafer, E. W. P. (1978). Brain responses while viewing television reflect program interest. *International Journal of Neuroscience, 8,* 71–77.

Schafer, E. W. P. (1982). Neural adaptability: A biological determinant of behavioral intelligence. *International Journal of Neuroscience, 17,* 183–191.

Scheibel, A. B. (1980). Anatomical and physiological substrates of arousal: A view from the bridge. In J. A. Hobson & M. A. B. Brazier (Eds.) *The reticular formation revisited.* New York: Raven Press.

Schwartz, A. S., Marchok, P. L., Kreinick, C. J., & Flynn, R. E. (1979). The asymmetric lateralization of tactile extinction in patients with unilateral cerebral dysfunction. *Brain, 102,* 669–684.

Schwent, V. L., Hillyard, S. A., & Galambos, R. (1976a). Selective attention and the auditory vertex potential. I. Effects of stimulus delivery rate. *Electroencephalography and Clinical Neurophysiology, 40,* 604–614.

Schwent, V. L., Hillyard, S. A., & Galambos, R. (1976b). Selective attention and the auditory vertex potential. II. Effects of signal intensity and masking noise. *Electroencephalography and Clinical Neurophysiology, 40,* 615–622.

Senba, K., & Iwahara, S. (1974). Effects of medial septal lesions on the hippocampal electrical activity and the orienting response to auditory stimulation in drinking rats. *Brain Research, 66,* 309–320.

Shagass, C., Roemer, R. A., Straumanis, J. J., & Josiassen, R. C. (1981). Intelligence as a factor in evoked potential studies of psychopathology. I. Comparison of low and high IQ subjects. *Biological Psychiatry, 16,* 1007–1030.

Shallice, T. (1972). Dual functions of consciousness. *Psychological Review, 79,* 383–393.

Shallice, T. (1982). Specific impairments of planning. *Philosophical Transactions of the Royal Society of London, Series B, 298,* 199–209.

Shaywitz, S. E., Cohen, D. J., & Shaywitz, B. A. (1978). The biochemical basis of minimal brain dysfunction. *Journal of Pediatrics, 92,* 2, 179–187.

Shekim, W. O., Kekirmenjian, H., Chapel, J. L., Javaid, J., & Davis, J. M. (1979). Norepinephrine metabolism and clinical response to dextroamphetamine in hyperactive boys. *Journal of Pediatrics, 95,* 389–394.

Shucard, D. W., & Horn, J. L. (1972). Evoked cortical potentials and measurement of human abilities. *Journal of Comparative Physiology and Psychology, 78,* 59–68.

Skinner, J. E., & Yingling, C. D. (1977). Central gating mechanisms that regulate event-related potentials and behavior: A neural model for attention. In J. E. Desmedt (Ed.), *Progress in clinical neurophysiology: Vol. 1. Attention, voluntary contraction and event-related potentials* (pp. 30–69). Basel: Karger.

Squires, N. K., Squires, K. C., & Hillyard, S. A. (1975). Two varieties of long latency positive waves evoked by unpredictable auditory stimuli in man. *Electroencephalography and Clinical Neurophysiology, 38,* 387–401.

Stamm, J. S., & Kreder, S. V. (1979). Minimal brain dysfunction: Psychological and neurophysiological disorders in hyperkinetic children. In M. Gazzaniga (Ed.), *Handbook of behavioral neurobiology: Vol. 2. Neuropsychology* (pp. 119–150). New York: Plenum Press.

Stein, S., & Volpe, B. T. (1983). Classical "parietal" neglect syndrome after subcortical right frontal lobe infarction. *Neurology, 33,* 797–799.

Straumanis, J. J., & Shagass, C. (1976). Relationship of cerebral evoked responses to "normal" intelligence and mental retardation. In D. V. Siva Sankar (Ed.) *Mental health in children,* (Vol. 2). Westbury, NY: PJD Publications (pp. 207–225).

Stroop, J. R. (1935). Studies of interference in serial verbal reactions. *Journal of Experimental Psychology, 18,* 643–662.

Stuss, D. T., Alexander, M. P., Lieberman, A., & Levine, H. (1978). An extraordinary form of confabulation. *Neurology, 28,* 1166–1172.

Stuss, D. T., & Benson, D. F. (1984). Neuropsychological studies of the frontal lobes. *Psychological Bulletin, 95,* 3–28.

Stuss, D. T., Benson, D. F., Kaplan, E. F., Weir, W. S., & Della Malva, C. (1981). Leucotomized and non-leucotomized schizophrenics: Comparison on tests of attention. *Biological Psychiatry, 16,* 1085–1100.

Stuss, D. T., Benson, D. F., Kaplan, E. F., Weir, W. S., Naeser, M. A., Lieberman, I., & Ferrill, D. (1983). The involvement of orbitofrontal cerebrum in cognitive tasks. *Neuropsychologia, 21,* 235–248.

Stuss, D. T., & Picton, T. W. (1978). Neurophysiological correlates of human concept formation. *Behavioral Biology, 23,* 135–162.

Stuss, D. T., & Richard, M. T. (1982). Neuropsychological sequelae of coma after head injury. In L. P. Ivan & D. Bruce (Eds.) *Coma: Physiopathology, diagnosis and management.* Springfield, IL: Charles C. Thomas.

Stuss, D. T., Sarazin, F. F., Leech, E. E., & Picton, T. W. (1983). Event-related potentials during naming and mental rotation. *Electroencephalography and Clinical Neurophysiology, 56,* 133–146.

Sutton, S., Braren, M., Zubin, J., & John, E. R. (1965). Evoked potential correlates of stimulus uncertainty. *Science, 150,* 1187–1188.

Suzuki, H., & Azuma, M. (1977). Prefrontal neuronal activity during gazing at a light spot in the monkey. *Brain Research, 126,* 497–508.

Tombaugh, T. N., Pappas, B. A., Roberts, D. C. S., Vickers, G. J., & Szostak, C. (1983). Failure to replicate the dorsal bundle extinction effect: Telencephalic norepinephrine depletion does not reliably increase resistance to extinction but does augment gustatory neophobia. *Brain Research, 261,* 231–242.

van Zomeren, A. H. (1981). *Reaction time and attention after closed head injury.* Lisse, Holland: Swets & Zeitlinger B.V.

Vaughan, Jr., H. G., Costa, L. D., & Ritter, W. (1968). Topography of the human motor potential. *Electroencephalography and Clinical Neurophysiology, 25,* 1–10.

Velasco, M., Velasco, F., & Olvera, A. (1980). Effect of task relevance and selective attention on components of cortical and subcortical evoked potentials in man. *Electroenceph-alography and Clinical Neurophysiology, 48,* 377–386.

Vinogradova, O. S. (1970). Registration of information and the limbic system. In G. Horn & R. A. Hinde (Eds.), *Short-term changes in neural activity and behaviour* (pp. 95–140). Cambridge, England: University Press.

Walley, R. E., & Weiden, T. D. (1973). Lateral inhibition and cognitive masking: A neuropsychological theory of attention. *Psychological Review, 4,* 284–302.

Walter, W. G., Cooper, R., Aldridge, V. J., McCallum, W. C., & Winter, A. L. (1964). Contingent negative variation: An electric sign of sensory-motor association and expectancy in the human brain. *Nature, 203,* 380–384.

Ward, M. M., Sandman, C. A., George, J. M., & Shulman, H. (1979). MSH/ACTH 4-10 in men and women: Effects upon performance of an attention and memory task. *Physiology and Behavior, 22,* 669–673.

Waterhouse, B. D., Moises, H. C., & Woodward, D. J. (1981). Alpha-receptor-mediated facilitation of somatosensory cortical neuronal responses to excitatory synaptic inputs and iontophoretically applied acetylcholine. *Neuropharmacology, 20,* 907–920.

Watson, R. T., Valenstein, E., & Heilman, K. M. (1981). Thalamic neglect: Possible role of the medial thalamus and nucleus reticularis in behavior. *Archives of Neurology, 38,* 501–506.

Weinberg, H. (1972). The contingent negative variation: Its relation to feedback and expectant attention. *Neuropsychologia, 10,* 299–306.

Wender, P. H., Wood, D. R., Reimherr, F. W., & Ward, M. (1983). An open trial of pargyline in the treatment of attention deficit disorder, residual type. *Psychiatry Research, 9,* 329–336.

Wickelgren, W. O. (1968). Effects of walking and flash stimulation on click evoked responses in cats. *Journal of Neurophysiology, 31,* 777–784.

Williams, J. T., Egan, T. M., & North, R. A. (1982). Enkephalin opens potassium channels on mammalian central neurones. *Nature, 299,* 74–77.

Woods, D. L., & Hillyard, S. A. (1978). Attention at the cocktail party: Brainstem evoked responses reveal no peripheral gating. In D. Otto (Ed.) *Multidisciplinary perspectives in event-related brain potential research.* Washington, DC: Environmental Protection Agency.

Woodward, D. J., Moises, H. C., Waterhouse, B. D., Hoffer, B. J., & Freedman, R. (1979). Modulatory actions of norepinephrine in the central nervous system. *Federation Proceedings, 38,* 2109–2116.

Wurtz, R. H., Goldberg, M. E., & Robinson, D. L. (1980). Behavioral modulation of visual responses in the monkey: Stimulus selection for attention and movement. *Progress in Psychobiology and Physiological Psychology, 9,* 43–83.

Wurtz, R. H., & Mohler, C. W. (1976). Enhancement of visual responses in monkey striate cortex and frontal eye fields. *Journal of Neurophysiology, 39*(4), 766–787.

Yingling, C. D., & Skinner, J. E. (1977). Gating of thalamic input to cerebral cortex by nucleus reticularis thalami. In J. E. Desmedt (Ed.), *Progress in clinical neurophysiology: Vol. 1. Attention, voluntary contraction and event-related potentials* (pp. 70–96). Basel: Karger.

Zihl, J., & von Cramon, D. (1979). The contribution of the "second" visual system to directed visual attention in man. *Brain, 102,* 835–856.

Zubin, J. (1975). Problem of attention in schizophrenia. In M. L. Kietzman, S. Sutton, & J. Zubin (Eds.), *Experimental approaches to psychopathology* (pp. 139–166). New York: Wiley.

CHAPTER 3

Attention and the Control of Cognition*

Michael I. Posner and Frances J. Friedrich

I. INTRODUCTION

The general field that studies the acquisition, representation and activation of knowledge is called *cognition*. The field of cognition may be broken down into separate cognitive systems that reflect such functions as object recognition, motor control, language processing, and attention. Among these cognitive systems, *attention* refers to the system that involves our ability to select among competing data so as to bias our memory, responses, or current thought toward some contents rather than others. Attention thus serves as an internal control or regulator of cognitive activity.

Attention may involve the selection of information either from sensory input or from semantic memory (Posner, 1978). Much of our information about such selectivity arises from information-processing experiments with normal people, but there has been some convergence of such experiments with studies of deficits arising from regional brain injury and with animal studies.

We now know that as people shift attention from one thought to another there are measurable changes in the selection of information relevant to that shift (Posner, 1982). These changes involve both facilitation and inhibition. They can be sufficiently time locked to external signals to allow precise measurement. Thus, we can trace the processing of a visual word through mechanisms specific to (1) the form of the input information, (2) the general characteristics of the orthography used, (3)

* Research reported here was supported in part by a grant from the Sloan Foundation to the University of Oregon in support of work in Cognitive Science and in part by a grant from IBM in the same area.

the phonological systems that are involved in the convergence of the visual and auditory input representing a single lexical item, and (4) the various levels of semantics that describe the network of connotative and denotative relationships to the input word. Each of these codes can be selected by the subject for entry into consciousness or as the basis of an external response. These findings from cognitive experiments are supported by evidence that acquired dyslexias can block from conscious processing visual or phonological codes but leave the subject able to deal with the semantics of the input (Coltheart, Patterson, & Marshall, 1980).

Attention is a broad field of investigation, but it is not coextensive with all aspects of internal processing. Although any level of the nervous system may be thought of as selective in the sense that cells at that level respond to only some range of information, there appears to be an enormous reduction in the amount of information that can occupy mechanisms related to awareness. Thus, much of the study of attention has to do with the mechanisms that underlie selection for conscious awareness. Midbrain systems that tune the cortex have their effect largely on mechanisms that subserve this highest level of selection (Posner, 1978). States of coma or sleep differ from the normal alert state in the ability of people to maintain this highest form of selectivity and to show an integrated response to the world around them. The amount of information that can occupy the subject's conscious attention at any given moment is extremely limited. Our ability to measure shifts of attention from one item or location to another provides the basis for studies of the neural systems that produce this highest level of selectivity. It is these systems on which we concentrate this chapter.

The goal of this chapter is to link brain processes to those aspects of attention that are important for education. This is a difficult goal and one that would be impossible if we tried to cover the full range of topics related to attention. Instead, we have attempted to select one simple model to illustrate the type of connection between brain systems and educational applications that we conceive to be possible. The model chosen for this purpose is the ability to select information from different places of the visual field.

After dealing with the selection of information in visual space in the next section, we argue that the same attentional mechanisms are involved in the selection of information from semantic memory and thus in such everyday life skills as reading and listening.

At the heart of our argument is the belief that there are two rather different languages available for discussing selectivity in the nervous system. One language comes from neuroscience studies and discusses primarily the location of different functions. The methods are largely designed to discover the parts of the brain that might be active or might change with attention or the effects of damage to a part of the brain on attention. A second language has arisen from cognitive psychology. Its emphasis is on the logical stages or elementary mental operations involved in a task. Most of the cognitive studies emphasize careful timing because they seek to understand the time course of information processing in the nervous system (mental chronometry). There is considerable dispute about the relationship of these two languages. Some believe they must remain independent alternative descriptions at different levels of analysis. Others believe that the cognitive theories will be replaced by neurophysiological ones as our understanding of the latter grow. The view taken in this chapter is what we call joint constraint. We seek to map the temporal stages of one language to the spatially distributed components of the other. Our hope is that an understanding at both levels will jointly provide better illumination of educational problems such as differences in learning ability, the effects of brain injury, or the degree to which conscious control of internal processes is possible.

II. SPATIAL ATTENTION

In the late 1800s the field of psychology was the science of consciousness. Frontiers of the discipline were at the entry of information to consciousness so that introspective reports would be possible. Fifty years of behaviorism has provided for psychology a number of objective techniques that allow exploration of material that is not conscious to the subject (Posner & Shulman, 1979). Only since the late 1970s have we begun to understand that the following fundamental issue can be explored by the behavioral methods of psychology: What processes of the nervous system lead to awareness and why? This question is important because information that arises to consciousness comes more easily under voluntary control and thus is more subject to the interventions of education (Posner, 1978).

Nearly every model of information processing has implicit within it a set of mechanisms that underlie conscious awareness of input. In Broadbent's 1958 model, the "p" system embodied the properties of the material of which the subject is aware; while in LaBerge and Samuel's (1974) classic paper on the skill of reading, a mechanism labelled "A" (attention) controlled the flow of information when pathways linking input to internal codes were not automatic. Although the term *consciousness* is rarely used in information-processing models, it is a common idea that much information goes on outside of awareness in automatic pathways and that only a certain portion of it is available to the subject's awareness. In an operational sense, we can define consciousness as the access to information-processing systems that allow the subject to make nonhabitual responses that are often indicated by verbal report.

It is of interest to understand how entry into consciousness might be governed by neural systems. For this goal, it is useful to define a very simple experimental situation that can be studied alike in normal and in brain-injured adults, in children, and in animals, including those for whom experimental neurosurgery and electrophysiology is possible. A simple task of this character is the ability of people and animals to orient to visual information either by movement of the eyes or by entirely covert changes. It is certainly well-known that eye movements affect the efficiency of taking visual information because only the fovea is capable of detailed pattern vision. Moreover, eye movements play a critical role in many cognitive tasks. However, eye movements are clearly not the mechanism that allows us to select information from semantic memory, from audition, or from some other sensory systems. For these functions, a covert mechanism is required. It is now possible to begin to outline some of the characteristics of this covert mechanism from studies of visual attention that are general to the selection of information and not specific to the visual system.

II.A. ORIENTING OF VISUAL ATTENTION

Our experiments have relied on the use of cues to induce subjects to turn attention to places in the visual field (Posner, 1980). We then examine the efficiency of detecting information from the cued position in comparison to detecting information from uncued positions. By a variety of methods, including reaction time and probability of reporting near-threshold stimuli, we have been able to show that while maintaining fixation it is possible to shift attention to places other than the line of sight. Such shifts are accompanied by improved efficiency, by detecting signals that occur at the expected position.

We have been able to show that in the case of luminance detection, the fovea plays no special role in routing information, although attention cannot be used to compensate for the fovea when acuity is important. Even more striking is the fact that shifts of covert attention can be sufficiently time-locked so that these changes in efficiency can be traced dynamically as attention is moved across the visual field. When attention is summoned by a peripheral cue, facilitation is found after 50 ms. That is, detection response times are more rapid at the cued location than elsewhere in the field. Moreover, the peripheral event also begins an inhibitory process that apparently modulates this increase in efficiency. Thus, if orienting is sustained at the cued position, the facilitation relative to uncued positions tends to drop out over time. If attention is drawn to some other place in the visual field, the place to which attention had previously been drawn will be inhibited with respect to other positions in the visual field. It is as though attention is held to check by a peripheral mechanism whose purpose is to aid in decoupling attention from its current locus. This combination of facilitation and inhibition is reminiscent of the agonist-antagonist tensions that govern muscle movements (Posner, Cohen, & Rafal, 1982).

The time-locking of attention to external signals allows testing of a number of theoretical positions about the relationship between selection of information and aspects unique to the visual modality. Our findings suggest that there are strong functional relationships between the shifts of visual attention and eye movements toward a peripheral stimulus, but there is no identity in the underlying physiological systems. That is, the mechanisms that underlie the shifts in visual attention are much more independent of the eye movement system and the fine structure of the fovea than one would expect if these mechanisms were uniquely visual (Posner, 1980). In general, we see the close functional relationship between attention movements and eye movements as similar to the relationship between eye movements and hand movements. Posner and Rothbart (1980) have also explored the significance of the functional relation between attention and eye movements found in adults for understanding the development of attentional mechanisms from birth. The extant data suggest that a protoattentional system present at birth develops a close functional relationship to foveal vision over the first few months of life. However, fine control of fixation and eye movements continue to develop over many years (Kowler & Martins, 1982).

II.B. NEURAL SYSTEMS

The exquisite time-locking of attentional mechanisms to cues and the simplicity of the experimental paradigms used allows comparison of results of normal human beings with those of neurological patients and nonhuman organisms. An impressive convergence of these results has begun to make clear that we should be able to obtain a knowledge of some of the control mechanisms of covert attention (Posner, Cohen, & Rafal, 1982). In neurology, a consequence of parietal lesions is known as visual neglect or hemispheric inattention (Mesulam, 1981).

This clinical result has led neuroscience investigators to examine in some detail the cellular properties of parietal neurons that might be related to problems of selective attention (Mountcastle, 1978; Robinson,

Goldberg, & Stanton, 1978). It has been shown that parietal neurons have many of the characteristics that one would expect of cells whose goal is to enhance information to which attention is directed. For example, such cells show selective enhancement when their receptive field lies in the neighborhood of the target either for an eye movement or for a shift of attention when the eyes are kept fixed. The close relationship of these cells to eye and hand movements in the surrounding environment is a striking characteristic of many of the parietal cells. However, it appears unlikely that these cells are intrinsically related only to movement itself because enhancement occurs in situations in which no movement is allowed. Thus, like our behavioral data, the neuroscience data suggests that selective enhancement of parietal cells is not intrinsically related to movement but is more related to an intention to use information from a spatial location.

The reports of neuroscientists of interesting properties of cells in the parietal lobe related to selective attention led us to examine the selective abilities of patients with parietal-lobe damage (Posner, Cohen, & Rafal, 1982). Our results confirm the neurological phenomenon of extinction and neglect and suggest that these two neurological syndromes are on a continuum with the effects that one gets in the normal person when attention is oriented to the wrong location. When a patient suffering from damage of the right parietal lobe has attention directed to the right visual field, information presented to the left visual field (contralateral to the lesion) is often completely undetected. This is called extinction in clinical neurology. If attention is miscued in normal persons, they also show a delay in detecting the target. Damage to the parietal lobe on one side seems to greatly magnify this normal difficulty so that under some conditions no covert orienting takes place and the target is simply not detected. However, when attention is properly aligned with the target, many patients show only a small or no deficit in the latency of target detection. The parietal lesion appears to interfere with the orienting of covert attention.

There is something of a paradox between the two neurological signs of parietal lobe damage called extinction and neglect. *Extinction* involves the loss of information from the side contralateral to the lesion when presented simultaneously with information ipsilateral to the lesion. This implies that subjects would be able to detect stimuli contralateral to the lesion without such simultaneous presentation. On the other hand, *neglect* suggests that subjects are relatively unable to direct attention to the side contralateral to the lesion even in situations when there is no stimulation on the side ipsilateral to the lesion.

We believe that the explanation of this paradox helps illustrate the complex links between a neurological mechanism that may be damaged by brain injury and an observed performance. In experiments involving extinction, the subject's attention is clearly directed toward the visual modality. When attention is riveted upon vision in this way, one finds that a single stimulus contralateral to the lesion, particularly if in motion, will be sufficient to summon attention. On the other hand, in many situations, including many neuropsychological tests, attention is not focused on vision. Thus, in most experiments on extinction, we are asking if a visual stimulus can summon attention when already directed toward vision, whereas in the study of neglect we ask, "Will a visual stimulus contralateral to the lesion summon attention when the current state of attention is uncontrolled?" If attentional mechanisms are general and not modality specific, one would expect that directing the subject's attention to vision will have a powerful affect on her or his orienting ability. Indeed, we (Posner, Cohen, Choate, Hockey, & Maylor, 1984) showed that when normals are required to count backwards, they showed a delay in orienting attention toward visual cues. If, as a consequence of parietal damage, stimuli are less able to pull attention toward themselves when they come from the side of the space contralateral to the lesion, it would be expected that orienting would not occur under conditions in which subject's attention is on something other than the visual system.

The clinical syndrome of unilateral parietal lesion may involve much more than an interference with the ability of stimuli to produce covert orienting. However, the clear interference with covert orienting suggests that the parietal lobe is an area of the brain of importance for the control of normal spatial orienting. These studies show how an internal mental operation studied by cognitive methods (covert orienting) can be linked experimentally to a neural system (parietal lobe). We believe that even a simple act of reading a single word involves many separate mental operations and that it may eventually be possible to link these components to neural systems. The studies of spatial orienting represent only a small step toward this difficult goal.

II.C. PATTERN RECOGNITION

It remains for us to provide some evidence that covert orienting and its neural systems relate in any important way to the cognitive skills that are the focus of this volume. We believe that the evidence is overwhelming that they do. In the first place, it seems very apparent that the ability of people to direct attention toward visual positions plays a very important role in individual development. Posner and Rothbart (1980) reviewed the evidence that flexibility of attention in terms of the ability to maintain or shift visual concentration are fundamental components present in infancy. Rothbart and Derryberry (1982) have used attentional self-regulation as one of the major components of infant temperament. Moreover, Keele, and Hawkins (1982) have shown that individual differences in the ability to shift attention are a systematic source of individual differences in adult performance.

There are relatively high correlations among different experimental paradigms that involve orienting of attention. While it is not yet known whether these individual differences are important in the performance of school subjects, their presence as a behavioral characteristic in early infancy and as an individual-differences trait in adulthood suggest that they may be an aspect of our ability to maintain and control concentration on school subjects.

While many of the studies that we have discussed so far involve orienting to a very simple stimuli such as changes in luminance, it has also been shown that basically the same processes are involved when spatial orienting involves the detection of visually presented language stimuli. For example, Posner (1980) reviewed several experiments in which subjects were required to signal the presence of a digit as distinct from a letter. Cues about location of the digit did improve performance when the digit occurred at the cued location and retarded performance at an uncued location, just as would be the case with luminance detection.

Similarly, Eriksen and Hoffman (1973) have shown that the position to which attention is directed in a complex field greatly enhances the recognition of items that are close to that position. More specifically, they demonstrated that the focus of attention is confined to a relatively limited contiguous area around the cue of approximately 1 degree. Within this 1-degree focus, irrelevant stimuli have powerful affects on performance, but outside of it they do not. Treisman (Treisman & Gelade, 1980; Treisman & Schmidt, 1982) has presented a detailed psychological theory suggesting that orienting of attention plays a particular role in a complex visual field in which different stimuli can be confused.

All of these experiments suggest that although our experiments have primarily involved very simple stimuli and have concentrated on luminance detection, the principles of attentional orienting that we have uncovered are general ones that extend through a variety of tasks. Particularly impressive along these lines is work by Chang (1981) showing that covert orienting of attention affects spatial selection in reading for meaning. The task is important both because of the obvious educational implications and because many of the analyses of attention in cognitive psychology have involved the presentation of visual language material. During reading, the span of perception is limited to approximately 10 items to the right of fixation and 3 to 4 items to the left of fixation (Rayner, Well, & Pollatsek, 1980). Hebrew readers have a reverse asymmetry. This asymmetry might be based on dominant direction of eye movements in reading, as if the tendency to move the eyes in one direction biases the person toward an increased concentration toward that side of space.

It has, however, been shown that reading can take place in a relatively efficient manner when information is presented only at fixation point (Potter, Kroll & Harris, 1980). If the right–left asymmetry in reading is a function of the eye movement system, there should be no asymmetry when the eyes remain fixed while reading. However, if the asymmetry arises from the linguistic nature of the task and is not necessarily related to the eye movement, one might expect the asymmetry to remain. Chang (1981) tested this idea by requiring subjects to read connected stories while maintaining fixation. Chang found a systematic bias toward the right side of visual space even when fixation was always maintained at the center. When words were presented upside-down, so that the direction of internal scan of the word would be right to left, there was clear evidence that the asymmetry reverses under this condition, giving a larger effective visual field to the left of fixation than to the right of fixation.

This experiment is important to our argument because it illustrates that covert attentional mechanisms operate during normal spatially directed tasks such as reading. We have shown that covert orienting is a mental operation that can be linked to certain underlying neural systems. The Chang study indicates that these same mechanisms can also account for specific aspects of performance during reading. Of course, only a small part of reading relates to the spatial nature of the task. Selection of the appropriate visual word must be accompanied by internal processes that convert the visual letters to semantics. We address these issues in the next section.

III. ATTENTION AND SEMANTIC MEMORY

We now turn to the question of the role of attention in cognitive systems involving language and semantic memory. To what extent do the principles of attention that have been demonstrated in the selection of information in visual space extend to the area of semantic memory and to the complex cognitive activities that dominate our daily lives?

Can we identify mechanisms that serve to control the flow and selection of information in semantic space?

The starting point for an analysis of this sort rests on an understanding of the kinds of information available within that semantic space. Thus, we first review evidence that sensory and semantic codes within the cognitive system are isolable and produce dissociations of functions in brain-damaged individuals. The next section addresses the issue of conscious and unconscious mechanisms: This distinction is a key factor in identifying the conscious attentional mechanisms that serve to select information appropriate to task performance and inhibit competing information. We emphasize the processing of verbal information throughout this discussion, with a particular focus on reading skills and the role of attentional mechanisms in the complex cognitive skills that are called into play during reading comprehension.

III.A.   CODING: SENSORY AND SEMANTIC PATHWAYS

Progress has been made in isolating separate coding systems within memory. Sensory codes, or information that is bound to a particular input modality, have been shown to persist in memory for relatively long periods (Hintzman, Block, & Inskeep, 1972; Kirsner & Smith, 1974). This was demonstrated in a study in which subjects made judgments about a series of words presented visually or aurally. Within the list, words were repeated either in the same or different modalities and with a varying number of intervening items. Using this technique, it is possible to separate benefit due to repetition *within* versus *across* modalities. The effects of within-modality repetition persisted with as many as 60 intervening items.

By providing evidence of repetition effects across modalities, the same study also demonstrates the existence of a modality-free coding system, a code that is common to input from either visual or auditory sources. The convergence of information from these two modalities at the point of a common name code is well-documented with both letters and words and with simultaneous and sequential presentation (Hanson, 1981; Posner, 1978; Sen & Posner, 1979).

Information from different modalities also converges on a common semantic coding system, by which meaning and categorical attributes are represented. Hanson (1981) showed that when subjects were asked to make judgments about category membership of a word in one modality, performance was facilitated if a different word from the same category was presented in the other, unattended, modality. Similar facilitation effects have been found under less semantically constrained conditions, for instance when an aurally presented sentence context precedes a visually presented word (Sen & Posner, 1979). The demonstration of a modality-free semantic code is perhaps not surprising intuitively; yet it provides an important addition to models of semantic processing derived from neuropsychological data. Cortical lesions often result in the dissociation of recognition abilities in different modalities. For instance, a patient with intact visual acuity may be totally unable to name a visually presented object or to indicate its function and yet may be able to immediately recognize the object if allowed to touch it or hear a characteristic associated sound. Evidence of a common semantic code from intact subjects, however, argues that this disconnection arises between a particular sensory representation and a single intact semantic representation.

Dissociations on this type, which follow brain injury, dramatize an important aspect of the organization of cognitive processes, that of the functional independence of different pathways to semantic memory. The condition of deep dyslexia is one of the most fascinating of these dissociations. In *deep dyslexia,* the phonological recoding of written language has been impaired and the semantic representation of a word appears to be accessed through a visual pathway. The performance of such a patient is characterized by semantic errors during reading (e.g., reading the word "dog" as "cat") and by a total inability to read pronounceable nonwords (Coltheart, Patterson, & Marshall, 1980). Although this condition has received considerable attention, cases of this sort are relatively rare.

Fortunately, it is possible to distinguish different routes to semantic memory in intact individuals as well. For instance, when the phonological code that is normally generated in reading is interfered with by requiring the reader to simultaneously repeat an auditory message, subjects show no impairment in semantic decisions about word pairs (Kleiman, 1975). Similarly, subjects are able to determine that phrases such as TIE THE NOT, which are meaningless in visual form while homophonic to meaningful phrases, are rejected as meaningless as quickly as nonhomophonic controls (Baron, 1973). A great deal of debate has surrounded the question of the necessity of phonological recoding in reading (e.g., Bradshaw, 1975; Coltheart, Davelaar, Jonasson, & Besner, 1977), and it appears that although semantic information can be activated without using a phonological route, a phonological representation may play an important role in the retention of verbatim information and in decoding complex syntactic structures (Davidson, 1978; Saffran & Marin, 1975). The demonstration that semantic information can be reached through separable pathways should not be used to suggest which pathway is more important; rather, the significance of this finding may lie in our ability to exploit multiple pathways to enhance the learning of reading and to remediate deficits that do arise.

III.B.   CONSCIOUS AND UNCONSCIOUS MECHANISMS

The notion that multiple codes may be active simultaneously following the presentation of a stimulus stands in sharp contrast to our subjective experience of the limitation in the amount of information that can be dealt with at one time. Indeed, a limit in processing capacity can be demonstrated quite readily by requiring an individual to carry out two operations at once (Posner, 1982). The limited capacity is manifest in the interference that these tasks produce.

The use of measurement techniques that monitor processes as they occur has enabled psychologists to separate automatic pathway activation from a central attentional mechanism that selects and coordinates information appropriate to the designated task. Whereas automatic pathway activation serves to facilitate the processing of items that share the same pathway, the limited-capacity mechanism associated with conscious awareness selects certain information at a cost to other information. It is this limited amount of selected information that reaches consciousness and that is manifest in responses to task demands. Chronometric techniques provide a sensitive means of demonstrating the selective nature of the central attentional mechanism through a cost–benefit analysis of processing time for an item presented under different conditions.

One demonstration of the separability of pathway activation and conscious attention in semantic memory was provided by Neely (1977). In a lexical decision task, Neely manipulated expectations about relationships between word pairs such that in some cases the expected relationship deviated from the usual semantic association. Thus the subjects were instructed that when a priming category such as "animal" was presented, they should expect to see a target word related to "a part of a building," such as "door." Neely found that when the interval between presentation of a priming word and a target was short, response time was facilitated for a target word that was a true semantic associate, regardless of whether that type of target was expected. As the interval between the prime and the target increased, unexpected targets began to show a cost (i.e., slower response times) even when they were true semantic associates. It appears that certain conscious expectations were generated and that these selection processes effectively inhibited responses to all other targets. Moreover, these results reveal an important difference in the time course of pathway activation and conscious attentional mechanisms. Benefit due to prior activation of pathways emerges very rapidly, while the inhibitory effect due to the limited-capacity conscious attentional mechanism accrues more slowly (Posner, 1970).

Priming effects of this sort have been found for word pairs that are related in a variety of ways, including shared-category membership, synonym pairs that share a common meaning, and words that have become linked through frequent association (Becker, 1980; Fischler, 1977; Neely, 1977). These principles extend, in fact, to the special case of lexically ambiguous words, in which a single word name has multiple meanings. Under conditions in which a priming context biases the interpretation of an ambiguous word toward a particular meaning, both meanings are simultaneously activated even though only one meaning is available to consciousness (Conrad, 1974; Killion, 1981). This effect is obtained even when the ambiguous word is masked so that the subject is unaware that a word has been presented at all, as Marcel (1980) has shown. However, Marcel went on to demonstrate that once a particular meaning has been selected for conscious processing, items related to the nonselected meaning are inhibited. Thus, rapid preconscious processing generates multiple codes and makes numerous semantic representations available to a control attentional mechanism, which functions to select and operate on a limited portion of this information.

III.C. STRATEGIES AND PATHWAY SELECTION

The nature of this selection process and the capability of the central attentional mechanism to preselect codes for conscious processing becomes an important issue precisely because mental operations differ greatly in the nature and amount of information they require for completion. The goals of a proofreader and a journal subscriber are certainly different even though they may face the same article. To what extent, then, can an individual employ specific intentional strategies in selecting among or coordinating available codes or, more precisely, to what extent can attention be shifted toward a particular type of internal representation in preparation for the information needed to carry out a task? Could, for instance, the central attention mechanism be preset to use a phonological code, thus inhibiting visual or semantic representations?

One approach to this question is to consider how the use of various types of information develop. Bradley and Bryant (1979), for instance, have argued that young children use different strategies in reading and spelling. It is not surprising that children can read words that they cannot spell, as the latter task generally involves more precision. However, Bradley and Bryant have also found that children frequently can spell words that they cannot read, and an analysis of the resulting errors has led them to hypothesize that young children use primarily visual information in reading and phonological information in spelling. The separate use of these two pathways tends to decrease with reading level, such that the more advanced readers are less likely to be able to spell words that they cannot read. It is interesting that remedial readers seem to preserve the independent use of visual and phonological information. These results suggest that what is lacking in the remedial reader may not be access to one pathway or the other, but the ability to shift from one type of information to another when the task demands it. Whereas normal readers begin to adopt a phonological strategy for reading as well as spelling, remedial readers do not. This is consistent with the common finding that poor readers have difficulty reading pronounce-able nonsense words (Frederiksen, 1978; Perfetti & Hogaboam, 1975). Presumably, if this independence hypothesis holds true, the remedial reader should perform as well as a normal reader in spelling regular words but should show a relative deficiency in the spelling of irregular words that require some memory of visual form.

The implication of these findings is that some beginning readers and poor readers have the capacity to use either visual or phonological infor-mation, but are unable to coordinate these codes or to shift between them within a given task. It is tempting to draw the inference from these suggestive results that modality-specific coding precedes cross-modal integration developmentally, and that unified or modality-free represen-tations exist only for the skilled reader. In apparent contrast, research with infants suggests that the earliest semantic representations may be made up of an integration of auditory, tactile, and visual dimensions (Gottfried, Rose, & Bridger, 1977; Meltzoff & Barton, 1980). In fact, the semantic representations of poor readers are undoubtedly derived from multimodal experiences with objects in the real world. But the acts of reading and spelling may represent special cases in the cross-modal coordination of codes. The semantic representation of language already exists for a child learning to read: The task at hand is to establish visual pathways that can access the existing phonological and semantic infor-mation and to develop reliable grapheme to phoneme correspondences.

Rozin and Gleitman (1977) have pointed out that attention is focused at the level of meaning for young children, while sounding out words requires an awareness of the relationship between individual letters and corresponding phonemes. Phonemic discrimination and categorization have been demonstrated in newborns (Eimas, Sequeland, Jusczyk, & Vigorito, 1971), but the ability to use this information in tasks that require conscious manipulation of these speech segments develops much later, at about the time children begin learning to read (Liberman, Shankweiler, Fischer, & Carter, 1974; Treiman, 1980). It is commonly found that delayed readers continue to have trouble in phonemic segmentation tasks. Thus, learning to read may provide an instructive case in the role of a central attentional mechanism: Although phonemic information is available, it must be selected and brought into awareness in order to link it to arbitrary visual symbols such as letters.

Skilled readers appear to be quite efficient in coordinating information from the various activated codes. Do these selection skills extend to being able to suppress irrelevant codes when this information interferes with performance? The answer to this question appears to be mixed. On the one hand, the name of a word interferes with naming the color of ink the word is printed in if the word is primed by a related word or if the word itself is a color name that is different from the ink color (Dyer, 1973; Warren, 1972). In this case the word name is activated and affects response selection even though it would be more efficient to suppress it. The size of this effect does appear to diminish somewhat between fourth- and sixth-grade reading level, which may indicate more control in the selection process (Schadler & Thissen, 1981). On the other hand, Hawkins, Reicher, Rogers, and Peterson (1976) have demonstrated that under certain conditions, subjects can shift from a phonological to a visual strategy in processing individual words. They briefly presented an item such as *sent* followed by a pair of words and asked subjects to indicate which of the pair they had seen. In some cases the pair was homophonic, that is, both members of the pair had the same pronunciation (e.g., "sent" and "cent"). For these pairs, use of a phonological strategy would interfere with correct recognition of the target word. When homophonic pairs were relatively rare in the list, interference did occur compared to nonhomophonic pairs, but when these pairs were frequent, subjects apparently shifted to a different processing strategy and performance on homophonic and nonhomophonic word pairs did not differ.

Context can also affect the size and nature of semantic priming effects. Becker (1980) has argued that different strategies are adopted in using semantic information, depending upon the relative strength of semantic relationships within a list of word pairs. Becker found that lists dominated by antonym pairs (e.g., GOOD/BAD) produced a strong benefit for related word pairs and little cost for unrelated pairs compared to a neutral control condition. In contrast, a list dominated by category names and their members (e.g., ANIMAL/COW) produced little benefit and greater cost. The strongest evidence in favor of a strategy argument in accounting for this difference is the fact that Becker found an antonym-like pattern for category member pairs when they were embedded in a list of pairs with a strong semantic relationship. Subjects appeared to shift their strategy for making use of semantic information depending upon the likelihood that it would be useful in making predictions.

Although there is evidence that attention can be shifted internally and focused on different codes for different tasks, individuals may differ in their preference for particular codes or, in fact, in their flexibility in shifting attention. For instance, some people tend to rely more heavily on phonemic information in reading while others focus on visual information (Baron & Strawson, 1976). In addition, reading flexibility has been characterized as the ability to shift strategies depending on the difficulty of the material, such that flexible readers read difficult text more slowly than easy material, while less-flexible readers proceed at the same rate regardless of text difficulty (Rankin, 1978). There is some evidence that this measurement of flexibility may be related to strategy selection in the use of semantic information in both the single-word priming task and in sentence processing (Eisenberg & Becker, 1982). Eisenberg and Becker argue that different strategies are available to all subjects and can be utilized under the proper conditions; however, individuals seem to differ in their ability to select and use a specific strategy to meet a specific task demand.

III.D. Text Comprehension

There has been an increased demand for "ecological validity" in the study of cognitive processes. Criticism has focused on the artificial constraints of the tasks used to isolate basic cognitive operations and the relevance of the results of these studies to more-complex activities. The relationship between reading flexibility and strategy selection in the use of semantic information discussed earlier provides one link between single-word recognition studies and more-complex text comprehension. In addition, there is some evidence that laboratory measures of attentional flexibility is correlated with performance on complex skills, such as driving a bus or flying an airplane, which demand frequent and rapid attention shifts (Gopher & Kahneman, 1971). The challenge to determine whether the attentional mechanisms that have been isolated in relatively simple laboratory situations function in similar ways in more-complex tasks has been met with the development of on-line techniques that allow us to monitor specific processes as they occur in the course of carrying out a complex activity.

The link between semantic priming effects for single-word recognition and priming effects in the course of sentence processing is particularly strong. Just as the presence of a semantic associate facilitates the processing of single words, so also do semantically related verbs or adjectives facilitate recognition of target nouns within sentences. Moreover, this benefit due to semantic context has been demonstrated for sentences presented both auditorily (Blank & Foss, 1978) and visually (Friedrich, 1980, Note 1). Thus the effects of semantic context that would be predicted from the results of basic cognitive research can be demonstrated in the course of text comprehension, and they have proved to be reliable across modalities.

The parallel between single-word recognition and sentence processing appears to extend to the operation of automatic and conscious attentional processes as well. For instance, when adults are asked to name a visually presented word, a cost–benefit analysis shows facilitation for words preceded by a related sentence context (relative to a neutral control), but not inhibition for words preceded by an unrelated sentence context (Stanovich & West, 1981). Increasing the interval between the context and the target word results in an inhibition effect, and children show both facilitation due to related contexts and inhibition due to unrelated contexts with short and long context–target intervals, under most conditions. It appears that adults normally can recognize words so rapidly that only automatic processes have an effect prior to naming, while for children the word recognition processes are slower and the slower-acting attentional mechanism has time to affect the naming process.

It may be possible to use these techniques to evaluate the role of still another level of comprehension processes, that of sentence integration. Preliminary work indicates that the facilitation for word meaning due to semantic relatedness operates independently of a higher-level process that checks the meaningfulness of a sentence as a whole (Kleiman, 1980). That is, there is a context effect due to the semantic relationship of a word within a sentence and another additive effect based on whether a word completes the sentence in a grammatically congruous manner. Incongruity tends to produce strong inhibition effects in adults (Fischler & Bloom, 1979); it may be that the attentional mechanism is set at a level of sentence meaningfulness and that lower-level effects due to the strength of the semantic relationship are produced through automatic processes.

Attentional strategies may in fact effect the manner in which sentences are encoded. Text can be read for a variety of purposes, ranging from general comprehensions to memorization of specific details. Instructions to recall a sentence verbatim will produce a different pattern of reading times than instructions to read for general comprehension

difficult but fundamental educational issue. Cognitive research indicates that the semantic structure available within a domain of knowledge are of central importance for skilled performance. It has been argued that even increases in a basic capacity like memory span during the years of childhood actually is a result of better ability to code digits and letters rather than a growing memory capacity (Chi, 1976). This view holds that skills learning involves the mastery of a finite amount of complex semantics that alters the memory system in such a way that a formerly naive person now shows the performance at a high level. This picture has little place for general systems important over a wide range of skilled activity. Yet much of what we have discussed in this chapter argues that attention is one such system, whose capacity is critical to the learning of material in a wide variety of domains. Moreover, attention would seem to be a general system that would benefit from training so that it might be shifted flexibly, maintained over time, and directed toward the critical elements of the skill to be learned. It is possible that training attention in one domain might produce an improvement that would transfer to other domains. If so, an understanding of the neural basis and psychological function of attention would be an important goal for educational research.

REFERENCES

Aaronson, D., & Scarborough, H. (1976). Performance theories for sentence coding: some quantitative evidence. *Journal of Experimental Psychology: Human Perception and Performance, 1,* 56–70.

Baron, J. (1973). Phonemic stages not necessary for reading. *Quarterly Journal of Experimental Psychology, 25,* 241–246.

Baron, J., & Strawson, C. (1976). Use of orthographic and word specific knowledge in reading words aloud. *Journal of Experimental Psychology: Human Perception and Performance, 2,* 386–393.

Becker, C. A. (1980). Semantic context effects in visual word recognition: An analysis of semantic strategies. *Memory and Cognition, 6,* 493–512.

Blank, M. A., & Foss, D. J. (1978). Semantic facilitation and lexical access during sentence processing. *Memory & Cognition, 6* (6), 644–652.

Bradley, H., & Bryant, P. (1979). The independence of reading and spelling in backward and normal readers. *Developmental Medicine and Child Neurology, 21,* 504–514.

Bradshaw, J. L. (1975). Three interrelated problems in reading: A review. *Memory & Cognition, 3*(2), 123–134.

Broadbent, D. E. (1958). *Perception and Communication.* London: Pergamon.

Chang, F. R. (1981). *Distribution of attention within a single fixation in reading: Studies of the perceptual span.* Unpublished doctoral dissertation, University of Oregon, Eugene.

Chi, M. T. H. (1976). Short-term memory capacity in children: Capacity or processing deficits. *Memory and Cognition, 4,* 559–572.

Coltheart, M., Davelaar, E., Jonnasson, J. R., & Besner, D. (1977). Access to the internal lexicon. In S. Dornic (Ed.). *Attention and performance* (Vol. 6). Hillsdale, NJ: Erlbaum.

Coltheart, M., Patterson, K., & Marshall, J. (Eds.). (1980). *Deep dyslexia.* London: Routledge and Kegan Paul.

Conrad, C. (1974). Context effects in sentence comprehension: A study of the subjective lexicon. *Memory & Cognition, 2*(1A), 130–138.

Davidson, B. J. (1978). *Coding processes during reading.* Unpublished doctoral dissertation, University of Oregon, Eugene.

Dyer, F. N. (1973). The Stroop phenomenon and its use in the study of perceptual, cognitive and response processes. *Memory & Cognition, 1*(2), 106–120.

Eimas, P. D., Sequeland, E. R., Jusczyk, P., & Vigorito, J. (1971). Speech perception in infants. *Science, 171,* 303–306.

Eisenberg, P., & Becker, C. A. (1982). Semantic context effects in visual word recognition, sentence processing and reading: evidence for semantic strategies. *Journal of Experimental Psychology: Human Perception and Performance, 8,* 739–756.

Eriksen, C., & Hoffman, J. (1973). The extent of processing of noise elements during selective encoding from visual displays. *Perception and Psychophysics, 14*(1), 155–160.

Fischler, I. (1977). Semantic facilitation without association in a lexical decision task. *Memory & Cognition, 5*(3), 335–339.

Fischler, I., & Bloom, P. A. (1979). Automatic and attentional processes in the effects of sentence contexts on word recognition. *Journal on Verbal Learning & Verbal Behavior, 18,* 1–20.

Frederiksen, J. R. (1978, January). A chronometric study of component skills in reading. (Report #3757, Technical Report No. 2). Bolt, Beranek & Newman, Inc., Boston.

Friedrich, F. J. (1980). [Sentence context effects on word recognition.] Unpublished raw data, University of Oregon, Eugene.

Gopher, D., & Kahneman, D. (1971). Individual differences in attention and the prediction of flight criteria. *Perceptual & Motor Skills, 33,* 1335–1342.

Gottfried, A. W., Rose, S. A., & Bridger, W. H. (1977). Cross-modal transfer in human infants. *Child Development, 48,* 118–123.

Graesser, A. C., Hoffman, N. L., & Clark, L. F. (1980). Structural components of reading time. *Journal of Verbal Learning and Verbal Behavior, 19,* 135–151.

Hanson, V. (1981). Processing of written and spoken words: Evidence for common coding. *Memory & Cognition, 9,* 93–100.

Hawkins, H. L., Reicher, G. M., Rogers, M., & Peterson, L. (1976). Flexible coding in word recognition. *Journal of Experimental Psychology: Human Perception and Performance, 2,* 380–385.

Hintzmen, D. I., Block, R. A., & Inskeep, N. R. (1972). Memory for mode of input. *Journal of Verbal Learning & Verbal Behavior, 11,* 741–749.

Keele, S. & Hawkins, H. (1982). Explorations of individual differences relevant to high level skill. *Journal of Motor Behavior, 14*(1), 3–23.

Killion, T. (1981). *Task effects in the processing of lexical ambiguity.* Unpublished doctoral dissertation University of Oregon, Eugene.

Kirsner, K., & Smith, M. (1974). Modality effects in word identification. *Memory & Cognition, 2*(4), 637–640.

Kleiman, G. M. (1975). Speech recoding in reading. *Journal of Verbal Learning and Verbal Behavior, 14,* 323–339.

Kleiman, G. M. (1980). Sentence frame contexts and lexical decisions: Sentence-acceptability and word-relatedness effects. *Memory & Cognition, 8*(4), 336–344.

Kowler, E., & Martins, A. J. (1982). Eye movements of preschool children. *Science, 215*, 997–999.

LaBerge, D., & Samuels, S. J. (1974). Toward a theory of automatic information processing in reading. *Cognitive Psychology, 6*, 293–323.

Liberman, I. Y., Shankweiler, D., Fischer, F. W., & Carter, B. (1974). Explicit syllable and phoneme segmentation in the young child. *Journal of Experimental Psychology, 18*, 201–212.

Marcel, A. (1980). Conscious and preconscious recognition of polysemous wards: Locating selective effects of prior verbal context. In *Attention and performance* (Vol. 8) (pp. 435–458).

Meltzoff, A. N., & Barton, R. W. (1980). Intermodal matching by human neonates. *Nature 1980, 282*, 403–404.

Mesulam, M. (1981). A cortical network for directed attention and unilateral neglect. *Neurology, 10*, 309–325.

Mountcastle, V. B. (1978). Brain mechanisms for directed attention. *Journal of the Royal Society of Medicine. 71*, 14–28.

Neely, J. H. (1977). Semantic priming and retrieval from lexical memory: Roles of inhibitionless spreading activation and limited-capacity attention. *Journal of Experimental Psychology: General, 106*, 226–254.

Perfetti, C. A., & Hogaboam, T. (1975). Relationship between single word decoding and reading comprehension skill. *Journal of Educational Psychology, 65*, 461–469.

Piontkowski, D., & Calfee, R. (1979). Attention in the classroom. In G. Hale & M. Lewis (Eds.), *Attention and Cognitive Development*. New York: Plenum Press.

Posner, M. I. (1970). On the relationship between letter names and superordinate categories. *Quarterly Journal of Experimental Psychology, 22*, 279–287.

Posner, M. I. (1978). *Chronometric explorations of mind: The Third Paul M. Fitts Lectures.* Hillsdale, N.J: Erlbaum.

Posner, M. I. (1980). Orienting of attention: the VIIth Sir Frederic Bartlett Lecture. *Quarterly Journal of Experimental Psychology, 32*, 3–25.

Posner, M. I. (1982, February). Cumulative development of attentional theory. *American Psychologist.*

Posner, M. I., Cohen, Y., & Rafal, R. (1982). Neural systems control of spatial orienting. *Proceedings of the Royal Society of London, Series B, 298*, 187–198.

Posner, M. I., & Rothbart, M. K. (1980). The development of attentional mechanisms. In J. Flowers & H. Howe (Eds.), *Nebraska Symposium on Motivation*. Lincoln: University of Nebraska Press.

Posner, M. I., & Shulman, G. (1979). Cognitive science. In E. Hearst (Ed.)., *The First Century of Experimental Psychology*. Hillsdale, NJ: Erlbaum.

Posner, M., Cohen, Y., Choate, L., Hockey, R., & Maylor, E. (1984). Sustained concentration: Active orienting or passive filtering. In S. Kornblum & J. Requin, (Eds.), *Preparatory States and Processes* (pp. 49–65). Hillsdale, NJ: Erlbaum.

Potter, M. C., Kroll, J. F., & Harris, C. (1980). Comprehension and memory in rapid sequential reading. In R. C. (Ed.), Nickerson *Attention and performance* (Vol. 8) (pp. 395–417). Hillsdale, NJ: Erlbaum.

Rankin, E. (1978). Rate of comprehension flexibility: A new measurement procedure. *Twenty-Seventh Yearbook of the National Reading Conference*. New York: Wiley.

Rayner, K., Well, A. D., & Pollatsek, A. (1980). Asymmetry of the effective visual field in reading. *Perception & Psychophysics, 27*, 537–544.

Robinson, D. L., Goldberg, M. E., & Stanton, G. B. (1978). Parietal association cortex in the primate: Sensory mechanisms and behavioral modulations. *Journal of Neurophysiology, 41,* 910–932.

Rothbart, M., & Derryberry, D. (1982). Development of individual differences in temperament. In M. Lewis & L. Taft (Eds.). *Advances in developmental psychology* (Vol. 1). Hillsdale, NJ: Erlbaum.

Rozin, P., & Gleitman, L. (1977). The structure and acquisition of reading. II. The reading process and the acquisition of the alphabetic principle. In A. S. Reber & D. Scarborough (Eds.), *Toward a psychology of reading. The proceedings of the CUNY conferences.* Hillsdale, NJ: Erlbaum.

Saffran, E. M., & Marin, O. S. M. (1975). Immediate memory for word lists and sentences in a patient with deficient auditory short term memory. *Brain and Language, 2,* 420–433.

Schadler, M., & Thissen, D. M. (1981). The development of automatic word recognition and reading skill. *Memory & Cognition.*

Sen, A., & Posner, M. I. (1979). the effect of unattended visual and auditory words on cross modal naming. *Bulletin of the Psychonomic Society, 13,* 405–408.

Stanovich, K., & West, R. F. (1981). The effect of sentence context on ongoing word recognition: Tests of a two process theory. *Journal of Experimental Psychology: Human Perception and Performance, 7,* 658–672.

Treiman, R. (1980). *The phonemic analysis ability of preschool children.* Unpublished doctoral dissertation, University of Pennsylvania, Philadelphia.

Treisman, A. M., & Gelade, G. (1980). A feature integration theory of attention. *Cognitive Psychology, 12,* 97–136.

Treisman, A., & Schmidt, H. (1982). Illusory conjunctions in the perception of objects. *Cognitive Psychology, 14,* 107–142.

Warren, R. E. (1972). Stimulus encoding and memory. *Journal of Experimental Psychology, 94,* 90–100.

CHAPTER **4**

The Role of Attention in Cognition*

Herbert A. Simon

In our progress toward understanding human thinking and information process, we will gradually, over the years, build bridges from the
neurological level of explanation over to the levels of basic information
processes with which Posner is mainly concerned, and of complex information processes with which I and some of my colleagues are mostly
preoccupied. At the complex end of that bridge, of course, are the cognitive processes we encounter in school learning. A volume like this one is
exceedingly useful in measuring, from time to time, the progress in our
bridge-building efforts.

I. THE MEANING OF ATTENTION

It might be useful, although perhaps elementary and even redundant
for the readers of this volume, to examine what we mean by attention
and what its role is in controlling behavior and internal cognitive processes. The authors of the preceding papers provided their definitions—
one of them reminded us of William James' (1890) well-known quota-
tion: "Everyone knows what attention is." Nevertheless, we might
pursue the definitional question a little further.

The concept of attention is of particular significance for an organism
that, apart from its sensory and motor organs, must carry out its thinking serially, rather than in parallel. Although there is still some disagree-
ment about the amount of parallel activity in human thinking, we might
agree that those processes that require attention can only go on one at a
time or a few at a time. We have a limited capacity for attention, which is
best modeled as a serial system.

It is interesting to raise the evolutionary question of why higher or-

* This research was supported by Research Grant MH-07722 from the National Institute
of Mental Health, and by a grant from Alfred P. Sloan Foundation.

ganisms generally evince this phenomenon of attention—why their thinking exhibits seriality and an attentional bottleneck. First—and this has been emphasized in the preceding chapters—such an organism needs a mechanism that will sustain its focus over some time on a particular problem context. Organisms are continually surrounded by a very rich and complex stimulus field, from which an enormous amount of information could be extracted each second. In the brains of higher organisms there is also stored a large amount of information that could be evoked at any moment, and thereby impact on, and influence, behavior. The organism needs a mechanism to guarantee that only a very small part of the potentially available stimulus information, and only a very small part of the information potentially available from long-term memory, is brought to bear on behavior during any short interval of time. In the absence of such a restriction, the organism would be buffeted by irrelevancies, and behavior would go off in all directions at once.

If I were to break out suddenly in Latin, that would be disconcerting both to the reader and to me. It is best that what little Latin remains stored in my brain not be evoked except in those rare instances when it becomes relevant to the problem that faces me. Attentional mechanisms enforce that relevance.

Second, on the positive side, a function of attention is to select out stimulus and memory elements that, though not active at the moment, *would* be relevant to the current problem context. Attention brings this information from the senses and from memory into the focus of attention, into the active processor.

A third, equally crucial, function of the attentional mechanisms is to allow a *shift* in focus and context: to break off the continuity of thought in order to respond to real-time requirements of the organism in adapting to its environment. Because bricks do fly through the air sometimes, it is good to be able to notice and dodge a brick even if you are not scanning the horizon for missiles when it comes flying. The attention mechanisms produce such interruptions when sudden, unexpected stimuli present themselves.

From a physiological standpoint, the eye can be regarded almost as two organs. The fovea is designed to transmit information that is in the focus of attention, while the periphery is designed to interrupt attention when urgent information comes from other directions. Thus, one important function of the visual system, and the same can be said of the auditory, is to provide a mechanism for interrupting the ongoing activity of an organism when what is currently being attended to can be postponed in order to deal with high-priority real-time needs.

This interrupting function of attention, which was not much discussed in the preceding chapters is also closely related to some of the emotions, and to the arousal mechanisms associated with emotion. Physiological psychology has paid a good deal of attention to this bridge, via arousal, between emotion and cognition. Lindsley provided a good account of it 40 years ago in the Stevens *Handbook* (1951). It is a theme that provides important linkage between the physiological and educational ends of the continuum represented in this volume.

Thus, both an evolutionary analysis of the functions that attention might perform in increasing the biological fitness of an organism, and the evidence that is provided by physiological research suggest that there are at least two clusters of mechanisms involved in attention: one producing attention shift through interruption, the other having to do with the filtering of information for relevance to the current context— what some researchers, like Anderson (1976), call "priming."

In their chapter, Posner and Freidrich also referred to two separate mechanisms in visual attention. They discussed covert attention and overt attention, although I do not believe they actually used the latter term. But I do not think the distinction they made is the same as the one that I have just developed. At least, I have not succeeded in providing for myself a mapping between the two.

The chapter by Posner and Friedrich focused primarily on selectivity, and they described attention as the system that enables us to select among competing data and to bias our recall from memory and our ongoing stream of thought toward some contexts rather than others. I am not sure whether they meant that description to encompass the interruption of ongoing attention and the selection of urgent messages that were irrelevant to the previous context.

II.   LEVELS OF EXPLANATION

Both the chapter by Picton *et al.* and by Posner and Friedrich illustrate beautifully the complementarity of neural and behavioral studies, and the way in which they can provide, and now are beginning to provide, clues for each other. Perhaps the younger among us cannot remember a time when they had little to do with each other, but that time lies not very far in the past. A partial exception was the study of brain damage and other brain abnormalities, which have always had to be studied, in the human organism at least, mainly through their behavioral manifestations.

One of the exciting pieces of information in the preceding chapters is about the strong bridges that are being built between the physiological and the behavioral with new techniques made possible by the CAT scanner and measures of brain metabolism, and our new capabilities for interpreting EEGs, particularly EEG responses to specific stimulus events. The chapter by Posner and Friedrich and the one by Wittrock extend our notions of complementarity to the behaviors that are especially relevant to education.

Another way of looking at the links between the physiological and the behavioral is to look at the things that are linked; and that leads immediately to the topic of levels of explanation, that is, the idea that there is a physiological level of explanation of human cognitive behavior, a level of explanation in terms of basic or elementary information processes, and a level of explanation in terms of complex information processes.

As a characterization of the world of psychology today, this description in terms of levels is rather accurate. It is even reflected in the sociology of our profession. Students earn their degrees from different departments and study different topics and develop different skills if they are interested in research at one of these levels than if they are interested in another. It is thought to be a real mark of courage, or foolhardiness, for a researcher to try to operate at two levels. There are separate literatures which we do not feel obligated to know in detail—or perhaps not at all—if they are not at our own level.

So it is a fact about research in cognition that these three levels exist. The more important question is whether it is healthy for scientific progress that they exist. That, of course, raises the question of what would constitute a satisfactory theory of cognition, a satisfactory explanation of human thinking. Let's look at the matter for a moment from the viewpoint of the educational level downward (or upward, if that is the way your map is oriented). How detailed a theory of attention at one level will be helpful in building a theory at the next higher level? This is the "who-needs-it?" question. Do we in fact need a physiological theory in order to explain cognition at the level of elementary information processes; and do we in fact need a theory of elementary information processes in order to understand how children learn to read or to spell or to do arithmetic?

A theoretical case can be made for sealing off the levels from each other, or nearly sealing them off. We have many successful instances of this in other sciences. The whole field of biochemistry does not wobble and shake every time physicists get a new idea about quarks. It is fortunate that it does not, because there is as yet little stability in the world of quarks. Yet we believe that quarks lie at the basis of elementary particles, particles at the basis of atoms, atoms at the basis of molecules, and so on. We are aware of the relations among the levels, but we can provide scientific explanations for phenomena at one level without understanding the underlying levels in detail.

Science, in fact, is something that can be hung from skyhooks; it does not always have to have a foundation from below. Nineteenth-century chemistry built a powerful theory for understanding chemical reactions and predicting them long before there was any kind of an atomic model beyond the idea that molecules were made of little, mostly structureless, balls.

The other side of the coin is that when the atomic model did reach a certain point of development—let us say, the stage of quantum mechanics in 1926 or therabouts—there began to be major leakage, so to speak, between the levels, and the atomic level began to have the important impact on the chemical level that it continues to have today. The whole new discipline of physical chemistry developed to deal with the linkage between the two levels.

So, I think a correct statement of the situation is something like this: sciences do tend to form hierarchies, where level in the hierarchy has to do with the degree of minuteness of the phenomena and the amount of detail we are concerned with, how microscopic a theory of the phenomena we want. For many purposes it is possible to build a macrotheory at some level of aggregation without knowing the details of the underlying microtheory.

We have a very clear understanding of this phenomenon of layering today derived from our experience with computer programming languages. One can become an expert programmer in PASCAL, LISP, FORTRAN, or some other higher-level language without knowing anything about assembly language or machine language, and certainly without having the slightest hint of what a transistor or a chip is as a physical or functional device. In fact, as the past four generations of computers show—each new generation built with completely different physical devices from the previous one—the programming level of computer behavior can rest on the most diverse physical underpinnings. Obviously, there is an almost complete sealing off of the physical microlevel of tubes or transistors, as the case may be, from the macroscopic level of programming languages.

Although, as the chemistry example shows, sealing-off of levels is never hermetic, the question is what details from below, if we knew them, would affect in a major way the theory at the macroscopic level. That is the practical question of the relation of all of the physiological and information-processing research to education.

Now, the answer might be different if our interests were, say, in the education of normal children in schools having a 30 to 1 student:teacher ratio from what it would be if we were interested in special education or one-to-one tutoring. It might turn out that for the typical school situation we would want a very rough-grained theory, and would be little concerned with the more microscopic levels. However, if we were dealing with children who had learning deficits, and particularly if those deficits were known or strongly suspected to derive from specific physiological deficits, then it might be of great importance to have a fine-grained physiological theory.

Consequently, my hunch is that the physiological research on cognition, and to a lesser extent the research on elementary information processes, will have its first impact, and perhaps its largest impact, on our work with children who have specific physiological problems. It may be a longer time before it will have significant impact on our ways of educating normal children. Perhaps it will never have such an impact, but "never" is a long time. People who make predictions about "never" usually turn out to be wrong.

III. THE EDUCATIONAL LEVEL OF THEORY

Let me now write from the viewpoint of the educational level of theory. I am only half-qualified to do that, because I have taught only in universities, and university teachers do not have to demonstrate professional competence in education—gifted amateurism is fully acceptable. So I am going to put on my professor's hat, instead of my researcher's hat, and try to summarize some of the things we can learn from the experience of teaching.

Most of us would agree that there is a very close connection between attention and learning. Crudely put, the zero-order approximation is simply: No learning without attention. There has even been some research to prove that. We know, for example, that learning does not happen during sleep—there's no use putting on earphones when you go to bed. I do not know of any evidence to refute the proposition that attention to something is a prerequisite for learning about that something. That is the zero-order theory.

The next approximation, the first-order theory, is that a person who attends for 8 seconds to a chunk (I am using the term *chunk* in the same technical sense that George Miller did in his famous "magical number seven" paper [1956]) will learn that chunk and will have it stored in long-term memory. There is an enormous amount of support for that hypothesis from the rote-learning literature, going back all the way to Ebbinghaus (1885/1913). The actual time might be 9 seconds or 7 seconds, but 8 seconds is a good round number that summarizes well the findings in the experimental literature. If you hold your attention on something for about 8 seconds, something is going to be stored in your brain, the kind of thing we now call a chunk, a familiar item.

Those are my zero-order and first-order theories of the relation between attention and learning. What they imply for education is that we should be focusing on how to gain and hold people's attention—how to get their attention applied to whatever it is we want them to learn. Teachers have believed that for quite some time. That is why we tell jokes in class, in order to get attention. (Sometimes there are better ways.)

A somewhat more sophisticated theory would claim that it is also important to consider what is learned. Most experienced teachers know that there is a fundamental difference, although it is still only partly understood, between rote learning and meaningful learning. If we knew how to secure differential attention, we would want to direct it in such a way that the resulting learning would be meaningful rather than rote (Katona, 1940).

Because *meaningful* and *rote* are very fuzzy words, long banned by behaviorism, let me give you at least an example of what I mean by them. There exist rather simple algorithms for solving single linear algebraic equations in one variable. Every child has to learn how to do that in about a week during his first year of high school. It's just the basic skill of being given $4x + 17 = 3x + 2$ and finding what x is.

The algorithm is not usually written out explicitly in the algebra textbook, but it could be written without any difficulty. But we all know that if it were written explicitly in the textbook, some students would suppose that what they ought to do is to memorize it. Having memorized it, they would be surprised that they could not solve any algebra equations.

We know that there is a difference between memorizing that algorithm and acquiring the ability to apply it when appropriate. By the distinction between *rote* and *meaningful* I mean just some such distinction between being able to store away sequences of words and to repeat them on demand and being able to deal with problem situations appropriately.

This leads to a next step. One thing we are learning today from research on complex tasks (e.g., how people solve physics problems or how they make chess moves), and particularly research on how experts do such tasks, is that when experts look at a problem situation in their domain of expertise, they immediately recognize familiar features in the situation, and these turn out to be the principal relevant features for correct handling of the situation (Larkin, McDermott, Simon, & Simon,

1980). I say "turn out to be." Of course, it is no accident; that is why they are experts. They have learned to recognize just those things that are, in fact, relevant to the task.

So the expert who looks at the equation $4x + 17 = 3x + 2$ says, "Oh, there's a 17 on the left-hand side before the equals sign. We have to get rid of that." Then he or she does something appropriate to get rid of it. But recognition of the relevant feature, the unwanted 17, is the first step.

One can argue convincingly from the research evidence that a large part of expert skill consists in recognizing these features of situations. This was the point of much of the research that William Chase and I did on chess experts: showing the experts' ability to recognize important features of chess positions, and to retrieve from memory appropriate responses stored in association with those recognitions (Simon & Chase, 1973). The chess grandmaster says, "Oh, there is an open file; I had better move my rook to it." Of course, he or she does not necessarily make that move, but she or he *always* notices that it is possible, and thinks about it as a possible action to take.

The hypothesis arises from this kind of research that a large component of expert skill resides in the ability to attend, upon seeing a stimulus in the domain of the skill, to the relevant parts of the stimulus; and, through that attention and the resultant recognition, to get access in long-term memory to the information that is required for executing the skill at that point.

Most of you know of the estimates that have been made of the number of patterns an expert might be able to recognize. The estimates always come out to be of the order of magnitude of 50,000, roughly the size of the natural language vocabulary of a college-trained person. A chess master can recognize 50,000 different little clusters of pieces on a chess board, and knows the sorts of things that ought to be done in response to the presence of these patterns (Simon & Chase, 1973).

From an educational point of view, we might argue that it is important for us to understand what the patterns are, in any discipline, that have to be discriminated and learned. And as educators, we have to understand how people can be induced to learn to attend better. If we look at current educational practice, and particularly at current textbooks, I think we will find that in most domains (I have looked mainly at science and mathematics textbooks) there is insufficient attention to the discriminative and recognition skills that are needed for expert task performance.

You have all experienced the professor who stands up at the beginning of the math class and starts writing a proof on the left side of the blackboard. The professor goes all the way across the board, and down in the lower right-hand corner finally writes "QED." You have followed every step and you know he or she has not cheated; every step follows by the laws of mathematics from the previous one. But at the end, you scratch your head and say, "What made Prof think of doing that?"

We are able to check the individual steps. But we lack the recognition capacity of noticing and attending at each step to that aspect of the stimulus that would tell us what step to take next. Attention and recognition play a key role in determining whether we understand what is going on, and are able to acquire the skill of constructing such proofs.

IV.   MOTIVATION FOR ATTENTION

I have not mentioned at all yet the topic relating to attention that is most often discussed by educators: What is there in it for the student? What is the motivation for attention? How do you induce students to attend?

One might even better say, "How do you motivate students to be *able* to attend? It is not clear that attention is a wholly voluntary action. The research we have heard reported in this session certainly does not suggest that attention is always voluntary.

We have a good deal of common-sense knowledge about attention, gleaned from our experiences as teachers. We believe that there is advantage from an educational standpoint in intrinsic over extrinsic motivation. That is, we believe that learning is facilitated if the stimuli that have to be attended to are interesting to the learner. We have various reasons for thinking that such intrinsic motivation may provide a more satisfactory basis for education than extrinsic motivation—"If you get an A on your report card, your allowance will be increased." We all know some of the theory and research on which this preference for intrinsic motivation is based.

If it is correct that we need intrinsic motivation to get the kind of attention that facilitates learning, then we need a theory about what makes things interesting. I would simply remark—not by way of criticism, for space was limited—that this aspect of attention did not receive very much attention in this volume.

The largest body of work on the determinants of attention was that done by Berlyne (1965). Berlyne showed that people (and rats) will give their most persistent attention to stimuli that are neither too simple nor too complex. When a stimulus is so simple (relative to the intelligence and previous experience of the organism) that there is nothing new in it, it will be boring and not attended to. When the stimulus is so complex that the organism cannot detect any pattern in it, there is also nothing to attend to, and it will be boring. These pieces of the theory of attention, and the relation between complexity and interest, would add another dimension to the topic as we have developed it in this volume, a dimension that is highly relevant for educational practice.

How detailed a theory of attention do we need for improvement of education? We might decide that we really did not need a neurological theory, but that we did need an information-processing theory. Or we might decide that we need only a theory of the complex processes, and we do not really need the layers below.

My guess is that we are going to opt, eventually, for all of these. We are not going to decide that there is one level on which we should focus exclusively. I cite two examples from the chapters in this volume, one of which has immediate methodological implications.

From Posner's report, we see that there is covert attention or selectivity in the response to visual stimuli even in the absence of eye movements. We do not simply look at whatever it is the fovea is pointed at, but we may look at a highly selective part of the stimulus that is within foveal vision. The methodological implication is that we should not depend on eye movements as a sovereign instrument for saying everything that has to be said about attention, even at the macro level.

The second example is the demonstration that there are several mechanisms having to do with attention, some of which may be under obvious voluntary control, and some of them quite involuntary. These two parts, the voluntary and the involuntary, may play quite different roles in the learning process.

V.   FINAL COMMENTS

In my comments, I have not mentioned the kinds of research that are closest to my own interest—computer modeling—and the relation of simulation research to the question of levels of theory. I would like to add just a footnote on that topic.

Suppose we are trying to model performance on school tasks, like solving physics problems (a principal current preoccupation of our research group [Larkin, McDermott, Simon, & Simon, 1980]) or spelling English words (on which my wife and I did some research a short time ago [Simon & Simon, 1973]). Suppose that we were trying to model these processes in a way that would be relevant to improving education in these subjects? How detailed would that model be? Would we need to construct a physiological model? Can we get away with a model that only goes down to the level of elementary information processes of the sort that Posner has discussed? Or can we even use a model that incorporates rather gross and complex information processes without analyzing them in detail?

I do not think we need to accept a doctrinaire answer to this question. We can usefully understand such processes at all three of these levels. For example, in the spelling case, with a rather aggregate and coarse model, we were able to predict rather accurately what spelling errors would be made with a word like "responsible." Moreover, from our detailed predictions of the spelling errors, we were able to draw some more general conclusions as to the value of certain kinds of educational procedures in improving spelling. Hence, modeling human performance in school subjects can give us some clues as to what help we could get from a coarse theory and when we might need one carried to a more detailed level.

REFERENCES

Anderson, J. R. (1976). *Language, memory, and thought*. Hillsdale, NJ: Erlbaum.

Berlyne, D. (1965). *Structure and direction in thinking*. New York: Wiley.

Ebbinghaus, H. (1913). *Memory* (H. A. Ruger & C. E. Bussenius, Trans.). New York: Teachers College. (Original work published 1885.)

James, W. (1890). *The principles of psychology*. New York: Holt.

Katona, G. (1940). *Organizing and memorizing*. New York: Columbia University Press.

Larkin, J., McDermott, J., Simon, D. P., & Simon, H. A. (1980). Expert and novice performance in solving physics problems. *Science, 208*, 1335–1342.

Lindsley, D. B. (1951). Emotion. In S. S. Stevens (Ed.), *Handbook of experimental psychology*. New York: Wiley.

Miller, G. A. (1956). The magical number seven, plus or minus two: Some limits on our capacity for processing information. *Psychological Review, 63*, 81–97.

Simon, H. A., & Chase, W. G. (1973). Skill in chess. *American Scientist, 61*, 394–403.

Simon, D. P., & Simon, H. A. (1973). Alternative uses of phonemic information in spelling. *Review of Educational Research, 43*, 115–137.

PART III

KNOWLEDGE ACQUISITION, REPRESENTATION, AND USE

CHAPTER 5

Biological Preprogramming for Language Learning?*

Lila R. Gleitman

Language is a paradigm case for understanding how humans represent, acquire, and use a complex cognitive system. It is particularly interesting for a discussion that brings neuroscientists and educators together with cognitive scientists. This is because language knowledge, as instantiated in every normal human, results from a complicated set of biologically preprogrammed capacities, significantly modulated by experience. Stated so generally, there can be no controversy about this claim. To believe that special biological adaptations are a requirement, it is enough to notice that all the children but none of the dogs and cats in the house acquire language. To that extent, language is learned "inside out" by organisms with specific mental endowments, and so surely is of some interest to neuroscientists. To believe that language is nevertheless learned, it is sufficient to note the massive correlation between living in France and learning French, and living in Germany and learning German. Because language is thus acquired "outside in" as a direct consequence of specific exposure conditions, it has prima facie interest for educators.

In the following discussion, I first present a schematic description of the language learning task, followed by a sketch of the kinds of argument often put forward in favor of significant biological preprogramming supporting that learning. Thereafter, I summarize the kinds of investigation that are being carried out by our own group of investigators. Finally, I will venture that these findings are of some ultimate interest to neuroscientists and educators.

* I was aided in writing this paper by Henry Gleitman, who read and criticized an earlier draft. I thank the March of Dimes Foundation for continuing support of the work described in this paper, under grants #12-25 and #12-113.

119

I.   ANALYSIS OF THE LANGUAGE LEARNING PROBLEM

Chomsky (1965) and other investigators (Pinker, 1979; Wexler & Culicover, 1980) have provided a schematic analysis of language learning; roughly, it looks like this:

1. The learner receives some sample utterances from the language.

2. He simultaneously observes situations: objects, scenes, and events in the world.

3. These utterance/situation pairs constitute the input to language learning. The learner's job is to project from the sample utterance/situation pairs a system, or grammar, that encompasses all sentence/meaning pairs in the language. This job includes, of course, learning the meanings and forms of words, for these affect the meanings of sentences. But it also includes as well learning the syntactic structures, for these affect the meaning of sentences even when the component words are held constant (i.e., *Caesar killed Brutus* and *Brutus killed Caesar* mean different things).

4. For learning to go forward, learners must have some means for representing the utterances and the situations to themselves in a linguistically relevant way. For example, though they receive utterances in the form of continuously varying sound waves, they must be disposed to represent these as sequences of discrete formatives such as phone, syllable, word, phrase, and sentence; and though they receive impressions of some single object, they must be disposed to represent it in various ways, such as 'Fido,' 'dog,' 'mammal,' 'physical object,' and not in other ways, such as 'undetached dog-parts.'

5. The learner must also have some strategies for manipulating these data in the interest of extracting the regularities that bind them.

6. She must have some perspective on the kinds of descriptive devices, or rule systems, that she is willing to countenance as statements of the regularities. To put this another way, different language learning "machines" (particular representational systems, with particular computational procedures) will construct different grammars, based on the same data.

7. Finally, learners must have some criterion that will lead them to stabilize on a particular conjecture about the grammar, to decide once and for all that the learning job is completed.

As presented, this analysis is neutral about many issues. For example, it is possible that tutors are required for some of these steps to be taken successfully—perhaps the learner requires the caretakers to say only very simple sentences, or sentences of restricted kinds, early in the learning period; and perhaps he requires reinforcement for correct performances and correction of errors made along the way. Depending on whether these additional conditions are met, quite different kinds of machine will be able to learn a human language. Therefore it is of some interest to examine the real input circumstances of children and the early generalizations they draw from these inputs. This may help to disentangle the kinds of internal and external resources learners recruit to crack the language code.

II. A SIGNIFICANT INNATE BASIS FOR LANGUAGE LEARNING

Three main kinds of argument favor the supposition that language and its learning are biologically preprogrammed. The first two derive from empirical study of learning: (1) language learning proceeds in uniform ways within a linguistic community, despite extensive variability of the input provided to individuals; and (2) the character of what is learned is not simply related to the input sample. A third argument is logical: (3) the child acquires many linguistic generalizations that experience could not have made available.

II.A.   UNIFORM LEARNING

Inquiry into language learning is constrained by one main principle. The right theory has to cope with the fact that everybody does it, by specifying a learning device guaranteed to converge on the grammar of any language to which it is exposed, in finite time, and in fair indifference to particulars of the sample data received (Wexler, 1982). This principle is based on the real world facts of the matter. Under widely varying environmental circumstances, learning different languages under different conditions of culture and childrearing, and with different motivations and talents, all nonpathological children acquire their native tongue at a high level of proficiency within a narrow developmental time frame. (This does not mean there are no differences in final attainment, but these differences pale into insignificance when compared with the samenesses.)

Moreover, there are very interesting similarities in the course this learning takes. Isolated words appear at about age 1 year, followed by two-word utterances at about age 2 years. Thereafter, sometime during the third year of life, there is a sudden spurt of vocabulary growth accompanied, coincidentally or not, by elaboration of the sentence structures. By about 4 years of age, the speaker sounds essentially adult, though his sentences tend to be quite short because the use of embeddings is limited, and though some item-specific information continues to come in through about ages 8 or 9 years. (By item-specific information, I have reference particularly to some features of derivational morphology, and significant growth of vocabulary.)

Summarizing, similarities in the pattern of learning are observed across individuals and across linguistic communities. As Lenneberg observed many years ago (1967), these uniformities in course of learning, despite vast differences in experience, are a first basis for conjecturing that language learning has a significant biological basis. Lenneberg adduced a good deal of further evidence tending to support such a claim; while each particle of this evidence is arguable, taken together his findings do begin to make a case. For instance, Lenneberg provided some normative evidence that the language acquisition process seems to be tied quite well to developments (e.g., the appearance of sitting, standing, walking, and jumping) that are known on other grounds to be maturationally dependent. Another finding of potential relevance had to do with the fact that children seem to be superior in language learning to adults. Lenneberg also made the claim that recovery from brain injury that implicates language is likely in children, but rare in adults. He conjectured that the capacity for language learning tends to wither away as the brain matures. To that extent, there would be a biologically sensitive period for language learning, or critical period.

The kinds of evidence adduced so far are so fragmentary, however, that they are consistent with quite distinct conjectures about what is learned and the basis for this learning. For example, global facts about perceptual and cognitive development rather than specific facts about an encapsulated language-learning mechanism in the head may be sufficient to describe some of them (Slobin, 1973; 1982). Moreover, there may be constraints on the input (e.g., the idea that simplest sentences are presented to the youngest or most primitive learners) that explain the similarities in the learning patterns even though casual inspection suggests great variability in that input. Thus rudimentary current evidence about learning is insufficient to support refined claims about how biology and experience interact to produce language knowledge. Exacerbating these difficulties, there are at present many contending descriptions of grammar—of what is finally learned. Given these disagreements about *what* is learned, it is hard to describe *how* it is learned. But in my view, some further evidence summarized below tips the balance of plausibility toward a biologically preprogrammed learning procedure much of which is specific to the language domain.

II.B. CHARACTER OF LEARNING; DISPARITIES BETWEEN INPUT AND OUTPUT

Closer inspection of the learning patterns suggests that the character of knowledge at various developmental moments is hard to reconcile with superficial properties of the input data. To be sure, the child learns from what she hears. But she does not directly copy these heard sentences, but makes systematic "errors." These errors can be understood, but only by claiming the learner filters the input data through an emerging system of rules of grammar, rules to which the learner is never directly exposed. (No one explains the language rules to the children. One reason is that the mothers don't explicitly know the rules. The other reason is that the children wouldn't understand the explanations.)

II.B.1. NONCANONICAL SENTENCES IN; CANONICAL SENTENCES OUT

Some convincing examples were developed by Bellugi (1967). One of her cases concerned interrogative structures. In simple sentences of English, auxiliary verbs appear after the subject noun-phrase, but before the verb (e.g., *I can eat pizza*). But in yes/no questions, the auxiliary precedes the subject (*Can I eat pizza?*). And in so-called *wh*-questions, this subject–auxiliary inversion appears again (*What can I eat?*), this time without the object noun-phrase (*pizza*) and with an initial *wh*-word (e.g., *what* or *when* or *who*) instead. The learner of English is exposed by his caretakers to many such *wh*-questions (about 10% of all the utterances he hears, on one estimate, Newport, 1977). Nevertheless, young learners generally do not reproduce these forms that they hear so often. Instead they produce a form that is virtually never spoken by adults, namely, *What I can eat?* or sometimes even *What can I can eat?* A related finding, also from Bellugi (1967), is that while over 90% of maternal auxiliaries in declaratives are contracted (e.g., *We'll go out now*), the child preferentially uses the uncontracted forms early in the learning period (*We will go out now*). The sense in which the child is learning the language from the presented environment of utterances is evidently quite abstract, in light of such findings.

There is a generalization that predicts these errors, as Bellugi pointed out: Children are biased toward canonical surface structure formats for their utterances (see also Gleitman & Wanner, 1982; Slobin & Bever, 1982). In the canonical declarative sentence of English, the subject does precede the whole verb-phrase, including its auxiliary. An abstract movement transformation reorders these elements in questions.[1] If it is supposed that the child acquires formation rules that underly the declarative first and countenances movement rules only later, this particular error is predictable. Similarly, it is possible to suppose that only the full canonical forms (*will*) of words like *'ll* are entered into the learner's lexicon. Contraction is achieved by a rule that operates on these abstract lexical representations under restricted circumstances. (For further discussion, see II.B.2.) In sum, it is certainly possible to explain why the young child does not behave exactly like her models, who contract and invert. One can invoke a bias toward canonical forms in the language being learned. But this, in turn, implies that the young learner has an ability to reconstruct the canonical forms for questions and for words like *'ll*. These canonical forms are related to the utterances she actually hears only by covert rules. Considering the tender age of humans who apparently can perform the complex data manipulations required to recover these canonical representations—quite effortlessly and unconsciously—it is likely that significant biological dispositions are guiding their analyses.

---

[1] Certain linguistic characterizations (see, e.g., Chomsky, 1965, for an early description) assume that interrogative sentences are at some level represented in a format whose phrase organization is just like that of declarative sentences, with the subject noun-phrase preceding the auxiliary and the object noun-phrase following the verb. A rule obligatorily applies to such structures, inverting the order of the subject and the auxiliary. But for those interrogatives beginning with a *wh*-word, there is an additional complication: The object noun-phrase is a question morpheme (*wh-*) joined with a pronoun (e.g., *-at* or *-en*, as in *what* or *when*)—that is, *I can eat what* or, following the inversion, *Can I eat what*. A further obligatory rule applies to such structures. The wh-word is moved to the left, yielding *What can I eat?*

One virtue of such an analysis is that it conforms transparently to the semantics of questions: *What can I eat* seems to be the way of querying (wh?) that unknown thing (-*at*), labelled by a noun-phrase, that can be eaten. Another virtue is that it materially simplifies the description of sentence form. For example, a reasonable generalization about many verbs, for example, *banish*, is that they must be followed by a noun-phrase: *John banished* sounds strange because it does not have such a following noun-phrase. But this generalization seems to be defeated in wh-questions where, indeed, *banish* does occur without a following noun-phrase: *Who did John banish?* The solution is that, at some stage of derivation, this sentence did have the noun-phrase, namely *wh-thing* or *what*, but that that noun-phrase was subsequently "moved." As I am now arguing, the facts about the speech of 2- and 3-year-olds lend independent plausibility to such conjectures about the mental representation of sentences. Thus, I believe, they bear on the psychological relevance of grammatical descriptions that do or do not countenance movement rules (compare, e.g., Wexler & Culicover, 1980; and Pinker, 1982).

II.B.2. OPEN CLASS–CLOSED CLASS

An even more general disparity between input and output, as Brown (1973), Gleitman and Wanner (1982), and many others have discussed, has to do with the differential pattern of acquisition of the so-called open-class and closed-class stock of morphological items (usually called *content* and *functor* words by psychologists). The distinction between these two classes is not easy to state formally (and in fact is partly controversial, see Kean, 1979 for the clearest explication). But technicalities aside, it is fairly clear. It has been known for some time that there are lexical categories that admit new members freely (i.e., new verbs, nouns, and adjectives are being created by language users every day— hence "open class"). Other lexical categories change their membership only very slowly over historical time (hence, "closed class"). The closed class includes the "little" words and affixes, the conjunctions, prepositions, inflectional and derivational suffixes, relativizers, and verbal auxiliaries. These examples given, it is obvious that the closed-class and open-class morphemes are different in many ways. They are restricted in semantic content (e.g., nobody's name is a preposition) and in syntactic function. They differ phonologically as well, i.e., closed-class morphemes are in most usages unstressed, some are subsyllabic, and many more become subsyllabic by contraction (e.g., *will* contracts to *'ll*).

Perhaps the most striking fact about early speech and the context in which it is learned is that open-class and closed-class materials are made available to the learner simultaneously, but these subcomponents of the morphological stock are incorporated into the child's speech at different developmental moments. The mother's speech consists of simple sentences like "The book is on the table," including the closed-class items *the, is,* and *on.* But there is a well-known stage of language learning, the so-called two-word or telegraphic stage, at which the output is "Book table," with all the closed-class items omitted. Thus the most primitive learners seem to have certain devices that allow them to filter out the closed class.

It is not obvious how to explain these developing speech patterns without begging the questions of language learning. For example, even if it were possible to say that the omitted items were the meaningless ones, which it emphatically is not, one wouldn't want to claim the child examines the semantics of closed-class words and on the basis of this, decides to omit them all. This would beg the question at issue: how the semantics of such items are arrived at in the first place. Ditto for a claim based on the syntactic functioning of closed-class items. Gleitman and Wanner (1982; 1984) conjectured that it is the special phonetic realization

of the closed-class items that renders them opaque to youngest learners—they are subsyllabic items or unstressed syllables. Differential attention to the unit *stressed syllable* in the incoming speech wave represents, we believe, one of the significant biases of young learners.[2]
Because of the child's selective attention to stressed syllables, the pattern of acquisition does not mirror the environment directly, but mirrors
the environment only as it is mediated by this preexisting bias as to how
to represent the sound wave. (See Fernald, 1984, for a full discussion of
acoustic-perceptual dispositions in infants, and the position that the
filtering effect of these predispositions plays a role in language learning.)

It is very interesting to notice that the distinction between the open-
class and closed-class morphological components is an organizing factor
in language use even after learning is complete. For example, speech
errors differ for the two classes and almost never involve an exchange
between an open-class and a closed-class item (Garrett, 1975); speed of
lexical retrieval is a function of word frequency for the open-class words
but not the closed-class words (Bradley, 1978); finally, the very definition of the distinction between Broca's and Wernicke's aphasia involves
a differential dissolution of these two subcomponents of language performance (Bradley, Garrett, & Zurif, 1979; Marin, Saffran, & Schwartz,
1976).

II.B.3. Lexical Selections

So far, I've noted selectivity of learning by the child in the syntactic
and morphophonological domains, which can account for differences
between what goes into the child's ear and what first comes out of his
mouth. The case for lexical-category acquisition is just as clear. Evidently, a learner hears verbs and adjectives as well as nouns early in life.
But the child's earliest words are overwhelmingly nouns that encode
simple concrete objects; verbs that encode activities tend to appear later,
and verbs that encode mental states later still; finally, adjectives, which
encode properties of things are later than all these others (e.g., Feldman,
Goldin-Meadow, & Gleitman, 1978; Gentner, 1982; Nelson, 1973). Similarly, certain syntactically rather than lexically encoded semantic-rela-
tional categories (e.g., "agent of the action," for instance *John* in *John eats*

---

[2] The specific acoustic correlates of primary stress in English include longer duration,
higher fundamental frequency, and intensity. For the arguments that follow to hold, it
would be necessary to show that related acoustic properties are available and exploited in
acquiring the nonstress-accent languages, and that these are the properties to which
infants are sensitive and which they reproduce in their first utterances (see Fernald, 1984,
for review of supportive evidence).

peas) uniformly appear early and others (e.g., "instrument of the action," for instance, *knife* in *John eats peas with a knife*) are uniformly later, again though examples of all of them appear in the child's data base—the caregiver's speech—from the beginning (Bloom, Lightbown, & Hood, 1975).

In sum, the child is clearly learning from what she hears (English from English, French from French) but the detailed properties of development are hard to describe as arising very simply or directly from the environment of heard utterances. Likely, global aspects of cognitive development will account for many of these learning patterns. For example, attention to concrete objects and physical activities before mental states and properties is unlikely to have specifically linguistic sources. But the morphophonemic and syntactic choices of novice language learners are less likely to be explained as deriving from general properties of cognitive development.

II.C. LANGUAGE KNOWLEDGE THAT EXPERIENCE COULD NOT PROVIDE

Another kind of argument for innate language-learning capacities comes from logical analyses by Chomsky (1975). These pertain to the learning of certain language properties that experience could hardly have made available. Taking one of his examples, consider that a distinction between higher and lower clause in a phrase structure configuration determines certain properties of movement transformations and of the reference of pronouns. (The characterization of the linguistic facts are perforce rough in this discussion, but will have to do for a sketch.) Specifically, consider again the movement of certain material in English yes/no questions. In the sentence *Is the man a fool?*, the *is* has moved to the left from its canonical position in declarative sentences, *The man is a fool*. But can any *is* in a declarative sentence be moved to form a yes/no question? It is impossible to judge from one-clause sentences alone. The issue is resolved by looking at more complex sentences, which contain more than one clause: It is the *is* in the higher clause, never the *is* in the lower clause, that moves to form yes/no questions from structures underlying, for example, *The man who is a fool is amusing* and *The man is a fool who is amusing*. This generalization explains the acceptability of yes/no questions such as *Is the man who is a fool amusing?* and *Is the man a fool who is amusing?* but the absence of *Is the man who a fool is amusing?* and *Is the man is a fool who amusing?* Whether *is* moves depends on its structural position in the sentence.

Notice that an alternative analysis—namely, serial order of the two *is*'s as opposed to structural position of the two *is*'s—could not explain the facts about English structure: In the examples just given, the moving *is* was once the first *is* in the sentence, but once the second. Learners apparently know that movement rules are structure-dependent, not simply serial-order dependent. To my knowledge, no child ever makes the mistake of saying "Is the man is a fool who amusing?" The important point here is that it is hard to conceive how the environment literally gives the required information to the learner. Surely, only the correct sentences, not the incorrect ones, appear in the input data. But the generalization required for producing new correct sentences is not directly presented, for no hierarchy of clauses appears in real utterances— only a string of words is directly observable to the listener. And certainly there is no instruction about clauses. Even if mothers know something explicit about these matters, which they don't, it wouldn't do much good for them to tell the aspiring learners that "It's the *is* in the higher clause that moves."

Many generalizations about sentence form turn on the same or related configural distinctions (though again the characterization being used here is rough and underestimates the complexity of the descriptive facts). To give one more example, coreference is possible when the pronoun precedes its antecedent but only if the pronoun is in a lower clause than the antecedent—that is, the man mentioned in the second clause could be the one who arrived in the sentence *When he arrived, the man danced* but not in the sentence *He arrived when the man danced*. Without special tutoring, and without an opportunity directly to experience the hierarchical structures, learners come to interpret this coreference correctly even in these hard cases.

As a final example, to explain what is finally learned, it has been necessary for Chomsky (and indeed, all syntacticians, to my knowledge) to postulate certain ghostly null elements in the representation of sentences. For example, a sentence I took up earlier was *What can I eat?* Many linguistics will transcribe this sentence as *What can I eat Ø*, as though some trace of its canonical phrase structure, with object noun-phrase following the verb were somehow still there in the question form. Many descriptive facts about English speech can be explained only by postulating such soundless, tasteless, odorless entities in the mental representation of sentences.

As one example, note that the item *is*, which can contract in many positions in English sentences, for example, *What's your name?*, in other positions cannot: One can say *I wonder who he is* but not *I wonder who he's*. Suppose that an abstract "trace" of the moved noun-phrase constituent appears in the underlying structure of this sentence, for example, *I wonder who he is* ∅. It can now be postulated that contraction is prohibited preceding the deletion site.

This claim is useful if and only if a large number of superficially distinct restrictions on contraction can be subsumed under the same generalization, and indeed this turns out to be the case. To give one more example, the same principle explains why one can use the *wanna* contraction of *want to* in *This is the rabbit who I wanna banish* but not in *This is the rabbit who I want to vanish*. Under an analysis similar to that given in the preceding section, there is a missing noun-phrase in each of these sentences: in each case a rabbit has disappeared. But that noun-phrase is missing from different places in the underlying representations of these sentences, a consequence of the fact that *vanish* is an intransitive verb (whose subject is missing) while *banish* is a transitive verb (whose object is missing). That is, the mental structure of these sentences is plausibly transcribed as *This is the rabbit who I want to banish* ∅ and *This is the rabbit who I want* ∅ *to vanish*. In each case, the trace, ∅, appears where once there was a rabbit. But only in the second case does the trace intervene between *want* and *to*. If it is contiguous *want* and *to* that contract to *wanna*, the real facts about restrictions on contraction are explained.

As a final demonstration of the power of this analysis, notice that *This is the rabbit who I want to visit* is ambiguous (as between *I want to visit the rabbit* and *I want the rabbit to visit*). This is because *visit* can be either transitive or intransitive and hence the rabbit could be missing from the subject or object position. But the *wanna* contraction would not be possible on the intransitive reading, as was just shown for *vanish*. Therefore, as predicted, *This is the rabbit who I wanna visit* is unambiguous: the missing rabbit was the object of *visit*. Young children honor these very abstractly described restrictions on contraction. This implies that mentally they are in possession of a descriptive device that involves something like these null elements though they never "heard" them.

Summarizing, it is hard to imagine how the environment instructs the learner that not serial order simply, but the hierarchical arrangement of clauses, determines properties of sentences and their interpretations, or that spirit-like null elements determine whether contraction is possible and, given the contraction, what the meaning must be of potentially ambiguous sentences. Yet errors on these properties are rare and perhaps nonexistent. This virtually errorless learning of structural properties of the language not transparently offered to experience—the poverty of the stimulus information—forms still another sort of argument that biases, this time biases in the formation and interpretation of configural structures underlying sentences, are required as explanations of how language organization is achieved by the child.

III. THE DEPRIVATION PARADIGM

During the last several years, my associates and I have looked at some natural cases where some of the components of the language learning situation are varied. We have operated by taking to heart the view that utterance/situation pairs are required input for language learning, as described in the schema for learning with which I began. Therefore we have looked at situations where this information is changed. Certain populations of learners allow us to see what happens if there is less or different information about the utterances; other populations allow us to see what happens if there is less or different information about the world. Symmetrically, certain populations are exposed to normal input data but differ from the normal in their current or final mental state. In these latter cases, we are asking what happens when different learning devices are exposed to the same data.

III.A. VARYING THE LANGUAGE SAMPLES

There seems to be quite general agreement that a learner exposed to random samples of the sentences of a language would be unable to converge on the grammar. The main difficulty is the richness of the incoming data, which would seem to support so bewildering a variety of generalizations, including wrong and irrelevant ones, that we would expect learners to vary extremely in the time at which they hit on the grammar of their language.

It is usually assumed, following findings from Brown and Hanlon (1970) that negative feedback, or correction, from the environment cannot be relied on to solve this problem. This is not so much that feedback for ungrammaticalness is never given, though Brown and Hanlon have shown it is rare. The main problem is that for a variety of structures and contents—such as those described in the preceding section—the child never errs in the first place, so no opportunity to correct, or to describe the learning as a consequence of such correction, arises. Another problem, as Brown and Hanlon showed, is that correction is given very often for matters other than grammaticalness of the child's utterances, for example their truth or moral propriety. Should the child construe all corrections, then, as grammatical corrections, he might falsely conclude that *ink-on-the-wall* is an outlawed phrase, rather than an outlawed act.

In light of these difficulties, most investigators assume that language learning is on positive examples only. Formally speaking, it is a lot easier to develop a mechanical procedure for learning from presented sample utterances if it is assumed that that procedure receives negative feedback when it makes a false generalization—that is, if it is told that some new sentence it tries out is not a correct sentence of the language being learned (for that demonstration, see Gold, 1967). Hence some proposals have considered whether restrictions or simplifications of sentences presented to novices can substitute for overt corrections.

III.A.1.   EFFECTS OF MATERNAL SIMPLIFICATION: THE MOTHERESE HYPOTHESIS

The paradox so far is that language learning is hard to describe given positive data only (a sample of the correct sentences) and yet all the real learners seem to do very well even though they receive only, or almost only, such positive data. A very popular response to this problem among developmental psycholinguists has been to suppose the environment provides detailed support for learning by ordering the input utterances (see the collection of articles edited by Snow & Ferguson, 1977, for many papers adopting this position). We have called this "the Motherese Hypothesis." It holds that caretakers present linguistic information in a set sequence, essentially smallest sentences to littlest ears.

In fact there is no doubt that adults speak quite differently to children than to adults, so the utterances heard by the children are not random selections from the adult language. The utterances to youngest learners are very short, slow in rate, and the like. Some investigators propose that this natural simplification from caretakers (whatever its source or motivation) plays a causal role in learning. Evidence favoring this hypothesis comes from Fernald (1982; 1984), who has shown that infants prefer to listen to the prosodically exaggerated forms of Motherese, which is used in every known culture: Apparently, as Fernald states, Motherese is "sweet music to the species." Gleitman and Wanner (1982; 1984) have proposed that these exaggerated prosodic cues can help an appropriately preprogrammed learner to reconstruct a global parse of the input sentences, a reconstruction that materially simplifies subsequent steps in the language-learning task.

But evidently there are limits on the work that Motherese can do for the learner. Particularly, it is hard to maintain the view that the preselection of syntactic types by caretakers can bear materially on the acquisition of grammar. Though restricting the sentence types may exclude certain hypotheses from being considered early, they may also make available hypotheses that would be insupportable given the full range of the language structures. As I described in the preceding section, the child would be unable to distinguish the serial order hypothesis from the structure movement hypothesis if all the input sentences were uniclausal (for discussion, see Chomsky, 1975, and Wexler & Culicover, 1980); if more complex sentences are offered, the serial order hypothesis fails on data. However, there is at least some surface plausibility to the idea that the mother first teaches the child some easy structures. After he learns these, she moves on to the next lesson. To help this idea go through, we would have to grant the caretaker some implicit metric of syntactic/semantic complexity so that in principle she could choose judiciously the sentences that might be good to say to learners. Here too there are some initial supportive findings: Caretakers' speech changes to some degree, in correspondence with the learner's age (Newport, 1977).

In our studies of the Motherese hypothesis (Newport, Gleitman, & Gleitman, 1977), we first collected extensive samples of maternal speech to young learners (age range 15 to 27 months). Rather to our surprise, the properties of this speech did not seem promising as aids to learning syntactic forms. The mothers' speech forms were only rarely (less than 10% of the time) canonical sentences, and they were neither uniform syntactically, nor more explicit in how they mapped onto the meanings, than the sentences used among adults. They *were* short and clear, but this hardly suggests anything very specific about how they reveal the syntax of the language.

But it is still possible that some less obvious properties of maternal speech are especially useful to learners. To study this, we revisited the original mother–child pairs 6 months after the first measurement (Newport, Gleitman, & Gleitman, 1977). Analyzing the child's speech at these two times, we were in a position to compute growth scores for each child on many linguistic dimensions. The question was which properties of the mother's speech at Time 1 had predicted the child's rate of growth on each measure, explaining her status at Time 2. (The correlational analysis used a partialling procedure that removed baseline differences among the learners.)

One interesting outcome of these studies was that a number of dimensions of learning rate were utterly indifferent to large differences in the speech pattern of the mothers. For example, the child's increasing tendency to express predicates (as verbs) and their obligatory arguments (as nouns) was not predictable from the particular speech forms presented. In contrast, in the age range studied, the child's progress with the closed-class morphology was a rather strict function of maternal speech style. For example, almost all the variance in rate of learning the English auxiliary verbs is predicted by the preponderance of yes/no questions in maternal speech (for replications of this finding, see Furrow, Nelson, & Benedict, 1979 and Landau & Gleitman, 1985). The effect of these is to place the closed-class items in first serial postion, with stress, and without contraction (e.g., *Will you pass the salt?* rather than *You will pass the salt, You'll pass the salt,* or *'Ll you pass the salt?*). Thus either, or both, positional biases or biases toward stressed syllables (as conjectured by Gleitman & Wanner) can be postulated for the child; and mothers whose usage gets through these child filters have children who learn the closed-class materials the faster.

Recall from the earlier discussion, however, that these environmental factors do not say much about *what* is learned. For one thing, as just stated, no known special properties of Motherese explain the learning patterns for open-class materials or their organization in the child's sentences. Further, the evidence is clear that children first learn to say declaratives with auxiliaries in *medial unstressed* position even though the environment favoring learning how to do so is hearing those auxiliaries in *initial stressed* position.

In sum, certain universal properties of natural languages (expressing the predicates and arguments of propositions, for example) seem to emerge in the child at maturationally fixed moments, and are insensitive to the naturally occurring variation among mothers. But elements and functions of the closed class, for children in this age range, seem to be closely affected by specifiable facts about the input. Even here, however, the environment exerts its influence only as the information it provides is filtered through the child's learning biases. For example the serial position, but not the frequency, of maternal auxiliary use affected the learning rate (for a general discussion of the Motherese hypothesis and its limitations, see Gletiman, Newport, & Gleitman, 1984).

Unfortunately, while these studies preclude certain strong forms of the Motherese hypothesis, they leave almost everything unresolved. First, the limited effects of environment on language learning that we found may be attributable to threshold effects of various sorts, to the attenuated sample, or to the measures or analyses used. These complaints (for which, see Furrow, Nelson, & Benedict, 1979) are fair even though they lose some force given the positive findings for the closed-class component. Nonetheless, there was a clear impetus for looking at cases in which the child's environment was more radically altered.

III.A.2.   THE CREATION OF LANGUAGE: ISOLATED DEAF CHILDREN

We therefore next studied a population grossly deprived of formal linguistic stimulation (Feldman, Goldin-Meadow, & Gleitman, 1978). These were six deaf children of hearing parents who had decided to educate their children orally, by having them taught to vocalize and lip read. Accordingly, in advance of the planned training period, the parents made no attempt to teach a manual language. More important, these parents did not *know* a manual language, so they were not in a position to present the easiest sentences first, the harder ones later. It has been observed that children in these circumstances develop an informal system of communicative gestures, called "home sign." It was the genesis of this system that we wished to study. Though many questions arise about how precisely we could analyze this exotic communication system, it is fair to say that the interpretive puzzles we faced are not materially different from those confounding the study of 2- and 3-year old English speakers, by adult English-speaking psycholinguists. In each case, one has to try to interpret the child's messages relying heavily on their real-world context of use (see Bloom, 1970). In doing so, one encounters the same perils and pitfalls as the language learner himself. We settled for using the methods traditionally employed in studying normal language learning. And we achieved about the same results, for early stages.

These linguistic isolates began to make single gestures (invented by themselves) at the same developmental moment that hearing learners of English speak one word at a time. Two- and three-sign sequences, encoding the same semantic/relational roles, appeared at the same age as hearing learners speak in two- and three-word sentences. To the (rough) extent that the words in these primitive sentences are serially ordered by young hearing learners according to these semantic roles, similar serial ordering of the same categories described the self-generated gesture system. It seems then that even if the environment provides no sample sentences, the child has the internal wherewithal to invent his own forms, to render the same meanings.

These results become more interesting when compared to the findings mentioned earlier, concerning the hearing learners. To the degree that the propositional forms and meanings appeared in indifference to variations in maternal input, these same properties appeared at the same time in the deaf learners, exposed to no formal language input at all. The closed-class subcomponent, responsive at this stage to variations in maternal input, did not appear at all in the signing of the isolated youngsters. The first suggestion here is that the closed class is laid down later, and in a different developmental pattern than other properties of the language system, an argument I made earlier based on quite different observational evidence (see Section II). The second suggestion is that the one subcomponent of the language system is more environmentally dependent than the other, and may not appear at all in some exposure conditions.

III.A.3. THE CREATION OF LANGUAGE: CREOLES FROM PIDGENS

A fascinating line of research (Bickerton, 1975; Sankoff & LaBerge, 1973) concerns the process of language formation among linguistically heterogeneous populations: pidgins, and their creolization. This work shows that there are very interesting overlaps between the rudimentary first attempts of young children learning an elaborated natural language, and the devices that appear early in the history of a new language. For example, at the first stages of both, the sentences are uniclausal, have rigid canonical phrase orders, etc. (for an admirable discussion that makes these connections to language acquisition research, see Slobin, 1977).

Most interesting of all in the present context, this work suggests that the final (phonological) steps in creating a closed-class morphology may be carried out by 5- to 8-year-old youngsters exposed to a pidgin as their first language. The pidgin itself characteristically contains only impoverished closed-class resources, again a property shared with the speech forms of all very young learners. The learners who hear a pidgin refine, grammaticize, and expand upon the open-class resources of the pidgin in late states of their learning. In a final step, these new resources are phonologically reduced by the learners, reproducing the destressed (and often contracted) closed-class morphology that is characteristic of fully elaborated languages (see Zwicky, 1976, for discussion of closed-class items, and their distribution in languages of the world).

A very similar development has been observed by Newport and Supalla (1980; forthcoming). They study adults who learned formal sign language (ASL) in early childhood from their deaf parents, and have shown that this learning is virtually identical to learning of spoken languages. But they also study mature deaf individuals who were isolated from ASL (and spoken language) during early childhood, the normal language learning period, either because of the oralist beliefs of their caretakers or because they acquired deafness later in life. That is, these investigators studied subjects like those of Feldman et. al., 1978, when they grew up. I have already noted that these isolated individuals develop a pidginized form of language, one that lacks complex embedding devices, closed-class items, and the like. Newport and Supalla have shown that, when these individuals are finally exposed to formal ASL, if later than about 12 years of age, they again learn a form of that language that is highly deficient in the ASL equivalents of closed-class morphology. They drop their own home sign pidgin, but they create a pidgin from the elaborated language to which they are now exposed. This is common in adult learners of any language.

Now the most fascinating result from these investigators is for deaf children of such first-generation deaf individuals. Keep in mind that these deaf signers who acquired the language relatively late are the ones who use a rather pidginized form of ASL. Their sentences, of course, form the basis for the second-generation deaf child's induction of ASL. Now (unlike the younger deaf isolates) these learners at approximately 4 and 5 years of age refine, expand, and grammaticize certain open-class resources, and create a closed-class morphology in the course of their learning. In a nutshell, for both the spoken pidgin of Sankoff and La-Berge and the gestural pidgin of Newport and Supalla, the first language-learning situation, carried out at the correct maturational moment, creates new resources out of the air, resources that are abstract and are the very hallmarks of fully elaborated natural languages.

III.A.4. SUMMARY COMMENTS

The evidence reviewed suggests that certain syntactic properties, though not all (those that involve the closed-class being the exception), appear in the learner in the same way even though the utterance samples vary. The studies of the deaf isolates suggest that there is no requirement for an experienced tutor who presents the easy sentences first to secure the first principles of natural language syntax. On the contrary, should the environment for first-language learning be deficient in the sample utterances, the learner will improve the language in the course of learning it.

III.B. VARYING THE INTERPRETIVE INFORMATION

There is more to the child's input than a sample of utterances—presumably it would be impossible to learn language just from listening to the radio. Specifically, in the logic sketched earlier, it was asserted—in agreement with most investigators, whatever their theoretical persuasions—that the child requires a real-world context that accompanies the speech events: some situation that he can interpret. In fact, many investigators assert that there is little mystery left in the language learning feat once it has been acknowledged that the child can interpret the extralinguistic world meaningfully (e.g., Bates & MacWhinney, 1982). However, it is not so easy to state just how "relying on meaning" *succeeds* in helping a child learn language.

One difficulty is that every object in the world can be described by many different kinds of words, a fact I alluded to earlier: The same object out there can be called *Felix*, a *cat*, a *mammal*, et cetera. On seeing the object then, the child still has a problem in determining the intended meaning of a word used to refer to it (the analysis of "basic level categories," e.g., Rosch, Mervis, Gray, Johnson, & Boyes-Braem, 1976, is sure to be of use in approaching such problems). Similarly, any given scene or event in the world can be described by many different sentences. For instance, scenes suitable to *The cat is on the mat* are just as suitable to *The mat is under the cat* and *Get that damn cat off the new mat*. Thus there is a considerable distance between meaningfully interpreting a scene and catching just how a heard sentence relates to it. To maintain the position that the scene helps the child learn, it will be necessary to provide the natural (perceptual and cognitive) analysis of the world that biases the learner to see cats-on-mats, not mats-under-cats, plus a conspiratorial agreement between mother and child such that the mother refer to scenes only in ways that match these biases, whatever they will turn out to be (for very useful discussions of the relations between language and perception, see Miller & Johnson-Laird, 1976, and Jackendoff, 1983). In addition, there will have to be a further conspiracy for marking specially any other intents for, after all, the grammar that is ultimately learned has to allow for the saying and comprehension of *mat-under-cat*.

A related problem has to do with how the utterance is to be analyzed, even assuming that the coconspirators have figured out how to be united on the interpretation. For example, suppose the mother says "Rabbit jumps" when the learner can see a rabbit jumping. And suppose, with Pinker, 1982, that the child believes things are to be the nouns, actions are to be the verbs. Even in these very favorable circumstances, there seem to be at least two choices the learner can make. She can suppose English is a noun or subject-first language, in which case *rabbit* is the required noun; or she can suppose English is a verb or predicate-first language, in which case *rabbit* is the required verb.[3] Given all this, it is hard to know how the child gets an initial grasp on the language.

Summarizing once again, all parties agree that language is learned in partial dependence on the real scenes that are there to be interpreted in the world. However, to my knowledge, nobody has succeeded in pro-

---

[3] A comeback to this supposed difficulty, of course is that, over many utterances that dissociate *rabbit* and *jumping*, a distributional analyzer can make the choice. But the semantic bootstrap notion has been put forward as a crucial step that precedes and renders possible subsequent distributional analysis; moreover, its very purpose is to relieve the learner of the burdensome tasks of storing and manipulating large quantities of data so as to dissociate, over the corpus as a whole, rabbits from jumping situations and jumping activities from rabbit objects.

viding the required cognitive-perceptual analysis of how scenes are to be interpreted against heard utterances.

Our approach (Landau, 1982; Landau & Gleitman, 1985) to these problems has been to look once more at differing environments in which language is learned. In the studies I have mentioned, the learner was in some ways deprived of information about language forms. What happens if the child is deprived of some opportunities to interpret heard utterances against the world of real objects and events? Surely, a blind learner suffers some such deprivations. Though he can hear, and touch objects, so can a sighted learner. A claim in the literature (Bruner, 1974–1975) is that a child learns which words refer to what—and hence their meanings—because, while listening, he follows his mother's gaze and pointing gestures. Even supposing (falsely) that the mother of a blind child names objects only when the child is holding them, in what sense could this be equivalent to gazing and pointing, in directing reference making?

In the light of these limitations on the blind learners' opportunities to discern the referents of many heard words and sentences, we have been surprised to discover that blindness hardly delays language onset; moreover, after the first few words are said, the pattern of linguistic development is virtually identical for sighted children and for neurologically intact blind children. This includes both the development of a lexicon, used appropriately to map onto the world, and the development of syntactic structure and the semantic–relational categories this describes. Apparently, receiving different, and less, interpretive information has no dramatic effect on overall acquisition rate or the character of that learning.

Some details of the blind child's learning are quite interesting. Landau and I expected to find the largest differences between blind and sighted learners in acquiring the visual vocabulary, words like *look* and *see*, for here the information base is maximally different from the normal. However, our blind subject used these words as early as do sighted children. In the education literature, such uses are called *verbalism*, often said to be detrimental to the child, who should be discouraged from use of the sighted vocabulary, lest he or she fall victim to "loose thinking."

But, on the contrary, the meanings the blind child came up with seem quite appropriate, though of course they map onto a different sensory world. Our sighted 3-year-old subjects, when told to "Look up," tilt their heads and orient their eyes upward—even though they are blindfolded during the testing. But the blind 3-year-old raises her hands, keeping the head immobile. It is not that the blind child simply conflates *look* and *touch*. For one thing, she responds to "Touch the doll, but don't look at it" by a tap or scratch on the doll, and then to "Now you can look at it" by exploring all of its surfaces manually. And in response to "Touch behind you" she touches her back, but in response to "Look behind you" she searches the space behind her.

On this and much related evidence, we think the blind English-speaking child has developed a distinction as made in French, between *toucher* and *tâter*, between manual contact, and apprehension by manual exploration. The question is whether the maternal contexts of use of the sighted terms is special, providing a basis on which the blind child could develop her special construals. Our finding is that no very superficial description of the contexts explains the learning. For one thing, the caretakers use *look* and *see* to their blind offspring in a surprising way: just as they do to their sighted offspring, i.e., to mean 'perceive' on some occasions (e.g., "Look at this boot"), to mean 'consider an event or state of affairs' on other occasions (e.g., "Let's see if granny's home," said while dialing the telephone) and to mean 'resemble' on others (e.g., "Oh, you look like a kangaroo in those overalls"). As these examples begin to show, it is not even possible to say that the mother of a blind child reserves the use of *look* and *see* to occasions when the listener has a relevant object in hand or close to hand—a generalization that potentially could explain how she settled on the interpretation 'explore or apprehend manually.'

To be sure, there is a correlational effect here: Usually the mother speaks of *looking* when her blind child is near some target object. But the trouble is that this situational factor is not very informative. This is because the mother says a goodly variety of simple verbs (e.g., *give, put, hold*) under the same circumstances: Because the child is blind, the mother most often talks of things nearby. But this means that many verbs cannot be discriminated from each other in terms of the nearbyness of things talked about. Rather, our conclusion in the investigations of the blind is that these children recruit several sources of information that jointly can be informative about which verb has which meaning. A contribution is made by the situational factors (e.g., *look* but not *get* or *come* is usually used when a target object is nearby). But a separate contribution is made by examining the constraints on the syntactic forms in which the different verbs participate. For example, notice that *give* is a verb that takes three noun-phrases, the first of which expresses the agent of the action, (*John gives Mary the ball*). But *look,* an inalienable perceptual activity, can express no agent—that is, it is semantically incoherent and syntactically anomalous to say *John looks Mary the ball.*

As a second example, since *see* is a perceptual verb and one can perceive events as well as objects, one can say *Let's see if the ball is on the table* (and not, e.g., *Let's hold if the ball is on the table*). That is, perceptual verbs accept sentential complements. We take the position that a child disposed by nature to analyze the varying syntactic formats can extract and differentiate the verb meanings, while a learner dependent on observation of linguistic circumstances alone has an insufficient basis for making these inductions. Considering the intricacy of the syntactic analyses required even of blind toddlers, we take their success as another argument for significant biological support of language learning.

III.C. VARYING THE ENDOWMENT OF THE LEARNER

The literature just sketched is consistent with a maturationally driven acquisition process, heavily dependent on specific linguistic and perceptual representations, with progress relatively independent of exposure time or type. If this position is correct, then organisms differently endowed should not be able to learn under anything like the same exposure conditions. For cats and dogs, however, there are many arguments much weaker than their lack of a language faculty that will serve to explain why they don't learn English. The case has been made more interestingly for primates by Premack and Premack (1983), for they have shown that chimpanzees have certain general conceptual wherewithal in common with humans and yet this does not allow them to function with syntactic categories like those of a human language. My colleagues and I have begun to look at special human populations to pursue this kind of issue.

III.C.1. LANGUAGE LEARNING IN DOWN'S SYNDROME (DS) RETARDATES

Fowler (1986) first examined the linguistic functioning of a small group of Down's syndrome (DS) adolescents who for 3 years had shown no further linguistic development—that is, they had arrived at some steady final state. They were selected for homogeneity on several measures of cognitive function (e.g., mental age [MA] about 6 years) and an anchor measure of language function (mean length of utterance [MLU] 3.0–3.5). This is the level usually achieved by normals between ages 2 and 3 years. It is important to note that these individuals differ extensively from one another in other aspects of cognitive functioning: for example, some of them were vastly better than others at primitive arithmetic, but this did not predict differences among them in language skill. Not only their gross language level as assessed by MLU, but also the internal properties of their language knowledge as assessed by a variety of standard instruments used by developmental psycholinguists, were found to be the same as that of $2\frac{1}{2}$-year-old normal controls. This similarity in the course and character of early language learning between normal and DS children has also been found by many others (e.g., Lackner, 1976; Lenneberg, 1967). Hence, it looks as if DS individuals may be a diminished case of the normal endowment. (In contrast, non-DS retardates we have studied differ both from the DS individuals and from each other in linguistic developmental patterning, making them a less likely group to study for the present questions.)

The important issue to Fowler, Gelman, and Gleitman had to do with the course of language development in the DS population, and so we instituted a longitudinal study of individuals whose IQ was about the same as the original adolescent group. This study is still underway, but a few generalizations are already apparent. These individuals began to speak very late, at about 5 years of age. But once language was manifest at all, their rate of growth was normal for some succeeding time. Correcting for the onset-time difference, those individuals who progressed beyond single word speech traversed Roger Brown's (1973) first four stages of language learning in the same absolute period of time required by normals. The internal structure of the knowledge at each interim measurement was identical to that of much younger normals traversing the same stages. However, at this point (MLU about 3.5), the learning of the retardates in the IQ range studied came to a halt. Perhaps the halt is permanent. It certainly extends for 2–3 years in the individuals we have so far observed, but we have to wait to see if they may start to learn once more. The adolescent population mentioned above suggests, however, that at least some DS individuals at this IQ level reach just such a ceiling of attainment, equivalent to that of 2-year-old normals, and then learn no more.

Summarizing, the interest of the longitudinal findings derives from two main points: (1) learning is not slow, but at normal pace, until some ceiling is achieved, often at a point very early in life; and (2) the character of knowledge is the same as for normals at the same stage of language development. The progress of the DS individuals, constrained as it is, suggests to us that a very low-level, automatic process is at work to determine the basic aspects of linguistic function.

III.C.2.   OTHER POPULATIONS

So far, the findings I have discussed suggest that language learning survives intact despite many differences in the exposure conditions, for example, exposure to a pidgin or an elaborated language, to speech that varies among individual mothers, to speech with diminished opportunity to observe the world (the blind case), or to no speech at all (the isolated deaf children). In contrast, a change in endowment has dramatic consequences for language learning. For the retardates, there is a very low ceiling on accomplishment. This motivates a search for yet other populations that would allow us to disentangle effects of biological status and effects of exposure.

One such population we are studying is children who differ in gestational age at birth (Landau & Gleitman, in progress). This work is still underway, and it has many technical problems, of which the worst is that prematurity is often accompanied by neurological defects that may be relevant to language attainment. We have attempted to control such variables, for example, by choosing only individuals whose birthweight was normal for their gestational age and who had no observable neurological abnormalities, but one should still be wary about the generalizations that can be drawn. Acknowledging this, our current findings do suggest that there is a stable effect of prematurity on language onset— that is, onset time is better predicted by time since conception (neurological status) than time since birth (exposure time).

Another potential source of evidence for the contribution of biology to language learning is the character of the learning process in those who are exposed late to a new language, for example, child second-language learners. If biological status bears a significant burden of explanation for the character of language knowledge, independent of exposure, we might expect both the rate and the patterns of learning to differ for second-language learners. This would help explain a very striking phenomenon. A 4-year-old foreign child, transported to America, requires only 1 year's exposure to speak English like a native 5-year old, who has had 5 years of exposure and practice. Of course another interpretation has to do with the fact that the emigre has priorly learned some other language. But a related, and again very large and striking phenomenon that escapes this defect has to do with native bilingualism. Many children are brought up in homes where two languages are spoken. Anecdotal evidence—but rather voluminous anecdotal evidence—suggests that the two languages are learned as fast as one; namely, at the level of peers learning a single one of the two languages. This is a pretty queer kind of learning, it seems. It can handle twice as much data without apparent strain—and handle the additional problem of disentangling two data bases, which, if confused, would yield an incoherent system. A theory in which induction from information provided in the environment is not the limiting factor on rate of acquisition could handle these facts (if they are real facts) rather easily: It would be the present expressive power of the learning machinery that is the limiting factor in language growth.

Experimental evidence on this topic is thin. Though there is an enormous literature on child bilingualism and second-language learning, generally it has not focussed on the kinds of issue I have considered in this chapter. There is only one study I know of that seems to attack them directly in the way that is required. That is Newport and Supalla's ongoing studies, mentioned earlier, of deaf individuals learning ASL at different ages. Because of oralist teaching methods and because deafness is often acquired late, there are cases of deaf individuals learning a *first* language at ages ranging from infancy to the late forties! They are left without a formal language until put in a situation where ASL is used. Newport and Supalla's preliminary findings are that the character of final knowledge of the manual language is predictable from the age of the learner at first exposure, independent of the number of years the individual subsequently used it. For example, as stated in an earlier section of this chapter, late learners fail to acquire the closed-class ASL morphology even after decades of exposure and everyday use. Such findings strengthen the case that the neurological status of the learner is dramatically implicated in what he or she can learn. In this case, evidence was provided supporting the lay impression that young children are better language learners than adults. Whether that evidence is strong enough to support Lenneberg's claim for a critical period similar to that involved in duck imprinting or bird song-learning remains for further investigation to determine.

IV. RELATIONS TO NEUROSCIENCE AND EDUCATION

If the picture I have drawn of patterns of language development is in essence correct, I suppose that it should in principle be possible to discover neurological correlates in the developing brain. Current linguistic theories postulate not only a distinct representation of language in the head (a "language organ," in Chomsky's wording, functioning as autonomously as, say, the liver), but a highly modularized system internal to language itself (Chomsky, 1981). It does not seem implausible to suppose that the regularities in development (and failures of certain populations to attain certain language milestones) are to be explained by relatively independent maturation of these subsystems. However, nothing in my reading of the literature suggests to me that linguistics, developmental psycholinguistics, and neuroscience are going to converge on such issues any time very soon. The generalizations from language development studies and the techniques available within neuroscience are simply too primitive.

Similarly, it is not at all clear that investigators of language learning have much to say that would be helpful to educators. Presumably the largest factors predicting successful education have to do with motivational and social issues to which language studies of the kind I have discussed do not and could not pertain. Nevertheless, because so much of school work seems to involve the teaching of language-related skills, it does seem that the task analyses developed by cognitive psychologists may have some general relevance.

To my mind, it seems at least indirectly useful for educators to realize that much of what is taught—and *should* be taught—about language to children is already known to the children implicitly. There is no doubt that the child of 5 or 6 years, just entering school, knows almost as much about language as she or he will ever know, school or not. For example, auditory discrimination of the sort relevant for language learning is in place at birth or shortly thereafter (Eimas, Siqueland, Jucsyzk, & Vigorito, 1971; Jucsyzk, 1980). One or two steps up, the rich phonological structures of a language are recruited in the speech forms of 5- or 6-year-olds in a way that is virtually adult. Children speak grammatically from about the age of 3 years, and the most complex syntactic structures the language has to offer are used freely and naturally by children from about age 4—whether or not they receive instruction in English grammar. As for meaning, it again seems clear beyond question that children know how to use the sentences that convey their thoughts, that refer appropriately to things, events, and scenes in the world, very early in life. To be sure, vocabulary acquisition continues for some time (but at a very diminished rate compared to that of young children).

The question arises, then, why the teaching of these matters that are already known to the learners? The facts I have just stated are incontrovertible, yet no sensible educator would change what he or she teaches in response to them. Presumably, this is because the child's manifest implicit knowledge is not enough to do many of the things society asks one to do with language. Primary among these, of course, is learning to read. Our own work on reading acquisition (Gleitman & Rozin, 1977; Rozin & Gleitman, 1977) and related work on metalinguistic knowledge (Gleitman & Gleitman, 1979; Gleitman, Gleitman, & Shipley, 1972) has been addressed to the question of the relation between implicit language knowledge (knowing *how* to do something, e.g., how to talk and comprehend) and explicit language knowledge (knowing *about* that knowledge in order to give conscious linguistic judgments, explicate verbal humor, etc.).

As every teacher knows, getting implicit knowledge explicit is no mean trick. No matter that the child says "bat" when he means 'bat' and "hat" when he means 'hat': It is still remarkably hard to get that child to realize that the former, but not the latter word, should be spelled with the letter *b* at the beginning. My colleagues and I were able to determine that the difficulty of such conscious linguistic tasks is related in a very stable way to the particular level of linguistic analysis required for its solution. The more highly processed representations of language are the easiest to bring to conscious attention and manipulate. As one example, many 5- and 6-year-olds are able to explain puns that turn on word meaning (e.g., "To find a lost dog, put your ear to a tree and listen to the bark") or logical representations of sentences (e.g., "Will you join me in a bowl of soup?"). But it takes a much older child to extract surface-structure ambiguities (e.g., the two interpretations of "John saw a man eating fish"; Hirsh-Pasek, Gleitman, & Gleitman, 1978). Much more important for the reading task, children are able to think about and manipulate word- and syllable-level representations of language much earlier in life than they can do the same for phoneme-segment representations of language (Liberman, Shankweiler, Liberman, Fowler, & Fischer, 1977; Rozin & Gleitman, 1977). These differential difficulties for young children, depending on the level of linguistic analysis, are reflected as differential difficulty of related tasks, even with well-educated adults (Gleitman & Gleitman, 1970), a fact that is probably related to the early invention of word and syllable scripts in human history, and the historically late development of the alphabet (Gleitman & Rozin, 1977).

These distinctions between implicit and explicit knowledge are consistent with perceptual representation and manipulation in other domains, so they are not really surprising (e.g., it is hard to think about what one is seeing at a level close enough to retinal stimulation so that one can draw in perspective). I think my collaborators would agree with me that though we were able to demonstrate differential patterns of development for implicit and explicit language knowledge, we were not able to explain—some Darwinian arm-waving aside—why these patterns are the way they are, or how to bring implicit knowledge into the consciousness of language users, and so render it explicit. Without explanation or remediation to offer, the reasons are compelling for not giving advice to educators, who do usually know how to draw out the pupils' implicit store of knowledge so they can inspect it and use it to solve new problems.

Without pretending any professional expertise in these matters, though, I venture that sometimes educators become so immersed in what children do not know that they lose sight of the rich language knowledge that youngsters already have before schooling begins. I believe that the best teaching methods will be those that specifically take advantage of this prior knowledge, that call the child's attention to what she or he knows, and build as directly as possible from that knowledge. The work of Gleitman and Rozin (1973; 1977) who tried to teach reading in terms of successively more abstract linguistic categorial representations of speech (first logographies, then syllabaries, and alphabets last of all) achieved results that provide some initial support for this kind of approach. In sum, while there is little technical support that developmental psycholinguists can offer to practicing teachers or educational theorists, I do think the one field can usefully support the other by documenting the language knowledge the kindergartner brings to school. Perhaps English grammar can be taught better—or at least more engagingly—by the teacher who is aware that the children know it already.

REFERENCES

Bates, E., & MacWhinney, B. (1982). Functionalist approaches to grammar in E. Wanner & L. R. Gleitman (Eds.), *Language acquisition: State of the art.* N.Y.: Cambridge University Press.

Bellugi, U. (1967). *The acquisition of negation.* Unpublished doctoral dissertation, Harvard University.

Bickerton, D. (1975). *Dynamics of a creole system.* New York: Cambridge University Press.

Bloom, L. (1970). *Language development: Form and function in emerging grammars.* Cambridge: MIT Press.

Bloom, L., Lightbown, P., & Hood, L. (1975). Structure and variation in child language. *Monographs of the Society for Research in Child Development, 40* (Serial No. 160).

Bradley, D. C. (1978). Computational distinctions of vocabulary type. Unpublished doctoral dissertation, Massachusetts Institute of Technology.

Bradley, D. C., Garrett, M. F., & Zurif, E. G. (1979). Syntactic deficits in Broca's aphasia. In D. Caplan (Ed.), *Biological studies of mental processes.* Cambridge: MIT Press.

Brown, R. (1973). *A first language: The early stages,* Cambridge: Harvard University Press.

Brown, R., & Hanlon, C. (1970). Derivational complexity and order of acquisition in child speech. In J. Hayes (Ed.) *Cognition and the development of language.* New York: Wiley.

Bruner, J. S. (1974/1975). From communication to language: A psychological perspective. *Cognition, 3,* 255–87.

Chomsky, N. (1965). *Aspects of the theory of syntax.* Cambridge: MIT Press.

Chomsky, N. (1975). *Reflections on language.* New York: Random House.

Chomsky, N. (1981). *Lectures on government and binding.* Dordrecht: Foris Publications.

Eimas, P., Siqueland, E. R., Jusczyk, P., & Vigorito, J. (1971). Speech perception in infants, *Science 171,* 303–306.

Feldman, H., Goldin-Meadow, S., & Gleitman, L. (1978). Beyond Herodotus: The creation of language by linguistically deprived deaf children. In A. Lock (Ed.), *Action, symbol, and gesture: The emergence of language*, New York: Academic Press.

Fernald, A. (1982). *Acoustic determinants of infant preference for "motherese"*. Unpublished doctoral dissertation, University of Oregon.

Fernald, A. (1984). The perceptual and affective salience of mothers' speech to infants, in C. Feagans, C. Garvey, & R. Golinkoff (Eds.), *The origins and growth of communication*, New Brunswick, NJ: Ablex.

Fowler, A. (1986). Down's Syndrome language: Syntax and morphology. In D. Cicchetti & M. Beeghley (Eds.), *Down's Syndrome: The developmental perspective*. New York: Cambridge University Press.

Furrow, D., Nelson, K., & Benedict, H. (1979). Mothers' speech to children and syntactic development: Some simple relationships, *Journal of Child Language, 6*, 423–442.

Garrett, M. F., (1975). The analysis of sentence production. In G. H. Bower (Ed.), *The psychology of learning and motivation* (Vol. 9). New York: Academic Press.

Gentner, D. (1982). Why nouns are learned before verbs: Linguistic relativity vs. natural partitioning. In S. Kuczaj (Ed.), *Language development: Language, culture, and cognition*. Hillsdale, NJ: Erlbaum.

Gleitman, H., & Gleitman, L. R. (1979). Language use and language judgment. In C. J. Fillmore, D. Kempler, & W. S-Y. Wang (Eds.), *Individual differences in language ability and language behavior*, New York: Academic Press.

Gleitman, L. R., & Gleitman, H. (1970). *Phrase and paraphrase*. New York: Norton.

Gleitman, L. R., Gleitman, H., & Shipley, E. F. (1972). The emergence of the child as grammarian, *Cognition, 1*, 137–164.

Gleitman, L. R., Newport, E. L., & Gleitman, H. (1984). The current status of the Motherese hypothesis, *Journal of child language, 11*(1), 43–80.

Gleitman, L. R., & Rozin, P. (1973). Teaching reading by use of a syllabary. *Reading Research Quarterly, 8*, 494–501.

Gleitman, L. R., & Rozin, P. (1977). The structure and acquisition of reading I: Relations between orthographies and the structure of language. In A. Reber & D. Scarborough (eds.), *Toward a psychology of reading*. Hillsdale, NJ: Erlbaum.

Gleitman, L. R., & Wanner, E. (1982). Language acquisition: The state of the state of the art. In E. Wanner & L. R. Gleitman (Eds.), *Language acquisition: The state of the art*. New York: Cambridge University Press.

Gleitman, L. R., & Wanner, E. (1984). Current issues in language learning. In M. Bornstein, & M. Lamb, (Eds.), *Developmental psychology: An Advanced Textbook*. Hillsdale, NJ: Erlbaum.

Gold, E. M. (1967). Language identification in the limit, *Information and Control, 10*, 447–474.

Hirsh-Pasek, K., Gleitman, L. R., & Gleitman, H. (1978). What did the brain say to the mind?: A study of the detection and report of ambiguity by young children. In A. Sinclair, R. J. Jarvella, & W. J. M. Levelt, *The child's conception of language*. Berlin: Springer-Verlag.

Jackendoff, R. (1983). *Semantics and cognition*, Cambridge: MIT Press.

Jusczyk, P. (1980). Auditory versus phonetic coding of speech signals during infancy, *Proceedings of the CNRS Conference*.

Kean, M. L. (1979). Agrammatism: A phonological deficit?, *Cognition 7*(1), 69–84.

Lackner, J. R. (1976). A developmental study of language behavior in retarded children. In D. M. Morehead & A. E. Morehead (Eds.), *Normal and deficient child language*. Baltimore: University Park Press.

Landau, B. (1982). *Language learning in blind children*. Unpublished doctoral dissertation, University of Pennsylvania, Philadelphia.

Landau, B., & Gleitman, L. R. (1985). *Language and experience: Evidence from the blind child*. Cambridge: Harvard University Press.

Lenneberg, E. (1967). *Biological foundations of language*, New York: Wiley.

Liberman, I. Y., Shankweiler, D., Liberman, A. M., Fowler, C., & Fischer, S. (1977). Phonetic segmentation and recoding in the beginning reader. In A. S. Reber & Don L. Scarborough (Eds.), *Toward a Psychology of Reading*, Hillsdale, NJ: Erlbaum.

Marin, O., Saffran, E., & Schwartz, M. (1976). Dissociations of language in aphasia: Implications for normal function. *Annals of the New York Academy of Sciences, 280*, 868–884.

Miller, G. A., & Johnson-Laird, P. N. (1976). *Language and perception*. Cambridge: Harvard University Press.

Nelson, K. (1973). Structure and strategy in learning to talk. *Monographs of the Society for Research in Child Development, 38*(1–2, Serial No. 149).

Newport, E. L. (1977). Motherese: The speech of mothers to young children. In N. J. Castellan, D. B. Pisoni & G. Potts (Eds.), *Cognitive theory* (Vol. 2). Hillsdale, NJ: Erlbaum.

Newport, E. L. (1982). Task specificity in language learning? Evidence from speech perception and American Sign Language. In E. Wanner & L. R. Gleitman (Eds.), *Language acquisition: The state of the art*, New York: Cambridge University Press.

Newport, E. L., Gleitman, H., & Gleitman, L. R. (1977). Mother, I'd rather do it myself: Some effects and noneffects of maternal speech style. In C. E. Snow & C. A. Ferguson (Eds.), *Talking to children: Language input and acquisition*, N.Y.: Cambridge University Press.

Newport, E. L., & Supalla, T. (1980). The structuring of language: Clues from the acquisition of signed and spoken language. In U. Bellugi & M. Studdert-Kennedy (Eds.), *Signed and spoken language: Biological constraints on linguistic form*. Dahlem Konferenzen. Weinheim/Deerfield Beach, FL/Basil/Berlin: Verlag Chemie.

Pinker, S. (1979). Formal models of language learning. *Cognition, 7*, 217–283.

Pinker, S. (1982). A theory of the acquisition of lexical interpretive grammars. In J. Bresnan (Ed.), *The mental representation of grammatical relations*. Cambridge: MIT Press.

Premack, D., & Premack, A. J. (1983). *The mind of an ape*. New York: Norton.

Rosch, E., Mervis, C. B., Gray, W. D., Johnson, D. M., & Boyes-Braem, P. (1976). Basic objects in natural categories. *Cognitive Psychology, 8*, 382–439.

Rozin, P., & Gleitman, L. R. (1977). The acquisition and structure of reading II: The reading process and the acquisition of the alphabetic principle. In A. Reber & D. Scarborough (eds.), *Toward a psychology of reading*, Hillsdale, NJ: Erlbaum.

Sankoff, G., & Laberge, S. (1973). On the acquisition of native speakers by a language, *Kivung, 6*, 32–47.

Slobin, D. I. (1973). Cognitive prerequisites for the development of grammar. In C. A. Ferguson & D. I. Slobin (Eds.) *Studies of child language development*. New York: Holt, Rinehart and Winston.

Slobin, D. I. (1977). Language change in childhood and in history. In J. Macnamara (Ed.), *Language learning and thought*. New York: Academic Press.

Slobin, D. I. (1982). Universal and particular in the acquisition of language. In E. Wanner & L. R. Gleitman (Eds.), *Language acquisition: The state of the art*. New York: Cambridge University Press.

Slobin, D. I., & Bever, T. G. (1982). Children use canonical sentence schemas: A crosslinguistic study of word order and inflections. *Cognition, 12*:3, (229–266).

Snow, C. E., & Ferguson, C. A. (Eds.). (1977). *Talking to children: Language input and acquisition*. New York: Cambridge University Press.

Wexler, K. (1982). A principle theory for language acquisition. In E. Wanner & L. R. Gleitman (Eds.), *Language acquisition: State of the Art*. New York: Cambridge University Press.

Wexler, K., & Culicover, P. (1980). *Formal principles of language acquisition*. Cambridge: MIT Press.

Zwicky, A. M. 1976, September 2. *On clitics*. Paper read at the Third International Phonologie-Tagung at the University of Vienna.

CHAPTER **6**

Education and Recent Research on Attention and Knowledge Acquisition

Merlin C. Wittrock

I. INTRODUCTION

I want to relate recent research in cognitive psychology and in neuro-psychology to recent research in education. The development of rela-tions-between education, cognition, and the brain is an old, nearly aban-doned activity, revived because of recent educationally significant research findings about cognitive and neural functions. Aristotle wrote that we remember information by forming images of it. We retrieve these images from memory by associating them with one another in order, according to the principles of similarity, contrast, and contiguity. In ancient Greece and Rome, teachers, students, and orators learned to remember and to retrieve ideas and information according to Aristotle's associationistic model of imagery in memory. In those ancient societies, an important part of higher education consisted of learning to remember speeches and answers to examination questions by constructing and ordering sequences of interactive images.

In recent times, associationistic models of learning, which omitted Aristotle's focus on memory and on thought processes, continued to influence education and educational research. The laboratory study of trial-and-error learning, reward, and reinforcement paralleled the wide-spread American emphasis in schools on practice, time to learn, behav-ioral objectives, and contingent reinforcement given to students imme-diately, frequently, and discriminatively. Teachers also imported into the schools the thoughts or models underlying these practices. As a result, behavioral objectives helped the teacher recognize student be-havior to reinforce more than they helped direct the student's or the teacher's attention. Reinforcement influenced student learning automatically, rather than by supplying affective and informational feedback which students could process and attribute to their own effort, luck, ability, or situational factors.

Especially since the mid-1960s or so, research on the processes of cognition and their neural substrates produced findings and models that provided new ways of looking at old problems of instruction and knowledge-getting. These models of cognitive and neural processes have led to a broad spectrum of educational research on attention, knowledge acquisition, process-oriented individual differences, and motivation. In the following paragraphs, I focus on the first two of these research areas. Then, I examine educational implications of some of the extensive work conducted in these fields. I focus on research in cognitive psychology because it has dealt directly with applied educational problems.

II. ATTENTION

When psychology emerged as a discipline over 100 years ago, attention was a centrally important, frequently discussed and studied topic. At that time, psychologists knew that human behavior could not be understood or predicted by studying only stimulus conditions. Attention appealed to them because it offered a way to study how people select stimuli and events, attach significance to them, and ignore other environmental events. Attention dealt with the difficult problem of how we choose what we will perceive and think about. William James (1890) wrote that attention is a cognitive process that enables us to choose "the sort of a universe" we will inhabit.

In recent research on cognitive psychology, including work by Donald Broadbent, Daniel Kahneman, and Michael Posner, selective attention continues to be a productive topic to study. In neuropsychology, including work by E. N. Sokolov on the orienting reflex, and by Karl Pribram on the phasic and tonic components of attention, new advances are also being made.

The educational implications of these two recent lines of research on attention interest a broad group of educational researchers. The models and empirical results of recent studies of attention suggest new ways to examine pedagogical techniques, such as questions asked by teachers and objectives given to learners, as well as learning problems and disabilities, such as hyperactivity, distractability, and mental retardation.

Models of attention explain some of the effects of adjunct or inserted questions upon knowledge acquisition. In this research, questions are inserted either before the paragraphs to which they refer, called prequestions, or after the paragraphs to which they refer, called postquestions. The inserted or adjunct questions ask for factual or conceptual answers. Compared with not asking questions, the inserted questions usually facilitate the acquisition of information related to the questions, and usually reduce the learning of information unrelated to the questions. Prequestions facilitate verbatim learning primarily, while postquestions facilitate learning more broadly (e.g., Boker, 1974; Swenson & Kulhavy, 1974). In the early studies in the 1950s, prequestions and postquestions were studied because of their relevance to the behavioristic models that emphasized practice and reinforcement of reading and reviewing the paragraphs.

In later studies, about 1965, attentional models were used to explain some of the findings of adjunct questions. Wittrock and Lumsdaine (1977) explained the results of many of the studies on adjunct questions with an attentional model. We maintained that inserted questions facilitate learning of relevant material and decrease learning of irrelevant material because the questions direct the learner's attention. The prequestions produce the narrowest learning because they can most effectively direct attention, coming before the paragraph is read. Postquestions direct attention less precisely and only in subsequent paragraphs because they appear and are seen only after the paragraph addressed by the question has been read. Although both types of questions function as reinforcers and stimulate practice and rehearsal, their effects seem more parsimoniously explained by an attentional model.

Rickards and Denner (1978) provide essentially the same explanation after an extensive review of studies on questions inserted into the text. Andre (1979) reviews the studies on higher-order, or conceptually rather than factually oriented, questions and also finds that they facilitate learning by directing attention. However, he argues that these results depend on the subject's perception of the reading task. If the subject is already attending and exerting effort, the adjunct questions will not facilitate learning. When the subject is poorly motivated, not well organized, or not highly able, the inserted questions have a better probability of facilitating the acquisition of knowledge. I agree and do not see that his qualification detracts from an attentional model. Rather his caveat implies that attention can be controlled by the learner as well as by external sources, which can be superfluous when the readers are properly attentive and motivated.

With research on the giving of behavioral objectives to learners, an attentional model also provides a plausible explanation of the findings. Duell (1974) tested and supported the prediction that behavioral objectives function by influencing the learner's selective attention. Kaplan and Simmons (1974) studied objectives given to learners either before or after the test they were asked to read. Material relevant to the questions, but not the specific answers to the questions, was learned better when the objectives came after the text. Duchastel (1979) gave objectives to college students reading selections on energy. The objectives enhanced free recall of the passage when they specified concepts of low structural importance in the text, which the author interpreted as support for a selective attention model. Their results regarding behavioral objectives are also parsimoniously explained by a selective-attention model.

These studies of inserted questions and behavioral objectives cannot eliminate alternative models. But they can and do support the relative utility of a selective-attention model.

In quite a different way, perhaps more familiar to researchers in neuropsychology, selective attention has been studied among retarded children and learning-disabled children (children of normal intelligence who achieve below expectations in school). Before discussing some of these studies, I should distinguish between short-term attention and sustained attention. McGuinness and Pribram (1980) present a model of attention that includes a short-term or phasic component, called arousal or the orienting reaction, indexed by changes in the galvanic skin response or by muscular movements, and a long-term or tonic component that maintains a set to continue previously established behavior.

Krupski (1980) reported on attentional processes in learning disabled and mentally retarded people. She reports that learning-disabled and mentally retarded children differ from normal children on voluntary sustained attention tasks, but not on tasks with low demands for voluntary sustained attention, nor on tasks involving involuntary short-term attention.

Tasks that involve voluntary attention prove difficult for mentally retarded people. For example, Krupski (1975) studied the reaction times of learning-disabled students to warning signals, which indexed involuntary attention, and to signals to act, which indexed voluntary attention. The mentally retarded students showed a normal reaction to the warning signals, but showed a less-than-normal reaction to the signal to act.

Mentally retarded individuals are also more distractible than normal children. Krupski (1979) observed retarded and nonretarded children working in a classroom. Retarded children 9–12 years old were more easily distracted than normal children in academic settings only. In nonacademic settings, the mentally retarded children sustained attention well. The results indicate that the ability to sustain attention relates to the type of task. The attention deficit noticed in academic situations does not necessarily indicate a deficit in capacity to attend.

Mentally retarded and learning-disabled children show a developmental lag in growth in selective attention. Hallahan and Reeve (1980) describe results growing from years of research on normal children's development in ability to recall relevant or central and irrelevant or incidental stimuli. From about age 5 years to about age 15 years, normal children increase in ability to recall central or relevant information, with a dramatic increase occurring at about age 12 to 13 years. However, ability to recall incidental information does not increase, or shows only a slight increase, across this same age span from 5 to 15 years. With other tasks, other researchers have found closely related results. The children seem to be learning to ignore incidental information, or perhaps to inhibit tendencies to attend to it. The result seems to be that by not attending to incidental materials, increased attention and processing can be given to relevant materials.

Hallahan and Reeve (1980) found that learning-disabled children demonstrate a 2- or 3-year developmental lag in development of ability to selectively attend. Several studies have investigated why these young learning-disabled children do poorly on serial-memory tasks. They do not, apparently, use rehearsal strategies as frequently as do normal children perhaps because, at least in part, they do not use language as proficiently as do normal children. One obvious educational implication is that learning strategies, including rehearsal strategies, might be taught to these children to remediate their developmental lag in selective attention. I return to this topic later. The point is that the developmental lag is probably in voluntary selective attention, and therefore might be remediated with appropriate instruction in verbal rehearsal strategies or in learning strategies.

Among children who are not learning disabled, selective attention sometimes presents a problem that might be remediated by training with verbal strategies. Paris, Lindauer, and Cox (1977) found that 7- and 8-year-old normal children can but rarely do spontaneously construct inferences about sentences they read as a way to achieve a goal, such as remembering what they have read. In this same study, children learned to construct stories from the sentences they read. Directing children's attention to the construction of stories facilitated comprehension and increased memory of the sentences. The construction of stories probably enhanced comprehension by facilitating the construction of relations across the sentences in the stories.

Willows (1974) also studied selective attention among normal children reading text. He gave sixth-graders, good and poor readers, either a standard double-spaced text typed in black ink or the same text with distracting words typed in red ink between the lines of the standard text. The inserted distracting text slowed the poor readers but not the good readers. More importantly, the surface structure of the inserted text distracted the poor readers while the meaning of the irrelevant text distracted the good readers. Apparently the good readers automatically decode text and focus their attention on it's meaning, but poor readers, to a greater extent, focus their attention on the text's visual characteristics in an effort to decode them. The red visual stimulus then distracts them.

Normal and learning-disabled children's attentional responses have also been studied using techniques, such as the evoked potential, developed in neuropsychology. Preston, Guthrie, and Childs (1974) presented words and light flashes to good and poor ninth grade readers. The children's reactions at 200 msec latency to the light flashes measured their attentional responses. Their reactions to the words measured their encoding responses. With the light flashes, but not with the words, the poor readers, compared with good readers, showed a lower-amplitude brain wave response at 180 msec latency, which implies a deficit in attention, but not in encoding or in construction of meaning (of the words). The implied deficit at this latency could be in involuntary or voluntary attention. However, the data are consistent with the hypothesis that some problems in learning in schools, such as the reading of words, involve deficits in selective attention, perhaps deficits in voluntary attention.

Again with the evoked potential technique, Conners (1970) found a − .60 correlation between reading achievement among third and fourth graders with reading disabilities and the amplitude of the left parietal lobe component at 200 msec latency (reflecting probable attention). These data also suggest a relation between attention and reading, this time among learning-disabled students.

Selective attention also provides a plausible explanation for many of the results observed in studies of hyperkinetic activity among children, which often responds well to stimulant drugs given in the proper dosage for the appropriate behavior and context. The so-called paradoxical effect of reduction in overt activity produced by a stimulant drug given to hyperactive children is probably a misnomer. These children are sometimes no more highly aroused than normal children. Instead they seem to have a flatter gradient of attention with respect to task-relevant distracting stimuli, and sometimes also to task-irrelevant stimuli (Bremer & Stern, 1976). They are relatively unable to inhibit responses to these task-relevant but distracting stimuli. The stimulant drugs seem to have their primary effect on selective attention, not on arousal. Conners (1970) confirmed this when he measured evoked potentials to auditory and visual stimuli. As a result, although arousal is increased somewhat by the stimulant drug, selective attention is enhanced and the hyperactive children concentrate their energies more effectively on the learning task in school. Perhaps their more-organized task-relevant behavior appears to the observer to indicate less activity because irrelevant and diffuse activity has been replaced by task-oriented effort. Rosenthal and Allen (1978) discuss further an attentional model of hyperactivity. The model implies that cognitive strategies, drugs, and other techniques that enhance selective attention reduce hyperactivity and enhance learning and memory of task-relevant information. Porges and Smith (1980) discuss the complexity of hyperactivity as a diagnostic category and the need to select cognitive, behavioral, and drug treatments according to the type of hyperactivity observed in the individual. Whalen and Henker (1976) present an attributional model of the effects of stimulant drugs on hyperactivity. The model implies that other treatments, such as cognitive intervention strategies, can with some children provide advantages over conventional medical procedures because they can lead to an internal attribution for controlling one's behavior.

Based on the ideas I have discussed, a large number of cognitive training programs designed to facilitate selective attention and self-control of impulsive responses have been developed. In some studies, cognitive, behavioral, and drug programs have been compared with one another. I do not discuss these comparisons of programs because the choice of treatment seems to depend on the particular problem, child, and context. Instead, I briefly describe cognitive programs that have produced effects that generalize to school tasks, such as reading or mathematics.

Douglas, Parry, Martin, and Garson (1976) developed a cognitive training program for hyperactive children that emphasized four methods: self-verbalization, modeling, self-monitoring, and self-reinforcement, all designed to teach children to control impulsive behavior, to selectively attended to task relevant stimuli, and to regulate their problem solving strategies. With 7- and 8-year-olds, they found that, compared with a matched control group, after three months of training on visual discrimination tasks the scores of the children increased on the matching Familiar Figures Test, which measures analytic ability, and on tests of organization and planning. The experimental group's scores on some reading achievement tests also increased, including oral comprehension and listening comprehension even though reading was not taught in this program.

Malamuth (1979) used cognitive techniques, similar to methods designed by Donald Meichenbaum, that were designed to improve self-management among poor readers who were not hyperactive. Sustained attention increased as a result of the training and reading scores also improved, which indicates the utility of cognitive training programs for some normal children with reading problems.

Cameron and Robinson (1980) taught three 7- and 8-year-old hyperactive children self-instructional and self-management skills that emphasized attending to the task-relevant aspects of each learning task. The three children increased in scores in mathematics, and two of them increased in measures of on-task behavior.

Camp (1980) describes her "Think Aloud" program, which is designed to teach self-control to impulsive and aggressive boys of early elementary school ages. The techniques she uses are similar to Meichenbaum's self-instructional procedures. The boys are taught to ask themselves four questions: (1) What is my problem?, (2) How shall I do it?, (3) Am I following may plan?, and (4) How did I do? After 30 training sessions the experimental group gained in scores on Wechsler Intelligence Scale for Children (WISC) IQ tests, Wide Range Achievement Tests, reading tests, and teacher ratings of interpersonal behavior. Again, this study shows a generalization effect to classroom and school-related variables, such as reading and social behavior.

In this brief section on cognitive training programs designed to facilitate attention and to control impulsive behavior, I have reported several of the more successful studies that I found in the literature. I have not reported the many studies that show no differences among the treatment groups because it is difficult to know how to interpret these studies. The studies that have shown gains in control of impulsive behavior have emphasized learning to attend to relevant stimuli, usually in verbal discrimination tasks; to inhibit impulses to respond immediately; and to develop a plan of action before responding. These relatively successful studies have trained children over extended periods of time, usually 2 months or longer. The results of these studies are encouraging because of their effects on sustained attention and reduction of impulsivity. The studies sometimes show transfer to school learning, such as to performance in reading and mathematics, although these transfer effects are not regularly obtained. The training effects seem to be mediated by a combination of processes that involve developing self-control over attention, inhibiting impulses, and planning actions.

In sum, research in attention has influenced education or educationally relevant research by suggesting new models and techniques that lead to instructional programs which can improve normal and learning disabled students' ability to control attention and to learn verbal discriminations and, sometimes, school subjects, such as reading and mathematics. The research and model-building in attention also provide a new explanation of the primary effects of adjunct questions inserted into text and of the effects of behavioral objectives given to learners. The commonly accepted explanation of these effects emphasizes attention and its control by the direction provided by the questions and the objectives. From these two distinct lines of research, attention in training programs for normal and learning-disabled children and attention as it functions in adjunct questions and objectives, I find support for believing that attentional models, as they have been studied and developed in cognitive psychology and in neuropsychology, have utility in educational research, in the remediation of some learning disabilities, and in the design of classroom techniques that involve uses of questions and objectives.

III.   THE ACQUISITION OF KNOWLEDGE

Ever since older generations have tried to organize and teach what they knew to younger generations, people have written about how knowledge is acquired. Is knowledge inherited, although perhaps not always remembered, as Plato wrote? If it is, then perhaps knowledge can still be taught by skillfully probing the learner's memory with questions, as Socrates did with the slave boy in the *Meno*. Perhaps knowledge acquisition involves a process of forming and storing an ordered sequence of interactive mental images, as Aristotle wrote in his essay on "Memory and Recollection." According to this model, one teaches learners how to relate familiar schemata to new and unfamiliar events and problems. One teaches them to construct relations between previously acquired knowledge and experience.

From ancient to modern times people who have studied knowledge acquisition have emphasized these themes introduced by Plato and Aristotle. Knowledge acquisition involves building relations between something old and something new, between organized memory and events, between schemata and new ideas or new experiences. The acquisition of knowledge also seems to involve building and storing an internal representation, an image, a proposition, a rule or a plan, for example, of what one has acquired. It might also involve revising one's previously acquired knowledge.

The nature of these internal representations and the active interplay between knowledge and experience continue to interest cognitive psychologists, neuropsychologists, and educational researchers. All of these people now share interests in conducting studies and in developing models of the cognitive processes learners engage in when they acquire knowledge. These processes include the verbal and imaginal transformations learners perform on information, the abstract and concrete relations they generate between experience and knowledge, the plans, learning strategies, and cognitive styles they employ to organize experience, and the attributions they make about the causes of knowledge acquisition.

Within this framework I focus on reading, especially reading comprehension, one area of research on knowledge acquisition that jointly interests researchers from several fields of cognitive science. I have already discussed research on attention in reading, which relates to research on acquisition of knowledge. Except incidentally, I do not discuss attention further. Neither do I discuss motivation and attribution, except to acknowledge the contributions research on these topics has made to understanding the importance of these congitive processes to instruction. Study of attribution processes indicates that learners are more likely to engage actively in processing information if they believe their efforts will help them to achieve goals they value. Reinforcement and success are not likely to be sufficient for sustaining these cognitive activities in schools unless the learners attribute at least some of their success to their own actions and effort.

To provide the flavor of cognitive research on reading and to tie the following discussion to the earlier sections of this chapter, I mention briefly two studies that demonstrate typical imagery and verbal techniques used in studies of reading. Mischel and Baker (1975) taught nursery school children to delay eating food by imagining it to be an inedible object, such as imagining a marshmallow is a white cloud. By manipulating attention through this imaginal transformation, the children were able to increase their delay of eating from about 6 minutes to about 14 minutes, the same length of time hungry graduate students, the control group, could delay eating without being taught the encoding strategy. Bower and Clark (1969) taught college students a verbal strategy that increased their retention of a serial list of words from about 20% to about 90%. The strategy was to put the words into sentences they generated, maintaining the serial order of the words in the sentences.

Similar imaginal or spatial and verbal strategies have been taught to children to increase memory and comprehension of materials they read. Bull and Wittrock (1973) taught elementary school students, 6th graders, to draw pictures (stick diagrams) of the vocabulary words they were to learn and remember. Compared to a control group who wrote and studied the definitions of the words, the children who drew their own simple pictures acquired more of the meanings of the words. Pressley (1976) also used an imagery strategy with children learning to read. He taught

8-year-olds to construct mental images of the sentences of a story. The imagery strategy enhanced comprehension and retention.

However, attempts to teach children who are less than 8 or 9 years of age to use imagery to facilitate reading comprehension or retention have not been successful. Apparently prior to this age, children cannot construct useful, relevant images, at least not without some help. Partial pictures, that is incomplete pictures, which children complete from knowledge about the text, do facilitate reading comprehension, however, among young children about 8 years of age, but not for kindergartners (Guttman, Levin, & Pressley, 1977).

Verbal strategies have been extensively studied in research on reading (Wittrock, Marks, & Doctorow, 1975). The strategies usually require the children either to relate their background or schema to the material they read, or to relate the parts of the text to one another. Doctorow, Wittrock, and Marks (1978) asked sixth graders either to read stories—the control group—or to read them and to generate summary sentences for each paragraph as they read it. In addition, some treatment groups were given headings for each paragraph. Across both ability levels of readers and across all stories and tests in two experiments with 488 individually, randomly assigned children, the generation of summary sentences sizably increased comprehension and retention. The combination of abstract paragraph headings (which we hypothesized would serve as cues for the readers' schema) and the construction of summary sentences (which we thought would stimulate generation of relations across sentences and perhaps between knowledge and the story) doubled comprehension. This study grew out of my model of generative learning and earlier research of ours.

In one of these earlier studies (Wittrock & Carter, 1975), we used word hierarchies developed by Gordon Bower. We asked college students either to generatively process the words, that is to construct relations among them, or to copy them. Retention of the words usually doubled with the generative processing instructions. Lutz and I (Wittrock & Lutz, in preparation) increased reading retention and comprehension by asking college students to construct either verbal analogies or summary sentences as they read a chapter in Rachel Carson's book, *The Sea Around Us*. Again self-generated images or verbal summaries facilitated reading. Scores on the Street test correlated positively with reading scores in the imagery condition, but not in the verbal analogy condition. Scores on the similarities subscale of the Wechsler Adult Intelligence Scale (WAIS) correlated positively with reading scores in the verbal analogy condition but not in the imagery condition. Although these data are tentative, they imply that different cognitive processes can be stimulated and used to construct meaning for text. Their effectiveness also relates to the learner's relative ability to use the verbal or imaginal strategies.

A wide variety of experimental and training studies have appeared to test predictions of cognitive models of reading and its facilitation, through asking students to construct verbal relations between the text and experience, or among the parts of the text. Kathryn Au (1977) taught native Hawaiian children, who often scored two standard deviations below the mean on standardized reading tests, to verbalize their own experience as the teacher read native Hawaiian stories to them. The first, second, and third graders expressed the story in their own words and recalled from experience several events that related to the story. After 1 year of instruction, the average percentile rank for the trained first graders was 69 on the Gates-MacGinitie Reading Test. The corresponding percentile ranks for each of three control classes of comparable but untrained first graders was 8, 21, 27. In the second grade, the corresponding percentile ranks were 42 for the experimental group and 10 or lower for the control groups. At the third-grade level, the experimental group scored 27 and the control group scored 7. Although in this applied context it is difficult to know the definite causes of the observed effects, perhaps these children can increase their ability to comprehend if they use their knowledge to generate relations for text as they read.

From quite a different perspective, the effects of generating relations between knowledge and the text was explored by Pichert and Anderson (1977). They asked college students to take the point of view of either a homebuyer or a burglar as they read a story about a house. The readers remembered better the information consistent with their perspective than with the alternative perspective. Apparently the relations constructed by the learners between the text and their knowledge depended on the perspective they brought to the story, or possibly to the features of the story drawn to their attention by the directions.

Constructing relations among the parts of the text has also been frequently studied. I previously mentioned that Paris et al. (1977) facilitated reading comprehension by asking 7- and 8- years-olds to construct inferences about sentences as they read. Apparently some verbal elaborations can be effectively constructed on request earlier than can imaginal elaborations.

Underlining a text is another way to facilitate construction of relations among its parts. With college students, Rickards and August (1975) found that retention of the text occurred best when the students underlined any words they wished and second best when they underlined words only of high structural importance. When they were asked to underline words of low structural importance to the text, their recall decreased below that obtained without underlining. When words were underlined for them by the experimenter, either words of high or low structural importance, recall was not influenced. Again, the transformation performed on the text by the reader influenced memory of what was read. When the operation was self-controlled and relevant to the structure of the story, recall increased. When the generative operation was inconsistent with the structure of the story, recall declined. When the operation was performed by others, recall was not sizably affected. We seem to be dealing with a useful variable that increases recall when it is used appropriately, decreases recall when it is used inappropriately, and leaves recall relatively uninfluenced when it is performed for the reader by someone else. There is a difference between directing the readers thought processes to relevant constructions, and providing those constructions for the readers.

Strategies for constructing relations among the parts of the text also seem to differ between good and poor readers. DiVesta, Hayward, and Orlando (1979) studied reading strategies used by sixth, seventh, and eighth graders. Running text was a strategy used by the poor readers, who seemed to take ideas in the linear order in which they are given. Searching subsequent text was a strategy used by good readers. They had goals that included comprehension of the text. They related its parts to one another and apparently they knew that their knowledge, not only the text, was relevant to understanding. They tended to read the information in the text to organize it and to relate their knowledge to it.

Meichenbaum and Asarnow (1978) report a study in which seventh and eighth graders with reading difficulties were taught to ask themselves questions about the story, its main events, sequence, and details, as they read it. The experimental group showed larger mean gains in reading achievement than did a control group not given the questioning strategy.

Linden and Wittrock (1981) taught fourth graders reading published text in the classroom to generate spatial and verbal elaborations as they read. Compared with a control group that read the passages without the instructions to generate these elaborations and with another control group in which the teacher was allowed to teach reading in any way she chose, the generative teaching procedure substantially increased reading comprehension ($p < .01$) from a mean of 17.7 to a mean of 28.6. Taken together, these studies imply that students do not always read actively, with the purpose of acquiring knowledge. However, at least sometimes they can be taught strategies that enhance their ability to construct relations between the text and their knowledge or between the text and their experience. When these strategies are learned and used, reading comprehension usually improves.

From research in cognitive psychology, the knowledge base of the learners—their schemata—is an important variable in reading. Dooling and Christiaansen (1977) told undergraduates that the story that they were reading either was or was not about a famous person, such as Helen Keller. The learners told the story was about a famous person used knowledge not in the story to construct information about the story, which sometimes led to errors of inference. Royer, Perkins, and Konold (1978) used a similar design and told undergraduates that the passage they read was either about a known famous person, such as Winston Churchill, or an unknown fictitious person. The readers told that the story was about a famous known person made many errors of inference about the person in the story. The errors were consistent with the readers' knowledge about the known famous person. Pearson, Hansen, and Gordon (1979) found that seventh graders with a greater knowledge of spiders learned more than children with a lesser knowledge about spiders from reading a passage about spiders, based on a test of inferential comprehension. Going beyond the text seemed to involve using knowledge relevant to the passage.

Throughout these studies of reading and reading comprehension, the researchers used models that have grown from research in cognitive psychology and neuropsychology. The emphasis in these studies on verbal and spatial processes, or analytic and holistic processes, has at least some roots in recently developed cognitive models of encoding and in neuropsychological models of cortical information processing, including research on the hemispheric processes of the brain.

These same cognitive and neuropsychological models, and the studies supporting them, also closely relate to educational interests in developing useful models and explanations of the processes and mechanisms in reading and in reading disabilities. To design reading instruction carefully, I would like to know the mechanisms and processes that I can stimulate to enhance comprehension. The number and the nature, verbal or spatial, analytic or holistic, of these processes interest me for the following reasons. At the very least, they put limits on the theoretical models I can construct, by indicating which of them probably will not be productive. An understanding of neural function can also provide an analogy for the psychological and educational functions that directly concern and interest me. Beyond analogies, cognitive and neural models provide a basic understanding of knowledge acquisition that can suggest alternative ways to teach and to instruct when customary techniques are ineffective, such as when reading disabilities occur.

In brief, neuroscience and cognitive science provide part of the context needed to understand and to model complex educational problems. These basic sciences do not provide educational implications in the usual sense of the word. Instead, they offer knowledge, on different levels, that enhance understanding of some of the complexities of education.

The method I have described for developing relations between neuroscience, cognitive science, and education differs from some common approaches to the construction of educational implications from scientific research. The differences occur because I believe that educational phenomena cannot be reduced to neural structure and physiological function. Nor can educational problems be overlayed directly onto research findings in neuroscience or in cognitive science. The reason is that each of these three areas—neuroscience, cognitive science, and educational research—represents different levels of study and understanding of education. Problems of teaching involve complexities not studied in these sciences. Trying to overlay one level of research directly onto a different level of study does an injustice to both of them and does not facilitate research or understanding in either field.

A more productive and more defensible use of neuroscience and cognitive science involves applying knowledge in these two fields to the building of educationally relevant models, based on a deep understanding of how people acquire knowledge. Without reducing education to neuroscience, one can come to understand problems of education at three distinct, yet related, levels of thought. From this multilevel context, one can more productively study with understanding some of the practical problems of teaching and learning. Educational researchers can then also better build enlightened models of some important educational phenomena, such as how people acquire knowledge in schools. These enlightened models promise to improve our chances of discovering useful information about educating people, and to concentrate and to accelerate our research efforts in productive directions.

IV. FOR THE FUTURE

The extensive research on neuropsychological and cognitive processes in reading and in reading disabilities cannot be examined here. Some of this research is presented in a book on reading (Pirozzolo & Wittrock, 1981) and in another book on the brain (Wittrock, 1980). In my chapters in those two books, I have written about the utility of neuropsychology research for the study of reading. The central theme I developed in those chapters was that the brain functions as a generator of plans, actions, and relations between knowledge and experience. Instruction and teaching facilitates these generations by providing relevant information when it is missing, by asking the learners to generate relations when they are able but do not spontaneously perform them, and by directing the generations when they are spontaneously performed.

For the future, at least several lines of research should be encouraged. Each of them involves close working relations between cognitive science and educational research; and each of them involves using and applying models of cognition growing from research in neuropsychology and cognitive psychology. First, we need collaborative and sustained research on the teaching of learning strategies, plans, and organizations of the thought processes used by students in acquiring knowledge. Some of this research is already under way. Second, and closely related to the first point, we need research that relates models of cognitive mechanisms involved in attention and knowledge acquisition to educational issues. A good example of this work is Eran Zaidel's (1977) model of lexical organization in the right hemisphere. Other examples deal with cerebral organization and reading disabilities.

We also need research on the development of cognitive processes. Much of our research on individual differences and cognitive development deals with aptitudes and variables, such as sex and IQ, that could be but are not process oriented. They do not help us greatly to understand the different ways people acquire knowledge by organizing experience. For example, we need to know more about the development of imagery strategies and verbal strategies. We need tests of what learning strategies children can use, upon request, at different ages. We also need to study what strategies we can teach to children at different developmental levels to facilitate their ability to control attention to acquire knowledge. Of course this kind of work is underway, but it could profit from closer ties between cognitive science and educational research, the goal that underlies all of my suggestions.

Last of all, it is time to move further from our modern behavioristic roots in our thinking about how cognitive systems function. We still write about information as if it were a stimulus that is transformed by a series of operations into a product. We seem to use a digestive system metaphor for cognition. But many biological systems, especially neural systems, operate differently. They are control systems. They do not transform input or stimulation into output. They generate signals, strategies, and plans that are sensitive to the reality that is perceived and that are useful for solving problems.

I do not know where this line of reasoning will lead, but I want to follow it. In my research on generative learning, I have begun the process. It has led me to reconceptualize the teaching of reading comprehension as a process of guiding learners' strategies, of directing learners' construction of relations between knowledge and information to be learned, and of controlling and directing learners' attention. It has caused me to think about studies and teaching procedures I would not otherwise have considered.

I am encouraged by the growing unity of interests occurring among people who study cognitive science. Their research findings and models of cognition can no longer be ignored by educational researchers. In the coming years I hope we will see many collaborative studies involving both of these groups of people in productive research on educationally significant issues and problems involving knowledge acquisition, attention, and development.

REFERENCES

Andre, T. (1979). Does answering higher-level questions while reading facilitate productive learning? *Review of Educational Research, 49,* 280–318.

Au, K. (1977, December). *Cognitive training and reading achievement.* Paper presented at the meeting of the Association for the Advancement of Behavior Therapy, Atlanta, GA.

Boker, J. R. (1974). Immediate and delayed retention effects of interspersing questions in written instructional passages. *Journal of Educational Psychology, 66,* 96–98.

Bower, G. H., & Clark, M. C. (1969). Narrative stories as mediators for serial learning. *Psychonomic Science, 14,* 181–182.

Bremer, D. A., & Stern, J. A. (1976). Attention and distractibility during reading in hyperactive boys. *Journal of Abnormal Clinical Psychology, 4,* 381–387.

Bull, B. L., & Wittrock, M. C. (1973). Imagery in the learning of verbal definitions. *British Journal of Education Psychology, 43,* 289–293.

Cameron, M. I., & Robinson, V. M. J. (1980). Effects of cognitive training on academic and on-task behavior of hyperactive children. *Journal of Abnormal Child Psychology, 8,* 405–419.

Camp, B. W. (1980). Two psychoeducational treatment programs for young aggressive boys. In C. K. Whalen & B. Henker (Eds.), *Hyperactive children: The social ecology of identification and treatment* (pp. 191–219). New York: Academic Press.

Conners, C. K. (1970). Cortical visual evoked response in children with learning disorders. *Psychophysiology, 7,* 418–428.

Di Vesta, F. S., Hayward, K. G., & Orlando, V. P. (1979). Developmental trends in monitoring text for comprehension. *Child Development, 50,* 97–105.

Doctorow, M. J., Wittrock, M. C., & Marks, C. B. (1978). Generative processes in reading comprehension. *Journal of Educational Psychology, 70,* 109–118.

Dooling, D. J., & Christiaansen, R. E. (1977). Episodic and sematic aspects of memory for prose. *Journal of Experimental Psychology: Human Learning and Memory, 3,* 428–436.

Douglas, V. I., Parry, P., Martin, P., & Garson, C. (1976). Assessment of a cognitive training program for hyperactive children. *Journal of Abnormal Child Psychology, 4,* 389–410.

Duchastel, P. (1979). Learning objectives and the organization of prose. *Journal of Educational Psychology, 71*, 100–106.

Duell, O. K. (1974). Effect of type of objective, level of test questions, and the judged importance of tested materials upon posttest performance. *Journal of Educational Psychology, 66*, 225–232.

Guttman, J., Levin, J. R., & Pressley, M. (1977). Pictures, partial pictures, and young children's oral prose learning. *Journal of Educational Psychology, 69*, 473–480.

Hallahan, D. P., & Reeve, R. E. (1980). Selective attention and distractibility. In B. K. Keogh (Ed.), *Advances in special education* Greenwich, CT: JAI Press.

James, W. (1890). *The principles of psychology:* Vol. I. New York: Henry Holt & Co.

Kaplan, R., & Simmons, F. G. (1974). Effects of instructional objectives used as orienting stimuli or as summary/review upon prose learning. *Journal of Educational Psychology*, 614–622.

Krupski, A. (1975). Heart rate changes during a fixed reaction time task in normal and retarded adult males. *Psychophysiology, 12*, 262–267.

Krupski, A. (1979). Are retarded children more distractible? Observational analysis of retarded and nonretarded children's classroom behavior. *American Journal of Mental Deficiency, 84*, 1–10.

Krupski, A. (1980). Attention processes: Research, theory, and implications for special education. In B. Keogh (Ed.), *Advances in special education* (Vol. 1). Greenwich, CT: JAI Press.

Linden, M., & Wittrock, M. C. (1981). The teaching of reading comprehension according to the model of generative learning. *Reading Research Quarterly, 17*, 44–57.

Malamuth, S. (1979). *Self-management training for children with reading problems: Effects on reading performance and sustained attention. (1979), Cognitive Therapy and Research, 3*, 279–289.

McGuinness, D., & Pribram, K. (1980). The neuropsychology of attention: Emotional and motivational controls. In M. C. Wittrock (Ed.) *The brain and psychology* (pp. 95–139). New York: Academic Press.

Meichenbaum, D., & Asarnow, J. (1978). Cognitive-behavior modification and metacognitive development: Implications for the classroom. In P. Kendall & S. Hollen (Eds.), *Cognitive-behavioral interventions: Theory, research, and procedures.* New York: Academic Press.

Mischel, W., & Baker, N. (1975). Cognitive appraisals and transformations in delay behavior. *Journal of Personality and Social Psychology, 31*, 254–261.

Paris, S. G., Lindauer, B. K., & Cox, G. L. (1977). The development of inferential comprehension. *Child Development, 48*, 1728–1733.

Pearson, P. D., Hansen, J., & Gordon, C. (1979, March). *The effect of background knowledge on young children's comprehension of explicit and implicit information* (Tech. Rep. No. 116). Urbana: University of Illinois, Center for the Study of Reading.

Pichert, J. W., & Anderson, R. C. (1977). Taking different perspectives on a story. *Journal of Educational Psychology, 69*, 309–315.

Pirozzolo, F. J., & Wittrock, M. C. (1981). *The neurophysiological and cognitive processes of reading.* New York: Academic Press.

Porges, S. W., & Smith, K. M. (1980). Defining hyperactivity: Psychophysiological and behavioral strategies. In C. K. Whalen & B. Henker (Eds.), *Hyperactive children: The social ecology of identification and treatment.* (pp. 75–104). New York: Academic Press.

Pressley, G. M. (1976). Mental imagery helps eight-year-olds remember what they read. *Journal of Educational Psychology, 68*, 355–359.

Preston, M. S., Guthrie, J. T., & Childs, B. (1974). Visual evoked responses in normal and disabled readers. *Psychophysiology, 11,* 452–457.

Rickards, J. P., & August, G. J. (1975). Generative underlining strategies in prose recall. *Journal of Educational Psychology, 67,* 860–865.

Rickards, J. P., & Denner, P. R. (1978). Inserted questions as aids to reading text. *Instructional Science, 1,* 313–346.

Rosenthal, R. H., & Allen, T. W. (1978). An examination of attention, arousal, and learning dysfunctions of hyperkinetic children. *Psychological Bulletin, 85,* 689–715.

Royer, J. M., Perkins, M. R., & Konold, C. E. (1978). Evidence for a selective storage mechanism in prose learning. *Journal of Educational Psychology, 70,* 457–462.

Swenson, I., & Kulhavy, R. W. (1974). Adjunct questions and the comprehension of prose by children. *Journal of Educational Psychology, 66,* 212–215.

Whalen, C. K., & Henker, B. (1976). Psychostimulants and children: A review and analysis. *Psychological Bulletin, 83,* 1113–1130.

Willows, D. M. (1974). Reading between the lines: Selective attention in good and poor readers. *Child Development, 45,* 408–415.

Wittrock, M. C. (1980). Learning and the brain. In M. C. Wittrock (Ed.), *The brain and psychology.* New York: Academic Press.

Wittrock, M. C., & Carter, J. (1975). Generative processing of hierarchically organized words. *American Journal of Psychology, 88,* 489–501.

Wittrock, M. C., & Lumsdaine, A. A. (1977). Instructional psychology. In *The annual review of psychology.* Palo Alto, CA: Annual Reviews.

Wittrock, M. C., & Lutz, K. (in preparation). *Reading comprehension and the generation of verbal analogies and summaries.*

Wittrock, M. C., Marks, C. B., & Doctorow, M. J. (1975). Reading as a generative process. *Journal of Educational Psychology, 67,* 484–489.

Zaidel, E. (1977). Lexical organization in the right hemisphere. In P. Buser & A. Rougeul-Buser (Eds.), *Cerebral correlates of conscious experience.* Amsterdam: Elsevier Press.

CHAPTER *7*

Memory and the Brain*

Larry R. Squire

I. INTRODUCTION

Neuroscience concerns itself with two great problems—the "hard-wiring" of the nervous system, and its capacity for plasticity. It is a guiding postulate of neuroscience that all behavior and mental activity is made possible by the brain's ten trillion or more neurons and by the signals produced by them. The problem of hard-wiring concerns (1) how the genome directs the formation of neurons and the anatomical connections among them, (2) how the electrochemical signals of neurons code information about the external and internal worlds, and (3) how the diverse functions of the brain (e.g., movement, regulating food and water intake, perceiving, feeling emotion, dreaming) are organized and localized. The problem of plasticity concerns how the organization of the brain can change under certain circumstances. The capacity for plasticity is a fundamental adaptive feature of organisms. Organisms inherit in the structure of their nervous systems many adaptations developed as a result of variation and natural selection operating during previous generations. Yet they also inherit the potential to adapt or change as the result of events occurring during their own lifetime. Because of this adaptation, the experiences of an organism can modify the nervous system and the organism later can behave differently because of these experiences. This ability to change gives organisms the capacity for learning and memory.

* A portion of this chapter appeared originally in *The Biology of Learning* (eds. P. Marler and H. Terrace), Springer-Verlag, 1984. The work reported here was supported by the Medical Research Service of the Veterans Administration, and by NIMH Grant, MH24600. I thank William Greenough, Morris Moscovitch, and Lynn Nadel for their helpful comments on an earlier draft.

171

Biological studies of plasticity concern phenomena as seemingly re-moved from real learning and memory as drug tolerance, synaptic sprouting after a brain lesion, enzyme induction, recovery of function after brain injury, and strictly synaptic events like facilitation and postte-tanic potentiation. These phenomena all reveal ways in which the brain can change after some event. They are interesting because it has seemed reasonable to expect that knowledge about how the nervous system manages these examples of plasticity might provide clues to how the nervous system accomplishes the special instance of plasticity that we call memory.

In 1950, Karl Lashley, a pioneer in experimental studies of brain and behavior, wrote pessimistically about the problem of memory.

> This series of experiments . . . has discovered nothing directly of the real nature of the engram. I sometimes feel, in reviewing the evidence on the localization of the memory trace, that the necessary conclusion is that learning just is not possi-ble. (Lashley, 1950, p. 477–478).

Since then, enormous technological growth in the neurosciences has made it possible to study the problem of memory in entirely new ways. In addition, exciting empirical and theoretical work has been accom-plished in the disciplines of behavioral neuroscience and neuropsychol-ogy. Keeping in mind the interdisciplinary spirit of this volume, the purpose here is to summarize and make some general points about memory and the brain, rather than to cite all pertinent findings or to support every statement with data. I try to show how the biology of memory is being studied fruitfully at several different levels of analysis, from the cellular to the neuropsychological, and how these different levels of inquiry can be mutually facilitatory. In addition, I try to show through a few examples how what is being learned can be expected to find relevance outside the neurosciences. Readers wishing more de-tailed coverage of the topic of neural plasticity and memory are directed to reviews and to the references therein (Greenough, 1984; Kandel, 1977; Squire, 1982b; Thompson, Berger, & Madden, 1983).

II. CELLULAR AND SYNAPTIC ANALYSIS OF MEMORY

One kind of question that is often asked about the biology of memory concerns its physical basis. What changes in the brain subserve learning and memory? How does the functional wiring diagram of the brain change so that different behavior results? What are the cellular and synaptic events responsible for changing the functional wiring diagram?

Although this kind of understanding must in the end depend on different experimental approaches in many animals, considerable information has come from study of one particularly interesting animal, *Aplysia californica* or sea hare. This marine snail, found in the intertidal waters of coastal California, was brought to neurobiological studies of learning and memory by Eric Kandel in the early 1960s. It seems fair to say that this animal has revolutionized neurobiology since that time because its nervous system is so amenable to cellular study. Its nervous system is distributed among nine separate ganglia, and the animal possesses a total of about 18,000 neurons. The optimal strategy in addressing cellular questions about memory is of course to study the simplest biological system that provides a chance of answering the question of interest. In the human brain, which has at least 10 trillion cells, the answers to many such questions are currently out of reach. But *Aplysia*'s individual ganglia have only 2000 neurons and many of them are so large that they can be seen by the naked eye. As a result, they can be named and identified from preparation to preparation, and the neuroanatomy (or wiring diagram) of this animal can begin to be worked out in some detail.

Largely as the result of work by Kandel and his colleagues at Columbia University, it has become possible to study at the cellular level some relatively simple forms of behavioral memory like habituation and sensitization (Kandel, 1976). *Habituation* refers to progressive diminution in the intensity of a response as the result of repeated presentations of a stimulus. *Sensitization* refers to the enhancement of the response to a stimulus as the result of strong stimulation with another stimulus. These forms of memory are *nonassociative*, in that they do not depend on pairing of stimuli or on forming associations between stimuli. Because both phenomena are nevertheless instances of how behavior can be changed by previous experience, they provide useful ways to study phylogenetically simple forms of memory.

Figure 7.1 shows the wiring diagram of the gill-withdrawal reflex, which has been the focus of the behavioral studies. The gill is a respiratory organ that is often externalized in calm ocean waters. In rough waters or during tactile stimulation in the laboratory with a jet of water, the gill withdraws into the mantle shelf. Gill withdrawal is controlled by six identified motor neurons and by 24 sensory neurons that make direct contact with the motor neurons via excitatory synapses. Interneurons are also present, receiving input from the sensory neurons and converging on the motor neurons. The gill withdrawal reflex habituates with progressive stimulation. It gradually comes to withdraw less vigorously, and it reappears after progressively shorter intervals.

After a training session involving 10 stimulations, memory of the

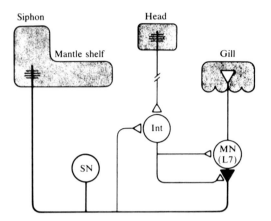

Siphon

Head

Mantle shelf

Gill

Int

MN
(L7)

SN

Figure 7.1 Simplified schematic representation of the neuronal circuit underlying short-term behavioral habituation and sensitization of the gill withdrawal reflex in *Aplysia*. The site of habituation is the synapse between the sensory neuron (SN) and the motor neuron [MN(L7)]. Activation of the interneuron (Int) pathway ending on the terminals of SN results in sensitization. (From Kandel, Brunelli, Byrne, & Castellucci, 1976.)

training event (as measured by behavior and by reduced excitatory post-synaptic potentials in the motor neurons), lasts for many minutes or a few hours. When training involves 40 stimulations, scheduled at 10 a day for 4 days, habituation lasts for a few weeks. Short-term habituation lasting minutes or hours is now known to depend on a change at synapses on the motor neurons, specifically on a decrease in transmitter release from the sensory (presynaptic) neurons. Habituation in this case does not involve build-up of inhibition, or postsynaptic changes in receptor sensitivity on the motor neurons, or destruction of synapses, or creation of new ones. Habituation involves only a decrease in synaptic efficacy along an already existing neural pathway from sensory neurons to motor neurons.

Sensitization, the opposite of habituation, can occur in this animal when a vigorous stimulus is applied to the head region. This results in an increase in synaptic transmission at the same aforementioned synapses, and can result in restoration of transmission when the synapses have previously been depressed by habituation. Sensitization is accounted for by the mechanism of presynaptic facilitation. The neurons responsible for it carry information from the head region and end on the terminals of the sensory neurons and increase the ability of the sensory neurons to release transmitter. It is known further that the neurons producing presynaptic facilitation release a transmitter substance, believed to be serotonin or a serotonin-like molecule, which results in turn in an influx of calcium into nerve terminals in the habituated pathway and an enhanced ability to release transmitter. Thus both short-term habituation and dishabituation have been analyzed at the cellular level with some success.

More recently, this same reflex has been shown to be capable of true associative learning, or classical conditioning, in that it can be modified by paired presentation of conditioned stimulus (CS) and unconditioned stimulus (US), but not by random or explicitly unpaired stimulation (Carew, Walters, & Kandel, 1981). The CS was a light tactile stimulation of the siphon, which causes gill withdrawal, and the US was strong electric shock to the tail. There now seems to be good reason for optimism that associative learning in *Aplysia* will be amenable to cellular analysis, and some success has already been achieved in this direction. In addition to *Aplysia*, other invertebrates have been used to good advantage as model systems for the cellular analysis of learning and memory, and these too promise to yield useful information about mechanisms of associative and nonassociative learning (Chang and Gelperin, 1980; Crow and Alkon, 1980; Davis and Gillette, 1978; Hoyle, 1979). At present, the number of available invertebrate systems seems sufficient to test the generality of newly discovered neural mechanisms, but not too small to risk missing major mechanisms used by invertebrates to accomplish learning and memory.

Some might wonder how knowing the specific kinds of synaptic events subserving information storage can be relevant to how memory storage occurs in animals with more complicated nervous systems. Yet, it seems reasonable, if not likely, that cellular mechanisms of learning and memory used by simpler organisms will be preserved in evolution. This does not deny that complicated vertebrate nervous systems may turn out to have mechanisms for accomplishing memory storage not exhibited by simpler organisms. In any case, it has become clear that work with simpler organisms has made it possible to think more concretely about the problem of memory. Some principles have been identified by which nervous systems can accomplish information storage, and it is sometimes possible to explore the applicability of these principles to more-complicated systems.

In more complicated nervous systems, tentative answers to questions about memory can be composed, but direct evidence is still elusive. When studying the vertebrate nervous system, it should be useful to keep in mind what has been learned about memory from the well-studied invertebrate cases. As we develop a clearer and fuller picture of memory storage in vertebrates, it seems prudent to check our progress against what has been described in invertebrates and where possible to test for generality.

For example, in the case of habituation and sensitization, memory storage occurs not by some exotic mechanism but by a relatively simple change in synaptic efficacy in already available neuronal circuitry. This fact becomes relevant when questions are raised about the localization and specificity of memory, which are fundamental to the study of memory in more complicated nervous systems. It has been a popular though as yet unproven idea that in vertebrates the specificity of memory is determined by where in the nervous system the relevant changes occur. The kind of change that occurs, which results in altered synaptic efficacy, does not code for different kinds of information. This idea presumes that the nervous system possesses such great diversity and specialization in its hard-wiring that information would be specific simply by virtue of the loci of the relevant changes.

Such a view is compatible with a lot of indirect data concerning the localization of memory in rat, cat, monkey, and human. Lashley's pessimism about localizing memory in the brain was based in large part on his famous observation that lesions in rat neocortex had similar disruptive effects on a maze habit regardless of the location of the lesions. Later, behavioral tasks other than maze learning were studied that clearly required the integrity of more-circumscribed brain regions. However, it has remained difficult to localize memory itself to any particular place in the brain. A likely reason for this is that those same lesions that could affect memory of a previously learned task usually have an additional effect of making an animal unable ever to learn the same task again. By this view, Lashley's observation can be attributed to the complexity of the maze-learning task for the rat. Memory for tasks that depend critically on many operations would be stored in a distributed fashion involving many brain loci. In this sense, it has seemed likely that memory might be localized in the same neural circuitry that supports the ability to perform the task that is to be learned (Squire, in press).

These ideas find support from *Aplysia,* where direct evidence is available on the issue of localization. Imagine the effect of making a lesion in a previously habituated animal in the area where sensory neurons make excitatory (and modifiable) connections on motor neurons controlling gill withdrawal. In this case, the animal would exhibit loss of the habituated response, to be sure, but it would also lose the ability to perform gill withdrawal—that is, it would lose the ability to perform the reflex that has been habituated. With this concrete example well established, it seems sensible to suppose as a starting point for experimental study that memory in complicated nervous systems also occurs as changes in neural pathways that are already specialized for the kinds of operations that are to be learned.

Another general idea about plasticity to emerge from invertebrate studies is the distinction between intrinsic and extrinsic systems (Krasne, 1978). *Intrinsic systems* consist of neural pathways that actually store information. In the case of habituation in *Aplysia,* the identity of the intrinsic system is clear, and the problem of localization has been addressed rather directly. *Extrinsic systems* consist of neural pathways that do not by themselves contain acquired information but that have the capacity to influence the development, maintenance, or expression of memory in intrinsic systems. In the case of *Aplysia,* an extrinsic system is responsible for sensitization, which occurs via heterosynaptic input to the sensory neurons that mediate habituation. The extrinsic system can restore inactivated—that is, habituated—synapses in the intrinsic system.

This concept of extrinsic system may have applicability to more complicated nervous systems. In particular, memory dysfunction observed in monkeys and humans following neurological injury or disease can be understood as a disruption of an extrinsic system, as is described in a later section. Some neuroscientists might object to use of the term *extrinsic* outside of the strictly synaptic meaning for which it was originally intended. In its more liberal usage, the concept of *extrinsic* applies to brain systems rather than to synapses, and has an analogous meaning to the synaptic one—that is, it identifies systems that can influence the development and maintenance of memory, but that do not by themselves contain stored information.

III. CANDIDATES FOR LONG-TERM BEHAVIORAL PLASTICITY

Whereas short-term mechanisms for changing behavior have been identified in *Aplysia* at the synaptic level, the cellular–synaptic basis of long-term behavioral change in *Aplysia* (e.g., long-term habituation) is incompletely understood. Long-term habituation could depend on a simple extension of the time course of the mechanisms responsible for short-term habituation. Alternatively, long-term habituation might involve additional mechanisms. Additional mechanisms might also be used by more complicated nervous systems, which have memory storage processes that can last for many years. In vertebrates, a variety of mechanisms have been identified as candidates for long-term memory. Although none of them has been linked directly to behavioral memory, there is no shortage of brain events to subserve long-lasting change.

In the 1960s and 1970s, it was common for discussion of long-term memory mechanisms to be limited primarily to biochemical hypotheses about how new protein synthesis and/or other macromolecules might be needed to establish lasting changes in synaptic efficacy. Due to more-recent empirical work, however, a variety of possibilities can now be considered in addition to strictly biochemical ones. In particular, experiments have resurfaced the old idea that morphological changes in brain might underlie long-term memory. In part because of the pioneering work of Mark Rosenzweig (cf. Rosenzweig, 1979) and his colleagues at Berkeley, and more recently William Greenough (Greenough, 1984) at the University of Illinois, it is now evident that the brain's architecture is exceedingly plastic—that is, it can be changed by experience. A considerable list of structural changes has now accumulated that can be linked correlatively to behavioral experience. For example, in rats reared in an enriched laboratory environment, (compared to rats reared in standard laboratory environments), one finds an increase in gross cortical weight and thickness; increased thickness of particular cortical layers, larger neuronal somata, an increase in the number of dendritic branches and in the length of dendritic branches, an increase in the diameter of synapses, changes in subsynaptic plate perforations (i.e., synapses with "holes" in them, like donuts, in which case changes occur as increases in the size of the holes and in the number of synapses with holes). Changes have also been observed in the number and shape of dendritic spines, which are contact points between neurons, and in the curvature of synapses. Importantly, many of these changes (e.g., cortical thickness, dendritic length) also occur in adults exposed to enriched environments, and some occur following training regimens in adults.

It is clear that morphological changes in neuronal architecture occur readily with differential experience and that such changes, if they are involved in memory, could provide a stable, enduring substrate for long-term storage. Another extremely interesting example of long-lasting plastic change is long-term potentiation, which can be demonstrated in hippocampus following brief electrical stimulation of an afferent pathway, and which culminates in morphological changes (Lee, Schottler, Oliver, & Lynch, 1980; Swanson, Teyler, & Thompson, 1982). Such changes might constitute final steps in a sequence of cellular events that begins with transient neurophysiological events and ends in structural change in neurons and altered connectivity between them. Because most cellular constituents are replaced at regular intervals, very long-lasting changes in synaptic connectivity (of the kind needed to subserve memory that persists for years) would seem to require changes in gene expression.

IV. BRAIN SYSTEMS AND MEMORY

A complete account of learning and memory must entail more than knowing the cellular details of how synapses change and knowing which cellular changes constitute memory storage. One wants to know as well how synaptic change is organized to express itself in learned behavior—that is, how memory is organized in the brain. Which regions of the brain are important? Is there one kind of memory or many? What is the flow diagram of information-processing events and how can these events be related to anatomy?

The biological analysis of memory thus involves much more than questions about the nature of relevant synaptic changes, though such questions are certainly of great interest. Indeed, in complex nervous systems, the neurobiological study of memory begins with questions about which brain systems participate in learning and memory, and where in the brain the relevant synaptic changes take place. In vertebrates, correlative neurophysiological information is becoming available about the development and neural organization of classical conditioning, as well as other forms of associative learning (Cohen, 1980; Disterhoft, Shipley, & Kraus, 1982; Gabriel, Orona, Foster, & Lambert, 1982; Thompson, Berger, Madden, 1983; Weinberger, 1982; Woody, 1982). Two fruitful model systems currently in use are classically conditioned heart-rate change in the pigeon (Cohen, 1980) and classically conditioned eyelid (and nictitating membrane) response in the rabbit (Solomon & Moore, 1975; Thompson, Berger, Cegavske, Patterson, Roemer, Teyler, & Young, 1976).

With such approaches, it has been possible in a preliminary way to localize in the ipsilateral cerebellum the memory trace for classical conditioning of the eyelid response (McCormick, Clark, Lavond, & Thompson, 1982). Rabbits given cerebellar lesions lose a previously established conditioned response (CR) without losing the unconditioned response (UR). That is not to say that everything the animal knows about its classical conditioning experience is in the cerebellum. Yet, essential neural changes that cause the CR to be elicited by the CS may occur there. This work provides the best evidence yet available concerning the localization of memory in a vertebrate. Another productive model system for the study of one kind of memory is the annual learning of bird song by the canary (Nottebohm, 1980, 1981), which depends on a well-studied brain circuit, and which involves seasonal increases and decreases in the volume of the critical brain regions.

Another approach to the study of memory in vertebrates has been to analyze behavioral memory with pharmacological or biochemical techniques to discover which neurotransmitter systems and metabolic events are involved. There is now considerable evidence for the idea that brain protein synthesis is necessary for the development of long-term memory (Agranoff, Burrell, Dokas, & Springer, 1978; Barondes, 1975; Davis & Squire, 1984). This and other aspects of the biochemistry of learning and memory have been addressed in a useful way by detailed studies of imprinting in the chick (Rose, 1977; Horn, 1981).

Particularly through the work of McGaugh and his colleagues, memory has come to be viewed as a dynamic and slowly developing process that can be influenced or modulated shortly after initial learning, by manipulation of specific transmitter systems (e.g., catecholamines), hormones (e.g., adrenocorticotropic hormone—ACTH), or other peptides. The importance of an event to an animal is often determined by what follows, for example, does the event predict pleasure or pain? That is, the value of information to an animal and whether or not information should be stored in memory depends in part on what occurs after information has been registered. It is therefore reasonable that memory storage can be affected by certain treatments administered after the time of learning, in a way that suggests modulatory influences on intrinsic, information-containing neural networks. It has been suggested that the effective treatments might amplify or dampen some of the normal physiological consequences of training (Gold & McGaugh, 1975). For example, in training motivated by footshock, hormones might modulate the physiological consequences of the footshock. If so, then studies of memory modulation can illuminate processes like reinforcement that influence memory formation.

The cholinergic system has also been identified as having possibly an important role in memory storage, both on the basis of animal studies (Detusch, 1971) and on the basis of studies of aging and dementia in monkeys and man (Bartus, Dean, Beer, & Lippa, 1982). Drugs that alter the efficacy of transmission at cholinergic synapses impair or facilitate retention, depending on the age of a memory, and they exert effects throughout the lifetime of a habit, not just shortly after learning. Considering such findings, Deutsch (1971) suggested that cholinergic synapses are sites of memory storage. Although this remains an interesting idea, it still rests on indirect evidence.

Since then, there has been enormous clinical interest in the possibility that Alzheimer's disease, the most common form of dementia, might selectively or disproportionately affect cholinergic neurons, at least in its early stages (Whitehouse, Price, Struble, Clark, Coyle, & DeLong, 1982). This finding has raised the hope that it might be possible to retard the memory loss associated with Alzheimer's disease by regimens of cholinergic drugs. So far, however, such efforts have been disappointing (Bartus et al., 1982). Readers wishing a more detailed review of the pharmacological aspects of memory may consult one of several reviews (Dunn, 1980; Martinez, 1983; Squire & Davis, 1981; Zornetzer, 1978).

Others have used experimental animals in the hope that a cognitive or

neuropsychological perspective might be brought to the biological analysis of learning and memory. Notably, O'Keefe and Nadel (1978) have
taken a broad theoretical approach to questions about which brain systems are involved and how memory is organized. Their approach emphasizes spatial knowledge and the notion that the hippocampus con-
tributes critically to memory functions by constructing a spatial map of
the environment—within which specific memories can be embedded.
Their work shows how the study of cognition in many species can
contribute to an understanding of brain and behavior. Descriptions of
the cognitive functions under study must be as accurate and complete as
descriptions of the brain systems subserving them.

V.   NEUROPSYCHOLOGY OF MEMORY

Neuropsychological studies potentially connect both cognitive psychology and philosophical inquiries about cognition to fundamental
neuroscience. Jerry Fodor wrote, "It was widely held that philosophers
ought to provide a survey of the conceptually coherent options, and that
there are, in fact, fewer of these than might be supposed" (1981, p. 2).
Neuropsychology aims to characterize the particular solution that the
brain uses to accomplish memory storage. It is empirical, inferential,
and aims at a level of abstraction that is biologically meaningful. It can
sometimes perform tests of hypotheses developed in cognitive psychology, thereby assessing the biological reality of psychological theory.
Conversely, neuropsychology can sometimes provide functional significance for neurobiological observations.

One strategy for addressing neuropsychological questions about
memory is to study human amnesia. It has turned out that the human
amnesic syndrome can sometimes occur as a relatively circumscribed
entity in the absence of other cognitive deficits, and such cases can be
instructive about how memory functions are organized in the brain (for
reviews, see Baddeley, 1982; Butters & Cermak, 1980; Cermak, 1982;
Hirst, 1982; Squire & Cohen, 1984; Stern, 1981). In addition, to the extent
that the neuropathology of these cases is known, and especially to the
extent that human amnesia can be mimicked in experimental animals
like the monkey, then it also becomes possible to learn something about
the identity of the brain regions that are involved in memory. These are
issues of which my colleagues and I have been particularly interested. In
the remainder of this chapter, I draw on work from our laboratory to
consider three aspects of amnesia that bear on questions about memory
and the brain: (1) the problem of classification; (2) retrograde amnesia
and memory consolidation; (3) the phenomenon of spared learning in

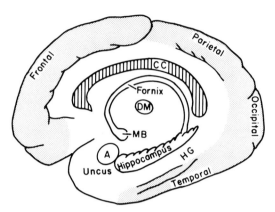

Figure 7.2 Schematic representation of the medial surface of one hemisphere, showing the hippocampus, fornix, mammillary bodies (MB), and other structures implicated in diencephalic and bitemporal amnesia. Amyg = amygdala; DM = dorsomedial nucleus of thalamus; HG = hippocampal gyrus.

amnesia; and (4) attempts to achieve an animal model of human global amnesia in the nonhuman primate.

V.A. The Problem of Classification

Amnesia occurs in many forms, sometimes as a strikingly selective disorder and sometimes as part of a broad spectrum of disorders. Amnesia itself has been linked to damage in medial temporal and diencephalic brain areas. A central question concerns what constitutes the core memory disorder. Are there some parts of the clinical picture that are optional, so to speak, in the sense that they need not always occur in amnesia? What parts of the clinical picture, if any, should be linked to damage outside the diencephalic and medial temporal regions? Another important question concerns whether the brain system damaged in amnesia can itself be fractionated, that is, do different parts of the system (e.g., the medial temporal and diencephalic regions) contribute differently to memory functions?

The core disorder in amnesia has been repeatedly redefined in recent years, as various commonly occurring deficits have been shown not to be obligatory. For example, Korsakoff patients (an example of diencephalic amnesia) have special difficulty making temporal order judgments (Squire, 1982a), they fail to release from proactive interference (Cermak, Butters, & Moreines, 1974; Squire 1982a), and they cannot predict accurately their own memory performance (Shimamura & Squire, in press). Yet these same deficits are absent altogether in other amnesic patients, whose impairment in learning ability is as severe as that seen in Korsakoff patients (Cermak, 1976; Squire, 1982a; Shimamura & Squire, in press). Even other patients with diencephalic amnesia do not always have these deficits. It seems most likely that the Korsakoff patient has more widespread neuropathology than many other amnesic patients and that this additional damage, for example in the frontal lobe, is responsible for aspects of their cognitive impairment.

A distinction within the core disorder has also been suggested, based on evidence that diencephalic and medial temporal amnesic patients differ in their rate of forgetting. A technique was used in which patients were given more exposure to stimulus material than were normal subjects—to equate performance at short learning–retention intervals. It was suggested originally that H. M., the well-studied amnesic patient with medial temporal lesions (Milner, 1972; Scoville & Milner, 1957), had a rapid forgetting rate and that Korsakoff patients had a normal forgetting rate (Huppert & Piercy, 1979). These findings were ambiguous because H. M. was more amnesic than were the patients with Korsakoff syndrome and because H. M.'s forgetting scores were not well matched to his control group. More recent results for H. M. using the same technique suggested that he forgets at a normal rate (Freed, Cohen, and Corkin, 1984). However, because H. M.'s amnesia is so severe, it remains a problem how to compare him to other patients. Forgetting rates are difficult to compare between subjects unless the severity of the memory impairment itself is similar.

This same method has also been applied to other groups of patients, who were amnesic to a similar degree and who could be given an equivalent duration of exposure to the stimulus material (the 120 pictures) during initial learning. In these experiments, patients with Korsakoff syndrome forgot at a normal rate, equal to that of alcoholic control subjects, and psychiatric patients receiving bilateral electroconvulsive therapy (ECT) forgot at an abnormally rapid rate (Squire, 1981). Under one experimental condition, ECT patients showed better retention than Korsakoff patients at 10 minutes after learning, but still forgot at a significantly more rapid rate (Figure 7.3). In addition, the diencephalic amnesic patient N. A. (Kaushall, Zetin, & Squire, 1981; Teuber, Milner, & Vaughan, 1968) forgot at a normal rate.

These findings provide a basis for placing case N. A. and Korsakoff patients in one category; and patients receiving bilateral ECT in a second category. Whether forgetting rates will consistently dissociate forms of amnesia depends on matching amnesic patients with respect to initial learning ability. Studies of experimental animals with identified surgical lesions will probably be needed to settle this issue.

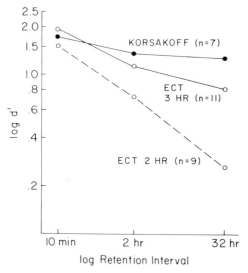

Figure 7.3 Normal forgetting by patients with Korsakoff syndrome and abnormally rapid forgetting by patients receiving ECT. All patients saw 120 pictures for 8 seconds each and then were tested for retention 10 minutes, 2 hours, and 32 hours later. The ECT groups learned either 2 hours or 3 hours after the last in a series of 4 to 6 bilateral treatments. The value d' is a measure of memory strength unaffected by response bias. Some of these results and results for normal subjects have been reported previously (Squire, 1981).

V.B. MEMORY CONSOLIDATION

Here, I consider the medial temporal region and its role in memory consolidation. *Memory consolidation* refers to the idea that memory changes with the passage of time after learning. Consolidation has been much discussed in the disciplines of experimental psychology, physiological psychology, and neuropsychology, though there has seldom been good agreement on what exactly it is or how long it lasts. My colleagues and I have suggested that memory consolidation best refers to a long-lived, dynamic process (Squire, Cohen, & Nadel, 1984). The basic idea that memory changes for a long time after learning was stated clearly many years ago.

> In normal memory a process of organization is continually going on,—a physical process of organization and a psychological process of repetition and association. In order that ideas may become a part permanent memory, time must elapse for these processes of organization to be completed. (Burnham, 1903, p. 396).

Our reasons for adopting this kind of view of memory consolidation and for relating memory consolidation to the medial temporal region are based on two key facts of retrograde amnesia. First, ECT typically causes a temporally limited retrograde amnesia, covering the period a few years prior to treatment without affecting the period prior to that time. Thus the susceptibility of memory to disruption can decrease for as long as a few years after learning. This aspect of the retrograde amnesia associated with ECT, together with similar, albeit less formal, observations in other forms of amnesia (Barbizet, 1970; Russell & Nathan, 1946), has led us to conclude that memory can change over long periods of time after learning, becoming resistant to disruption as a result of this change.

Second, case H. M., an example of medial temporal amnesia, has consistently been described as having a retrograde amnesia of 1 to 3 years, and good memory for earlier time periods. Recent tests suggest that his memory deficit extends as far as 11 years prior to surgery for some kinds of material (Corkin, 1984). The facts of case H. M. connect these ideas about memory consolidation to the medial temporal region. The medial temporal region cannot be a site of storage for all memories because H. M. recalls memories that were acquired more than 3 years before the onset of his amnesia. It appears instead that the medial temporal region has a necessary role in the formation and development of memory. We have supposed that at the time of learning, the medial temporal region establishes a relationship with memory storage sites elsewhere in the brain, primarily in neocortex. This interaction is required for as long as a few years after learning in order for memory to develop and be maintained in a normal way. There need be nothing special or fixed about this length of time, because many or most memories do not endure as long as a few years. Accordingly, the role of the medial temporal region in the consolidation of memory is presumed to continue so long as information is being forgotten, during the reorganization and stabilization of what remains. This gradual process strengthens and makes more coherent those elements of memory that are not lost through forgetting, thereby enabling stable memory representations to be maintained across time (Squire, Cohen, & Nadel, 1984).

There is abundant evidence for slow biological processes that, like consolidation, require time, for example, the development of the nervous system itself. We have supposed that the slow process in which the medial temporal region participates—that is, memory consolidation—is not determined at the outset nor is it relentlessly gradual or automatic. Rather, it is best understood as a dynamic process affected by rehearsal and association and by subsequent memory storage episodes. These events would influence the fate of recent, and unconsolidated, memories by remodeling the neural circuitry underlying the original representation. During consolidation, some parts of the original representation would be lost through forgetting while those that remain would become more stable and more coherent. The representation of an event thereby changes over time and eventually is able to support memory storage and retrieval in the absence of the medial temporal region.

Two prominent signs of the amnesia associated with ECT—rapid forgetting and temporally limited retrograde amnesia—can both be understood as a disruption of consolidation. Indeed, the crucial idea that these particular kinds of anterograde and retrograde amnesia are linked has been explored by computer simulation (McClelland & Rummelhart, 1983). The simulation showed that a deficit in the same hypothetical mechanism produced both rapid forgetting of new information and temporally limited retrograde amnesia. In the absence of a consolidation process that maintains, reorganizes, and stabilizes memory representations, if learning were attempted, information should be forgotten at an abnormally rapid rate. Disruption of consolidation also results in the loss of recently acquired, as-yet-unconsolidated memory. The shorter the interval between learning and the disruption, the greater the loss. Unless previously acquired memory is fully consolidated, it should be lost at an abnormally rapid rate during the period of disruption. If the function of the medial temporal region were restored (e.g., after the transient disturbance caused by ECT), the elements that remained in memory should continue to consolidate. The extent to which past memory should recover would therefore depend on how long the disruption was present. The longer that the disruption persists, the longer should be the permanent retrograde amnesia present after the disruption subsides.

V.C. PRESERVED LEARNING

Knowing what amnesic patients can do well is as important to questions about memory and the brain as knowing what they cannot learn. This kind of information is needed to define the scope and limits of amnesia and helps characterize the function of the affected brain regions. It is now known that amnesia is a selective deficit and that the role of the medial temporal region and of the diencephalic midline in memory functions is narrower than once believed.

The traditional view of amnesic patients had been that they can acquire perceptual-motor skills, but cannot learn much else. During the last 10 years, however, investigators have compiled a considerable list of nonmotor tasks that can be accomplished by amnesic patients, sometimes in normal fashion (Cohen, 1981; Weiskrantz, 1978; Wood, Ebert, & Kinsbourne, 1982). A particularly good example is mirror-reading, (i.e., reading words reversed in a mirror), which has been studied extensively in normal subjects by Paul Kolers (1976, 1979). Working with three kinds of amnesic patients, Neal Cohen and I showed that the capacity to learn the mirror-reading skill developed at an entirely normal rate over a period of 3 days and then was retained at normal levels for 3 months (Cohen & Squire, 1980). Yet, many of the patients did not remember

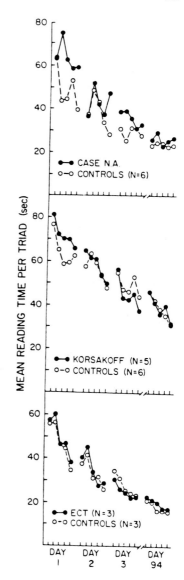

Figure 7.4 Acquisition of a mirror-reading skill (e.g., [bedraggle-capricious-grandiose] by patient N.A., patients with Korsakoff syndrome, and patients receiving bilateral ECT). The skill was acquired at a normal rate and retained at a normal level 3 months later (Cohen & Squire, 1980).

having worked at the task before, and all were amnesic for the particular words that they read. (See Figure 7.4.)

These results have suggested a distinction between information based on skills or procedures and information based on specific facts or episodes. Both diencephalic and medial temporal patients seem to be capable of acquiring the skills needed for mirror-reading, but they cannot acquire facts about the world that would ordinarily be acquired by using these skills—that is, the fact that they had been tested or the ability to recognize as familiar the words that they had read. The view that amnesia selectively spares skills has also been proposed by Moscovitch (1982). The distinction drawn here is reminiscent of others that have been proposed between kinds of knowledge (e.g., knowing-how and knowing-that [Ryle, 1949]; memory without record and memory with record, [Brunner, 1969]; procedural and declarative knowledge [Winograd, 1975]).

These ideas have considerable relevance to questions about how memory is organized in the brain (Cohen, 1981; Squire & Cohen, 1984). The distinction between skills or procedures and facts or episodes appears to be honored by the nervous system, in that the brain accomplishes memory storage so as to distinguish prominently between two kinds of knowledge. Procedural knowledge can be acquired independently of the brain regions affected in amnesia. The medial temporal region (and the diencephalic structures affected in amnesia) are not needed for the acquisition and maintenance of procedural knowledge. These structures are critical, however, for the acquisition and consolidation of declarative knowledge, i.e., knowledge that provides an explicit, accessible record of individual previous experiences, a sense of familiarity about those experiences, information about the time and place of their occurrence, and facts about the world derived from these experiences.

Considering what is known about the cellular or synaptic basis of information storage in simpler nervous systems, it seems reasonable to suppose that procedural learning is phylogenetically primitive, and that it occurs as on-line changes or as tuning in already existing neural circuitry. *Procedural knowledge* is implicit and accessible only by engaging in or running through the skills in which the knowledge is embedded. By this view, habituation, sensitization, and some forms of classical conditioning are procedural. They should not require participation of the medial temporal region, and they should not be subject to consolidation. These forms of learning can occur without knowledge of the specific instances that led to a change in behavior and without knowledge that learning has occurred. It is not yet known whether these forms of learning can be acquired normally in amnesia.

By contrast, declarative knowledge requires the participation of the diencephalic midline and the medial temporal region and is subject to consolidation. *Declarative knowledge* includes the facts and data of conventional memory experiments. It is directly accessible and affords recognition that an event happened previously. It includes both specific information about time and place (episodic knowledge) as well as general information (semantic knowledge), which though not specific to time and place is nevertheless obtained in the course of specific experiences. Indeed, one of the consequences of consolidation might be to extract and integrate the semantic knowledge acquired through different time-and-place experiences.

The idea that procedural knowledge might be so specific as to include certain kinds of classical conditioning (and the attendant CS–US contingencies) implies that the skills or procedures that can be acquired in amnesia can be quite specific. The process of activation (Mandler, 1980) or perceptual fluency (Jacoby, 1982) is relevant to this question. When a word is presented for study, its features are automatically activated, and the probability is raised of detecting the same word later or producing it when given a cue. *Activation,* as studied in priming and certain other tasks, is to be distinguished from the ability to recognize a word as one previously presented, as measured by conventional memory tests. Rozin (1976a) suggested that activation, or what he termed a "hot-tubes" effect," might occur normally in amnesia. Thus, a test cue might elicit a word if the trace of that word were sufficiently activated by recent use. If this formulation is correct, then amnesic patients should be able to show rather specific benefits of prior experience, even if they acquire no awareness of what they have learned or of what they know.

One example of such a finding comes from a study of word-list learning (Graf, Squire, & Mandler, 1984). Amnesic patients and control subjects saw 3-letter word stems that could be completed to form any of 10 common words. When the instruction was to complete each word stem with a word from a recently studied list, amnesic patients performed more poorly than control subjects. They also performed poorly on other conventional memory tests—that is, free recall and recognition. However, different results were obtained when the subjects studied a list, but then at retest were not explicitly told that they were in a memory experiment. Instead they were asked to complete the word stems with the first word that came to mind. The probability of completing word stems by chance to form target words was 9.5%. In this condition, amnesic and control subjects performed identically, completing almost 50% of the word stems to match target words. Thus, despite their deficit on conventional memory tests, one kind of test condition shows that amnesic patients are influenced normally by previously presented words. Similar claims for amnesic patients have been made by others (Jacoby & Witherspoon, 1982; Warrington & Weiskrantz, 1978).

The question inevitably arises as to whether the problem of amnesia is a problem of storage or a problem of access. The finding that patients can show knowledge of individual words by generating them from word stems, while failing in conventional memory tests, might be taken to favor the view that these patients have stored the necessary information but do not have access to everything they have learned about the words. Similarly, the finding that patients can read mirror-reversed words without recognizing the words as familiar could be taken to mean that they have stored the requisite information but do not have access to all of it. However, it is possible as well in these cases that not all the information available to normal subjects has been stored by amnesic patients. For a variety of reasons, my colleagues and I have favored this latter view that the amnesic deficit is a failure to develop and maintain some part of the synaptic connectivity that ordinarily constitutes memory representations (Squire, 1982b; Squire, Cohen, & Nadel, 1984). In this sense, we view amnesia as a storage deficit, and not just a problem of access. The deficit cannot be a simple access problem because in bitemporal amnesia, premorbid memory is available that was acquired many years previously.

The storage–retrieval question is larger and harder to settle than it might first appear to be. Indeed, the storage–retrieval dichotomy has its roots in a long-standing debate about whether normal forgetting itself is a matter of changes in storage—that is, actual reversal of some of the synaptic events that originally subserved memory, or changes in retrieval or accessibility. It seems reasonable that the synaptic events underlying both forgetting in normal subjects and rapid forgetting in amnesia are likely to be similar. I suggest that both normal forgetting and rapid forgetting depend at least in part on an actual loss or reversal of synaptic change. In *Aplysia,* forgetting of habituation is reflected in a return to baseline of the synaptic changes originally responsible for habituation. Neurobiological evidence of this kind was needed to show conclusively that for *Aplysia,* loss of habituation is a matter of a change in storage. For this reason, the storage–retrieval issue in other animals is an issue that will require neurobiological evidence to settle entirely.

Bitemporal amnesia reflects a failure of the medial temporal region to establish and maintain stable memory representations. If the storage view of amnesia is correct, then without the medial temporal region, some of the synaptic connectivity that was originally present in a representation is lost. The role of the medial temporal region in maintaining synaptic connectivity is formally similar to that of an extrinsic system, in the sense that memory is not stored in the medial temporal region itself but depends on a maintained interaction during consolidation between this region and distributed memory storage sites. The participation of the medial temporal region seems to be required for memory to become organized, schematized, and related to other material in memory. The consolidation process must occur for storage to be maintained (and retrieval accomplished) independently of the medial temporal region.

V.D. ANIMAL MODELS OF HUMAN GLOBAL AMNESIA

Until recently, the known behavioral effects of medial temporal or diencephalic lesions in experimental animals like the monkey seemed difficult to relate to work with human patients. One thing that may have contributed to this difficulty was uncertainty about which tasks should be used to assess memory. The question of task seems particularly critical because the amnesic syndrome in humans is now known to apply to a narrower domain of learning and memory than previously thought. Accordingly, one must select only particular tasks to study amnesia in monkeys. Work with monkeys can contribute a good deal when it is done against a background of the neuropsychological facts obtained from human amnesia. These two domains of investigation are mutually facilitatory. Human amnesic cases can provide extensive information about the nature and number of memory disorders. Monkeys can be prepared with precise lesions and can be studied with tests that are rigorously analogous to the human tests. In this way one can hope to bridge neurology and neuroanatomy and to relate function to brain structure with a precision that would be very difficult to obtain from human cases alone.

In the monkey, several tasks are available that appear to test memory just as human memory is tested in studies of amnesia. The best studied of these tasks is delayed nonmatching to sample (Gaffan, 1974; Mishkin & Delacour, 1975). Here the monkey is given sets of paired trials, always with unique stimuli. First the monkey sees a novel object which it displaces to obtain food. Then, seconds, minutes, or even hours later, the monkey sees two objects side by side—the original one and a new one. To obtain food reward, the monkey must displace the novel of the two objects. Normal monkeys learn to perform this task and can then demonstrate differential behavior toward old and new objects (i.e., recognition memory) across long intervals. In contrast to this task, which requires recognition of a familiar object, and which human amnesic patients cannot master, other tasks can be identified that appear to depend substantially on skill learning. Visual discrimination learning in the monkey, which is acquired gradually across days, seems to be an example of such a task (Squire & Zola-Morgan, 1983). (See Figure 7.5.)

With tasks like these, considerable headway has been made toward identifying the brain regions that are damaged in amnesia. In humans, the neuropathology is seldom known in the same patients who are extensively studied, and the lesions that the patients have are often the result of insidious disease (e.g., Korsakoff syndrome) or brain injury (e.g., case N.A.), where undoubtedly some damage occurs to brain regions in addition to those responsible for the memory impairment. Thus, after 100 years of neuropathological cases, there is still uncertainty as to which brain regions are responsible for diencephalic amnesia. The

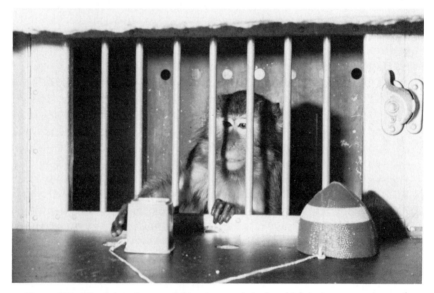

Figure 7.5 The delayed nonmatching to sample task, which tests memory in monkeys in an analogous way to tasks that are sensitive to human amnesia. (Top) The monkey displaces a single object, presented alone, to obtain a raisin reward. (Bottom) After a delay, which can vary from seconds to hours, the monkey sees the original object and a novel one. The monkey must displace the novel object to find a raisin reward. A different pair of objects is used on every trial.

mammillary bodies and the dorsal medial nucleus have received the most attention (for reviews, and various points of view, see Mair, Warrington, & Weiskrantz, 1979; Squire & Zola-Morgan, 1983; Victor, Adams, & Collins, 1971). Similarly, in spite of a continuing interest in the hippocampal formation, there is still uncertainty about which temporal lobe structures are responsible for bitemporal amnesia. With monkeys, however, precise lesions can be made, and memory can be assessed with carefully selected tasks. Study of bitemporal amnesia, in particular, has been informative in the past few years. Readers interested in more detailed coverage of this material are referred to reviews (Mishkin, Spiegler, Saunders, & Malamut, 1982; Squire & Zola-Morgan, 1983).

In the case of bitemporal amnesia, Mishkin (1978) has suggested that conjoint hippocampus–amygdala damage may be required to produce the syndrome that has been studied so extensively in case H.M. and other patients. This view, if correct, would force a revision of the traditional and widespread belief that damage to hippocampus alone can cause amnesia. So far, this idea is based on work with monkeys and the delayed nonmatching to sample task, and more studies using other tasks are needed. Neuropathological information from a well-studied case of human amnesia has shown that a bilateral lesion limited to the hippocampus can cause a substantial, disabling amnesia, albeit one less severe than that exhibited by case H. M. (Zola-Morgan, Squire, & Amaral, in press). Work with monkeys should be able to determine what specific damage in addition to hippocampus is needed to produce the severe kind of amnesia exhibited by H. M.

Horel (1978) suggested that neither the hippocampus nor the amygdala are involved in amnesia. He reviewed the existing data, arguing that the traditional view is not so well supported as might be thought. Instead, he suggested that the critical area is the temporal stem, a band of white matter lying adjacent to hippocampus. This view must now be discounted, however, because monkeys with temporal stem lesions are not amnesic (Zola-Morgan, Squire, & Mishkin, 1982). Current evidence also tends to minimize the role in memory of the fornix, a major efferent tract of the hippocampal formation that projects in part to the mammillary bodies (Squire & Zola-Morgan, 1983; Zola-Morgan, Dabrowska, Moss, & Mahut, 1983). If this interpretation turns out to be correct, then attention should be directed to brain regions that receive caudal projections from the hippocampal formation, for example, entorhinal cortex and area TH–TF.

With additional studies, it should be possible to identify with certainty which structure or structures can be damaged to cause bitemporal amnesia. This same investigative approach can also be used to address the

Bartus, R. T., Dean, R. L., Beer, B., & Lippa, A. S. (1982). The cholinergic hypothesis of geriatric memory dysfunction. *Science, 217*, 408–417.

Bruner, J. S. (1969). Modalities of memory. In G. A. Talland & N. C. Waugh (Eds.), *The pathology of memory* (pp. 253–259). New York: Academic Press.

Burnham, W. H. (1903). Retroactive amnesia: Illustrative cases and a tentative explanation. *American Journal of Psychology, 14*, 382–396.

Butters, N., & Cermak, L. S. (1980). *Alcoholic Korsakoff's syndrome: An information processing approach to amnesia.* New York: Academic Press.

Carew, T. J., Walters, E. T., & Kandel, E. R. (1981). Classical conditioning in a simple withdrawal reflex in *Aplysia californica. Journal of Neuroscience, 1*, 1426–1437.

Cermak, L. S. (1976). The encoding capacity of a patient with amnesia due to encephalitis. *Neuropsychologia, 14*, 311–326.

Cermak, L. S. (Ed.). (1982). *Human memory and amnesia.* Hillsdale, NJ: Erlbaum.

Cermak, L. S., Butters, N., & Morcines, J. (1974). Some analyses of the verbal encoding deficit of alcoholic Korsakoff patients. *Brain and Language, 1*, 141–150.

Chang, T. J., & Gelperin, A. (1980). Rapid taste aversion learning by an isolated molluscan central nervous system. *Proceedings of the National Academy of Science, 77*, 6204–6206.

Cohen, D. H. (1980). The functional neuroanatomy of a conditioned response. *Neural mechanisms of goal-directed behavior and learning* (pp. 283–302). New York: Academic Press.

Cohen, N. J. (1981). *Neuropsychological evidence for a distinction between procedural and declarative knowledge in human memory and amnesia.* Unpublished doctoral dissertation, University of California, San Diego.

Cohen, N. J., & Squire, L. R. (1980). Preserved learning and retention of pattern analyzing skill in amnesia: Dissociation of knowing how and knowing that. *Science, 210*, 207–209.

Corkin, S. (1984). Lasting consequences of bilateral medial temporal lobectomy: Clinical course and experimental findings in H. M. *Seminars in Neurology, 4*, 249–259.

Crow, T. J., & Alkon, D. L. (1980). Associative behavior modification in Hermissenda: Cellular correlates, *Science, 209*, 412–414.

Davis, H. P. & Squire, L. R. (1984). Protein synthesis and memory: A review. *Psychological Bulletin, 96*, 518–559.

Davis, W. J. & Gillette, R. (1978). Neural correlate of behavioral plasticity in command neurons of *Pleurobranchaea. Science, 199*, 801–804.

Deutsch, J. A. (1971). The cholinergic synapse and the site of memory. *Science, 174*, 788–794.

Disterhoft, J. F., Shipley, M. T., & Kraus, N. (1982). Analyzing the rabbit NM conditioned reflex arc. In C. D. Woody (Ed.), *Conditioning: Representation of involved neural functions,* New York: Plenum.

Dunn, A. J. (1980). Neurochemistry of learning and memory: An evaluation of recent data. *Annual Review of Psychology, 31*, 343–390.

Fodor, J. (1981). *Representations,* Cambridge, MA: MIT Press.

Freed, D. M., Cohen, N. J., & Corkin, S. (1984). Rate of forgetting in H. M.: A reanalysis, *Society for Neuroscience Abstracts, 10*, 383.

Freud, S. S. (1901). *The psychopathology of everyday life* (standard ed. 6) (p. 69). London: Hogarth Press.

Freud, S. S. (1930). *Civilization and its discontents* (standard ed. 21). London: Hogarth Press.

Gabriel, M., Orona, E., Foster, K., & Lambert, R. W. (1982). Mechanism and generality of stimulus significance coding in a mammalion model system. In C. D. Woody (Eds.), *Conditioning representation of involved neural function,* New York: Plenum Press.

Gaffan, D. (1974). Recognition impaired and association intact in the memory of monkeys after transection of the fornix. *Journal of Comparative and Physiological Psychology, 86,* 1100–1109.

Gold, P., & McGaugh, J. L. (1975). A single-trace, two-process view of memory storage processes. In D. Deutsch & J. A. Deutsch (Eds.), *Short-term memory* (pp. 355–378). New York: Academic Press.

Graf, P., Squire, L. R., & Mandler, G. (1984). The information that amnesic patients do not forget. *Journal of Experimental Psychology: Learning, Memory, and Cognition, 10,* 164–178.

Greenough, W. T. (1984). Possible structural substrate of plastic neural phenomena. In G. Lynch, J. McGaugh, & N. Weinberger (Eds.), *Neurobiology of learning and memory* (pp. 470–478). New York: Guilford Press.

Hirst, W. (1982). The amnesic syndrome: Descriptions and explanations. *Psychological Bulletin, 91,* 435–460.

Horel, J. A. (1978). The neuroanatomy of amnesia: A critique of the hippocampal memory hypothesis. *Brain, 101,* 403–445.

Horn, G. (1981). Neural mechanisms of learning: An analysis of imprinting in the domestic chick. *Proceedings of the Royal Society of London (Biol.), 213,* 101–137.

Hoyle, G. (1979). Instrumental conditioning of the leg lift in the locust. *Neuroscience Research Program Bulletin, 17,* 577–586.

Huppert, F. A., & Piercy, M. (1979). Normal and abnormal forgetting in organic amnesia: effect of locus of lesion. *Cortex, 15,* 385–390.

Jacoby, L. L. (1982). Knowing and remembering: Some parallels in the behavior of Korsakoff patients and normals. In L. S. Cermak (Ed.), *Human memory and amnesia* (pp. 97–122). Hillsdale, NJ: Erlbaum.

Jacoby, L. L., & Witherspoon, D. (1982). Remembering without awareness. *Canadian Journal of Psychology, 32,* 300–324.

Kandel, E. (1976). *Cellular basis of behavior.* New York: Freeman.

Kandel, E. (1977). Neuronal plasticity and the modification of behavior. In J. M. Brookhart, V. B. Mountcastle, E. R. Kandel, & S. R. Geiger (Eds.), *Handbook of physiology,* (Vol. 1) (pp. 1137–1182). Bethesda, MD, American Physiological Society.

Kandel, E. R., Brunelli, M., Byrne, J., & Castellucci, V. (1976). A common presynaptic locus for the synaptic changes underlying short-term habituation and sensitization of the gill withdrawal reflex in *Aplysia. Cold Spring Harbor Laboratory Symposium on Quantitative Biology* (Vol. 40). *The Synapse* (pp. 465–482). Cold Spring Harbor, NY:

Kolers, P. A. (1976). Pattern-analyzing memory. *Science, 191,* 1280–1281.

Kolers, P. A. (1979). A pattern-analyzing basis of recognition. In L. S. Cermak, F. I. M. Craik (Eds.), *Levels of processing in human memory* (pp. 363–384). Hillsdale, NJ: Erlbaum.

Krasne, F. B. (1978). Extrinsic control of intrinsic neuronal plasticity: An hypothesis from work on simple systems. *Brain Research, 14,* 197–216.

Lashley, K. S. (1950). In search of the engram. *Society of Experimental Biology Symposium: No. 4. Physiological mechanisms in animal behavior* (pp. 454–482). Cambridge University Press.

Lee, K., Schottler, F., Oliver, M., & Lynch, G. S. (1980). Brief bursts of high-frequency stimulation produced two types of structural change in rat hippocampus. *Journal of Neurophysiology, 44,* 247–258.

Mair, W. G. P., Warrington, E. K., & Weiskrantz, L. (1979). Memory disorder in Korsakoff's psychosis: A neuropathological and neuropsychological investigation of two cases. *Brain, 1023,* 719–783.

Mandler, G. (1980). Recognizing: The judgment of previous occurrence. *Psychological Review, 87*, 252–271.

Martinez, J. L. (1983). Endogenous modulators of learning and memory. In S. Cooper (Ed.), *Theory in psychopharmacology* (Vol. 2). New York: Academic Press.

McCormick, D. A., Clark, G. A., Lavond, D. G., & Thompson, R. F. (1982). Initial localization of the memory trace for a basic form of learning. *Proceedings of the National Academy of Science, 79*, 2731–2735.

Milner, B. (1972). Disorders of learning and memory after temporal lobe lesions in man. *Clinical Neurosurgery, 19*, 421–446.

Mishkin, M. (1978). Memory in monkeys severely impaired by combined but not by separate removal of amygdala and hippocampus. *Nature, 273*, 297–298.

Mishkin, M., & Delacour, J. (1975). An analysis of short-term visual memory in the monkey. *Journal of Experimental Psychology, 1*, 326, 334.

Mishkin, M., Spiegler, B. J., Saunders, R. C., Malamut, B. L. (1982). An animal model of global amnesia. In S. Corkin, K. L. Davis, J. H. Growdon, E. Usdin, & R. J. Wurtman (Eds.), *Toward a treatment of Alzheimer's disease.* New York: Raven Press.

Moscovitch, M. (1982). Multiple dissociations of function in amnesia. In L. Cermak (Ed.), *Human memory and amnesia* (pp. 337–370). Hillsdale, NJ: Erlbaum.

Nadel, L., & Zola-Morgan, S. (1984). Toward the understanding of infant memory: Contributions from animal neuropsychology. In M. Moscovitch (Ed.), *Infant memory* (pp. 145–172). New York: Plenum Press.

Nottebohm, F. (1980). Brain pathways for vocal learning in birds: A review of the first 10 years. In J. M. Sprague & A. N. Epstein (Eds.), *Progress in psychobiology and physiology and psychology* (Vol. 9). New York: Academic Press.

Nottebohm, F. (1981). A brain for all seasons: Cyclical anatomical changes in song control nuclei of the canary brain. *Science, 214*, 1368–1370.

O'Keefe, J., & Nadel, L. (1978). *The hippocampus as a cognitive map.* London: Oxford University Press.

Rose, S. P. R. (1977). Early visual experience, learning and neurochemical plasticity in the rat and the chick. *Philosophical Transactions of the Royal Society of London, Series B. 278*, 307–318.

Rosenzweig, M. R. (1979). Responsiveness of brain size to individual experience. Behavioral and evolutionary implication. In M. E. Hahn, C. Jensen, & B. Dudek (Eds.), *Development and evolution of brain size: Behavioral implications* (pp. 263–294). New York: Academic Press.

Rozin, P. (1976a). The psychobiological approach to human memory. In M. R. Rosenzweig & E. L. Bennett (Eds.), *Neural mechanisms of learning and memory.* Cambridge, MA: MIT Press.

Rozin, P. (1976b). The evolution of intelligence and access to the cognitive unconscious. In *Progress in psychobiology and physiological psychology, 6*, 245–280.

Russell, W. R. & Nathan, P. W. (1946). Traumatic amnesia. *Brain, 69*, 280–300.

Ryle, G. (1949). *The concept of mind.* London: Hutchinson.

Schacter, D. L. & Moscovitch, M. (1984). Infants, amnesics, and dissociable memory systems. In M. Moscovitch (Ed.), *Infant memory* (173–216). New York: Plenum Press.

Scoville, W. B., & Milner, B. (1957). Loss of recent memory after bilateral hippocampal lesions. *Journal of Neurology, Neurosurgery, and Psychiatry, 20*, 11–21.

Shimamura, A. P., & Squire, L. R. (1986). Memory and metamemory: A study of the feeling-of-knowing phenomenon in amnesic patients. *Journal of Experimental Psychology: Learning, Memory, and Cognition,* in press.

Solomon, P. R., & Moore, J. W. (1975). Latent inhibition and stimulus generalization of the classically conditioned nictitating membrane response in rabbits (Oryctolagus cuniculus) following dorsal hippocampal ablation. *Journal of Comparative and Physiological Psychology, 89,* 1192–1203.

Squire, L. R. (1981). Two forms of human amnesia: An analysis of forgetting. *Journal of Neuroscience, 1,* 635–640.

Squire, L. R. (1982a). Comparisons between forms of amnesia: Some deficits are unique to Korsakoff syndrome. *Journal of Experimental Psychology: Learning, Memory, and Cognition, 8,* 560–571.

Squire, L. R. (1982b). The neuropsychology of human memory. *Annual Review of Neuroscience, 5,* 241–273.

Squire, L. R. (1984). The neuropsychology of memory. In P. Marler & H. S. Terrace (Eds.), *The Biology of Learning* (pp. 667–685). Dahlem Konferenzen. Berlin, Heidelberg, New York, Tokyo: Springer-Verlag.

Squire, L. R. (in press). Memory and Brain. Oxford Univ. Press: New York.

Squire, L. R., Cohen, N., & Nadel, L. (1984). The medial temporal region and memory consolidation: A new hypothesis. In H. Weingarter & E. Parker (Eds.), *Memory consolidation,* Hillsdale, NJ: Erlbaum.

Squire, L. R., & Davis, H. P. (1981). The pharmacology of memory: A neurobiological perspective. *Annual Review of Pharmacology and Toxicology, 21,* 323–356.

Squire, L. R. & Cohen, N. J. (1984). Human memory and amnesia. In G. Lynch, J. McGaugh, N. Weinberger (Eds.), *Neurobiology of learning and memory* (pp. 3–64). New York: Guilford Press.

Squire, L. R., & Zola-Morgan, S. (1983). The neurology of memory: The case for correspondence between the findings for man and non-human primate. In J. A. Deutsch (Ed.), *The Physiological Basis of Memory* (2nd ed.) (pp. 199–268). New York: Academic Press.

Stern, L. D. (1981). A review of theories of human amnesia. *Memory and cognition, 9,* 247–262.

Swanson, L. W., Teyler, T. J., & Thompson, R. F. (1982). Hippocampal long-term potentiation: mechanisms and implications for memory. *Neurosciences Research Program Bulletin 20,* 613–765.

Teuber, H.-L., Milner, B., & Vaughan, H. G. (1968). Persistent anterograde amnesia after stab wound of the basal brain. *Neuropsychologia, 6,* 267–282.

Thompson, R. F., Berger, T. W., Cegavske, C. F., Patterson, M. M., Roemer, R. A., Teyler, T. J., & Young, R. A. (1976). The search for the engram. *American Psychologist, 31,* 209–227.

Thompson, R., Berger, T., & Madden, J. (1983). Cellular processes of learning and memory in the mammalian CNS. *Annual Review of Neuroscience, 6,* 447–492.

Victor, M., Adams, R. D., & Collins, G. H. (1971). In F. Plum & F. H. McDowell (Eds.), *The Wernicke-Korsakoff syndrome.* Philadelphia, PA: Davis.

Warrington, E. K., & Weiskrantz, L. (1978). Further analysis of the prior learning effect in amnesic patients. *Neuropsychologia, 16,* 169–177.

Weinberger, N. M. (1982). Sensory plasticity and learning of magnocellular geniculate nucleus of the auditory system. In C. D. Woody (Ed.), *Conditioning: Representation of involved neural function.* New York: Plenum.

Weiskrantz, L. (1978). A comparison of hippocampal pathology in man and other animals. *Functions of the Septo-hippocampal System* (CIBA Foundation Symposium, No. 58). Oxford: Elsevier.

Whitehouse, P. J., Price, D. L., Struble, R. G., Clark, A. W., Coyle, J. T., DeLong, M. R. (1982). Alzheimer's disease and senile dementia: Loss of neurons in the basal forebrain. *Science, 215,* 1237–1238.

Winograd, R. (1975). Frame representations and the declarative-procedural controversy.

In D. Bobrow & A. Collins (Eds.), *Representation and understanding*. New York: Academic Press.

Wood, F., Ebert, V., & Kinsbourne, M. (1982). The episodic-semantic memory distinction in memory and amnesia: Clinical and experimental observations. In L. Cermak (Ed.), *Human memory and amnesia* (pp. 167–193). Hillsdale, NJ: Erlbaum.

Woody, C. D. (Ed.). (1982). *Conditioning: Representation of involved neural function*, New York: Plenum.

Zola-Morgan, S., Dabrowska, J., Moss, M., & Mahut, H. (1983). Enhanced preference for perceptual novelty in the monkey after fornix sections, but not after hippocampal ablations. *Neuropsychologia, 21,* 433–454.

Zola-Morgan, S., Squire, L. R., and Amaral, D. (In press). Amnesia and the medial temporal region: enduring memory impairment following a bilateral lesion limited to field CA1 of the hippocampus. *Journal of Neuroscience.*

Zola-Morgan, S., Squire, L. R., & Mishkin, M. (1982). The neuroanatomy of amnesia: Amygdala-hippocampus vs. temporal stem. *Science, 218,* 1337–1339.

Zornetzer, S. F. (1978). Neurotransmitter modulation and memory: A new neuropharmacological phrenology? In M. A. Lipton, A. DiMascio, & K. F. Killan (Eds.), *Psychopharmacology: A generation of progress* (pp. 637–649). New York: Raven Press.

CHAPTER 8

Integrating Three Perspectives on Learning

Susan F. Chipman*

I. INTRODUCTION

No one believes in magic. We are quite certain that the anatomy and physiology of the brain provide the underlying mechanisms of the human mind. Yet, much about the relationship between neural functions and the phenomena of mind remains mysterious. Occasional findings can shake our confidence in what we think we know. "Is your brain really necessary?" asked an article in *Science* (Lewin, 1980), reporting the existence of individuals in whom hydrocephalus has reduced the cortex to a very thin layer lining the skull without apparent detriment to normal function. One such person had an IQ of 126 and had earned a first-class honors degree in mathematics from a British university.

It is no wonder, therefore, that Squire begins his chapter in this volume by stating that there are two great problems in neuroscience: the problem of describing the *hard-wiring* of the brain as it localizes and organizes various functions and the problem of understanding *plasticity*—how the organization of the brain can change and adapt. As the case just described illustrates, the links that are made between the study of the brain, of cognitive function, and of education processes are tenuous and open to challenge. There is considerable merit to the argument that these are quite separate domains, distinct levels of scientific expla-

* The author is Program Manager for Personnel and Training Research, U.S. Office of Naval Research and was formerly Assistant Director of the National Institute of Education for Learning and Development. The opinions expressed herein are the author's own and do not necessarily represent the official policy or position of the Office of Naval Research or of the National Institute of Education.

203

nation that can be legitimately and productively pursued without reference to each other. Yet each field—neuroscience, cognitive science, education—addresses problems so complex and difficult to untangle that it can use help from whatever source. These fields can be seen as offering three different perspectives on a common scientific problem: explicating the nature and process of human mental function. They can provide independent, converging sources of evidence that increase our confidence in scientific conclusions. The strategy of this volume was to select topics in the study of human intellectual function that have been of some interest to all three fields so that the potential for fruitful interaction could be considered.

Neuroscience is concerned with the hardware of the mind, the mechanisms that carry out the functions of the mind. To the extent that it attempts to relate the structures and chemical activities it describes to function and behavior, it requires a sound characterization of those functions. Cognitive science (cognitive psychology, linguistics, artificial intelligence, etc.) is primarily concerned with delineating those functions—describing the codes in which experience is represented, the mental operations that transform and make use of that information, and the abstract programs that control action. The example of the modern digital computer—in which the same hardware subserves the purposes of many programs—has shown us that studying hardware need not provide much insight into the functions being performed. On the other hand, neuropsychological work provides much valuable information about the separability of intellectual functions that might otherwise have been thought inseparable. Education, which is partially a practical field and partially a distinctive research enterprise, is primarily concerned with the production of intellectual change through management of experience. Its emphasis on change is greater than that of the other two fields, and its time perspective is typically longer. For example, a learning experiment conducted by a psychologist is likely to last for an hour or 2 at most, while a researcher in mathematics education may conduct a teaching experiment over a period of months. Neuroscientists may study change in the brain or recovery of function after damage over a relatively long period of time, but generally the experience of the organism during that period is uncontrolled, or controlled only in very gross terms. In some cases, education may provide demonstrations of the unexpected possibility of change that are of interest to the other fields. The claims made for infant stimulation programs for Down's syndrome children would be such an example if they prove to be true.

In addition to these points of connection that penetrate the barriers between the fields, there are parallels in the great questions that animate the fields. For neuroscience, according to Squire, these are the questions of hard-wiring and plasticity. In cognitive science, there is the distinction between what is innate and what is acquired, between what might be the unchanging, constant elemental processes in cognition and what can be constructed, taught, or learned from that foundation. The postulated *language acquisition device* (Chomsky, 1965, 1980) that has emerged as linguists have attempted to account for the learning of language is clearly thought of as something that is hard-wired by the human genetic program (Fodor, 1983). In education, the concern is with plasticity—the essence of the educational enterprise. Still, the possibility of built-in limitations on or predilections toward learning remains a background concern. It is particularly salient, of course, when educators attempt to deal with students who do not learn effectively from the usual school experiences.

These connections and parallels among the fields point to the promise of positive interaction, but they have also tempted many to draw fallacious conclusions in one field from the results in another. For example, hard-wiring tends to be identified with notions of innateness and immutability despite the demonstrations of neural plasticity that should caution against that identification. In this discussion chapter, I consider the opportunities for positive interaction among the fields that are brought out by the three preceding chapters and then suggest ways that this positive interaction might be enhanced. I then discuss some of the unfortunate ways in which neuroscience is being viewed as having implications for education and suggest ways in which these negative aspects of the interaction between fields might be minimized.

The preceding three chapters are grouped around the very general topic of knowledge acquisition. Squire considers memory from the perspective of neuroscience, emphasizing evidence for different kinds of memory. Gleitman discusses the evidence for a biological and maturational component in language acquisition, an example of a unique human skill that has been the focus of much fruitful interaction between neuroscience and cognitive science. Wittrock discusses research that aims to enhance the acquisition of the declarative knowledge that schools emphasize. Here, a discussion of each of these chapters serves as an occasion to consider what related work tells us about productive interaction between the fields.

II. THREE FACETS OF KNOWLEDGE ACQUISITION

II.A. MEMORY

Memory is an extremely broad, commonsense concept. There is a sense in which almost any change in behavior consequent on experience can be called memory, as Squire's chapter illustrates. Neuropsychological work has proved helpful in drawing distinctions within this very broad concept. Today, for example, the distinction between short-term memory for information and long-term memory is generally accepted. However, not so long ago it was argued that the characterization of short- and long-term memory as a single process was a simpler, more parsimonious theory (Melton, 1963; Postman, 1964). Arguments over the legitimacy of the distinction turned upon similarity or dissimilarity in the rules that govern the storage and forgetting of information over short and long periods of time. Thus, a decisive outcome was difficult to obtain. In their important theoretical paper on human memory, Atkinson and Shiffrin (1968) characterized Milner's reports (1959) on the effects of hippocampal lesions as "perhaps the single most convincing demonstration of a dichotomy in the memory system." Milner reported that patients with bilateral surgical lesions in the hippocampus seem to be incapable of adding new information to their long-term memory storage even though they retain old knowledge and skills and also perform well on tests of short-term memory. Atkinson and Shiffrin noted that a similar pattern of performance had been observed for a long time as Korsakoff's syndrome.

Current work with amnesic patients appears to confirm the validity of another important theoretical distinction among types of memory or knowledge. This is the distinction that opposes skills or procedures to facts or episodes. Ryle (1949) called it the distinction between knowing how and knowing that. More recently, cognitive scientists have applied the labels procedural and declarative knowledge (Winograd, 1975). It has been known for a long time that amnesic patients can learn motor skills, but the list of skills that they can acquire is growing. For example, they can acquire the skill of mirror-reading at a normal rate and retain it normally without being able to recall either their prior experience in the task or the words that they have read. Still more surprisingly, they can learn to solve the Tower of Hanoi puzzle, a 31-move problem, without "remembering" it.

Squire notes that these findings describe a type of learning that may be similar to the learning that occurs in early childhood. He points to the developmental phenomenon of infantile amnesia, the unavailability of memory for events that occur early in life. Because of this parallel, the suggestion has been made that the hippocampal system does not become functional for some time after birth (Nadel & Zola-Morgan, 1984). It might prove fruitful to pursue these hypotheses by comparing learning in these patients more systematically to the Piagetian concept of sensorimotor intelligence as characteristic of very young children. Sensorimotor intelligence involves practical perceptual and motor adjustments to things in the environment, without symbolic representations or symbolic manipulations of them (Flavell, 1963).

In his chapter, Squire describes a finer distinction that is now emerging between two types of memory deficits. In experiments that equated the recognition level for pictures after 10 minutes, the patient H.M., with lesions of the hippocampus, was found to forget much more rapidly than Korsakoff syndrome patients, who forgot at a normal rate. Patients receiving electroconvulsive shock therapy also forget at a very rapid rate, as do monkeys with lesions including both the hippocampus and the amygdala. Monkeys with lesions of the medial thalamus, like Korsakoff syndrome patients, are amnesic, but forget at normal rates. This suggests to Squire that the two regions of the brain make essential but fundamentally different contributions to normal memory functions. He believes that the hippocampal region is somehow involved in the process of consolidation of memory by which memory somehow changes over a long period of time to become more stable and coherent.

It is interesting to see how Squire draws upon both cognitive science and the most reductionist aspects of neuroscience in order to further explore and interpret his findings. Because changes in the structure of synapses have been shown to underlie the changes in reflex responses of the sea hare, Squire hypothesizes that the capacity for learning that remains in amnesic patients is similar, that such memory may be localized in the same neural circuitry that supports the ability to do the tasks. Needless to say, the behavioral experiments that are serving to distinguish among groups of amnesic patients and to delineate their capacities and incapacities are drawing upon a rather substantial cognitive research tradition. A particularly interesting example of this is the demonstration of normal "activation" effects of previously presented words on the performance of amnesic patients in a word completion task. One would not have thought of such a task without knowing of recent cognitive research. Thus, it provides a particularly clear example of the way neuroscience depends on cognitive science for assistance in specifying the functions of neural structures.

Squire's speculations about the nature of memory consolidation also

seem to draw upon both traditions. He suggests that the medial temporal region (hypothalamus, etc.) is necessary for memory to become organized, schematized, and related to other information in memory. He
views memory consolidation as a dynamic process affected by rehearsal,
association, and subsequent memory storage episodes. These are clearly
cognitive notions. On the other hand, he also characterizes memory
consolidation as a dynamic and slowly developing process that can be
influenced or modulated shortly after initial learning by manipulation of
specific transmitter systems, hormones or other peptides. At one time, it
appeared that there might be distinct stages of memory consolidation
differentiated by the susceptibility of disruption by different treatments.
More recently, however, such research has been reinterpreted. The time
after training for which a treatment has an effect is now considered to be
a measure of the treatment's general severity or effectiveness rather than
an indicator of a separate and distinct memory consolidation process
affected by that treatment (Gold & Zornetzer, 1983). It is not obvious
how these physiological views of memory consolidation link to the cognitive notions or how one would demonstrate that hypothetical parallels
between the physiological processes and the cognitive are valid. At the
end of his chapter, Squire reveals that it still is not certain precisely
which brain structures are responsible for the memory effects he has
described—because of the uncertainties that surround the study of human brain lesions. Thus, evidence from neuroscience has been making
important contributions to our understanding of memory, but it seems
no more solid, no less susceptible to reinterpretation than the psychological evidence.

II.B. LANGUAGE

Gleitman's chapter presents the case for a biological and maturational
component in language acquisition. One of the major arguments making up this case is the common pattern of language acquisition. For
nearly all children, language learning follows a strikingly similar time
course, despite substantial variation in the language input to which they
are exposed. There are strong indications that there are critical periods
in human development when language development, or specific aspects
of language development, will occur. Lenneberg (1967) pointed out that
recovery from language loss caused by brain injury is likely to occur in
young children, but is rare in adults. Both Lenneberg and Gleitman
noted that the delayed language acquisition of Down's syndrome children tends to halt in adolescence before acquisition in complete. Lenneberg attributed the cessation of learning to a biologically determined end

to the period in which language learning is possible. Gleitman, on the other hand, seems to suggest that these children lack the inborn capacities that support the later stages of language acquisition. Surprisingly, she and her associates have determined that language acquisition in these children proceeds at a rapid, normal rate after its very late start and then stops short of full development.

Many, including Lenneberg, have observed that young children appear to be more capable than adults of second-language learning. Gleitman reports that late learners of a language tend not to acquire the closed-class function words in a complete manner, even after years of practice. More strikingly still, 5 to 8 year-old youngsters exposed to pidgin as their first language seem to invent and supply the closed-class morphology that the language itself lacks. That is, there seems to be an ideal maturational moment for this particular advanced aspect of language acquisition.

The postulated innate *language acquisition device* (LAD) is a major feature of modern linguistic theory. Much of Gleitman's research and much of her chapter are devoted to the description of the LAD. She presents several of the key lines of argument for the existence of a LAD. In general, it is argued that the combination of the observed linguistic exposure and a simple learning mechanism is insufficient to explain the observed features of language acquisition. The child's linguistic output differs from the linguistic input in interesting ways. Children conform appropriately to linguistic rules about permissible transformations of sentences and contractions that depend upon the hierarchical structure of utterances, not upon their serial order. Thus, they seem to be supplying the correct hierarchical organization from their internal resources. Similarly, Gleitman argues convincingly that the information available to the child about the mapping between simple sentences and the perceptual circumstances being talked about is insufficient to permit a decoding especially for blind children.

Taken together, these arguments suggest that an innate program for language learning may be very complex, providing many detailed kinds of information that aid in the interpretation and transformation of linguistic input. However, that apparent complexity may simply result from our failure to penetrate the secrets of language acquisition. Gleitman (along with Wanner and others) speculates that the child's selective neglect of closed-class words may result from the fact that they are unstressed in adult speech. It seems possible that the other aforementioned linguistic mysteries could have relatively simple explanations of the same kind. It is quite plausible, for example, that stress or other prosodic features signal the structural features of sentences that govern grammatical rules. Thus, the LAD could be much simpler than Gleit-man's arguments seem to suggest. Perhaps it consists of little more than the perceptual apparatus for the analysis of phonemes (Eimas, Siqueland, Jucsyzk, & Vigorito, 1971) and a mechanism sensitive to stress. To those of us who have completed our first-language acqui-sition, the critical features of auditory input that aided acquisition may have become nonsalient. Perhaps our capacity to generate the appropriate hypotheses about the language acquisition process is therefore as limited as our capacity to acquire new languages seems to be.

In principle, Gleitman concludes, it should be possible to discover neurological correlates to these patterns of language development in the developing brain. There may be relatively independent maturation of the subsystems that account for various aspects of language compe-tence. But she does not expect to see the evidence within the next century.

Despite Gleitman's pessimism, the history of interaction between neuroscience and psychology or linguistics has been long and fruitful. Indeed, the two classic aphasias, Broca's and Wernicke's, that initiated the efforts to localize cognitive function in the brain separate, as Gleit-man points out, the closed- and open-class words. This lends support to the reality of a rather fuzzy linguistic classification of words that is derived from complex arguments.

It may be instructive to quickly review the history of interaction be-tween the study of language and neuroscience. There are those who would go so far as to say that language is better analyzed by aphasia than by linguists because the structure of performance is directly re-vealed in its breakdown, rather than having to be inferred through complex arguments and evidence (Brown, 1980). The validity of this enthusiastic claim is somewhat open to doubt. In 1971, for example, Pribram was complaining that there was great confusion concerning the effects of brain injuries upon language function. He attributed this con-fusion to confusion in the way in which language competence is de-scribed by investigators. The original model of language function that was used by Wernicke in the 1880s was extremely simple, differentiating input or comprehension functions from output functions. It was soon recognized that there were limitations in this account because victims of Broca's aphasia did have comprehension problems. Indeed, Pribram (1971) expressed doubts about whether Broca's aphasia—as originally described—is actually observed. For such reasons, Broca's achievement has been characterized as predominantly in the domain of neuroanat-omy (Caplan, 1980): Broca established that the convolutions of the brain were not random and meaningless, but had a relatively consistent relation to functions.

Clearly, one cannot claim that neuropsychological work has contributed to the analysis of linguistic function in a direct and powerful way. However, the rich variety of ways in which brain injury separates linguistic functions that might otherwise be regarded as a seamless whole (see Gardner, 1975) has been widely known. No doubt this knowledge has provided a general background against which linguistic theory has developed, influenced in ways that would be difficult to trace. Certainly, the evidence of neuropsychology legitimizes theories that break down language competence into many interacting components. However, the evidence has not been used in detailed ways to develop linguistic theory because it has not been categorized and described in terms that are linguistically meaningful—it was not collected by persons whose primary interest was in language.

More recently, linguists have examined the language of brain-injured patients with great analytic care. The result has been substantial change in the characterization of language deficits. Kean (1980), for example, has asserted that the linguistic deficits of Broca's aphasia can be described effectively in terms of a linguistic theory of the language generation process. In the component of grammar that describes the generation of a phonological representation, the words and parts of words that are deleted by these patients can be differentiated from those that are not. Unlike the earlier, cruder description contrasting substantive to functional words, Kean's account correctly predicts, for example, that some prepositions (function words) like "beyond" will be retained while others will be omitted. Her account makes strong predictions about what will be observed in other languages with different structural characteristics so that it can be tested. Of course, when such hypotheses are confirmed, they lend the strength of truly independent evidence to the linguistic theories that generated them. For neuropsychology, the evidence is likely to appear less confusing when more-appropriate descriptive categories are developed—when the functions whose neurological correlates are sought have been appropriately defined. It turns out, for example, that Broca's aphasia patients are insensitive in comprehension to the meaning conveyed by the same class of words and inflections that they omit in production (Bradley, Garrett, & Zurif, 1980).

A similar, but still more substantial, change has occurred in our understanding of the linguistic effects of removing the left cerebral hemisphere at an early age. Traditionally, and surprisingly, this operation was thought to result in normal language development, perhaps accompanied by a small overall depression of intellectual ability (Lenneberg,

1967). However, a more sophisticated psycholinguistic testing of such subjects has shown that they are weak in processing syntactic information (Dennis & Kohn, 1975; Dennis & Whitaker, 1977). It appears that they infer sentence structure from meaning rather than using syntax as a clue to meaning. In addition, these individuals have difficulty accessing words via rhyming cues. This suggests that some specific mechanisms normally contributing to language competence have been lost. Nevertheless, the clinical impression is that such persons are linguistically normal. The classic conclusion that the young brain is quite flexible in reallocating functions seems to remain valid.

Whether or not they arise from the same processes that provide such flexible adaptation to damage, there are also significant and orderly individual differences in the areas of the brain that subserve language functions. Bogen (1980), a neurosurgeon, has commented upon this variability, which he refers to as a probabilistic distribution of aphasic symptoms in relation to areas of the brain. Left-handed persons (Gloning, 1977) and females (McGlone, 1977) do not show the same pattern of lateralization of language functions as is considered typical (of right-handed males). Yet, this does not result in language deficiencies. Therefore, substantial progress in understanding the language deficits associated with brain damage is accompanied by continuing mysteries and much speculation about the processes by which functions come to be allocated to specific brain loci.

II.C. LEARNING SUBJECT MATTER

Wittrock's chapter is primarily concerned with externally and internally controlled strategies that affect the success of students in reading and studying to learn school subject matter. There is a very substantial, if not entirely consistent, literature on the usefulness of questions and other adjunct aids in learning (see Reder, 1980). Wittrock points out that these aids can be viewed as controllers of attention, or of processing effort, during reading. Wittrock describes how cognitive analyses of the processing done by good readers and effective students can be used to design instructional interventions that help less-able students to direct their processing efforts for more effective learning. For example, students have been instructed to construct mental images of the story they are reading, to generate summary sentences, or to verbally relate the content of a text to their previous knowledge. All of these strategies have sometimes been successful, But Wittrock also touches upon the limitations of this approach: Younger students sometimes do not seem to be able to implement the suggested strategies. Indeed, Brown and her associates have shown that both young children and many junior college students have difficulty in selecting the main ideas in paragraphs (Brown & Smiley, 1978). Such students cannot profit from instructions to concentrate their attention on the main ideas, but they can be helped by more-detailed instruction in specific strategies that will help them locate the main ideas and construct summaries (Brown & Day, 1983).

Of course, such concerns become more salient in discussing the problems of students who have severe difficulties in learning. Wittrock notes that defects of attention are considered to be a major source of difficulty for learning disabled and mentally retarded students—particularly in academic settings and tasks. But does the problem lie in not knowing what is worth attending to, or in maintaining an intention—however simple—long enough to carry out the act, or in simple alerting and orienting? *Attention* in the sense of knowing how to plan and control one's own cognitive processes may be quite different from the simpler alerting, arousal, and visual orienting aspects of attention that are typically the focus of neuropsychological research. A particular problem with attention to academic tasks suggests the first explanation. Wittrock cites evidence that points in each of these directions. Of course, each of these problems might occur separately or in different combinations in different individuals.

It is evident that research on the nature of the problems of learning disabled students needs to be structured and guided by a clearly stated model of all the processes involved in the performance of interest. Furthermore, clearcut conclusions are unlikely as long as school or clinical classifications, rather than theoretical taxonomies, are used as the foundations of research. The present state of confusion is illustrated by the diverse recommendations for treatment that Wittrock describes. The implication that drugs such as amphetamines and instruction in cognitive strategies are alternative treatments for the same problem seems implausible. If a student has no idea what content merits attention, it is unlikely that a drug thought to facilitate attention will be immediately helpful as the sole treatment. Undoubtedly, however, emotional and physiological states can interfere with the execution of cognitive strategies that we are otherwise capable of carrying out. Persistent defects in low-level attentional processes might well prevent the acquisition of any complex strategies.

Aside from its specific content, Wittrock's chapter is interesting for its assertion about the way that research tends to have its impact upon education—that educational change is mediated by a change in the broad conceptual framework that educators bring to the solution of educational problems. Thus, he points to a general relation between neuro-

psychological models of information processing in the brain hemispheres and the educational interest in utilizing and contrasting verbal
and spatial processes, or analytic and holistic processes.

These connections are extremely weak. The juxtaposition of the chapters by Squire and Wittrock suggests that it is possible to formulate
more-important research questions that link these concerns much more
tightly. Can a person who learns without any apparent memory of the
learning experience itself acquire or use a learning strategy? Can that
person learn to learn? Perhaps a learning strategy can also be acquired
without conscious memory of or insight into its use. If so, we might gain
understanding of individual differences in the use of learning strategies.
The investigation of learning in brain-damaged individuals might be
helpful in clarifying the functional distinctions that need to be made in
understanding the strategic control of learning processes. Such improved understanding would provide clearer guidelines to educators in
designing effective educational experiences. Correspondingly, the cognitive research on these control functions suggests new questions that
should be asked by neuropsychologists.

The links between cognitive and educational research are much
tighter than the link between neuroscience and education. Wittrock's
own experiments are informed by an extensive knowledge of cognitive
research. Yet, I think, one can still see the effects of the barriers between
fields, which are penetrated—if at all—by the consolidated conclusions
of a body of research. One can also see from those experiments the
potential benefit of a more thoroughgoing use of developments and
methods from a neighboring field. Those experiments, with considerable success, relied on verbal instructions to induce the desired cognitive
strategies in students. Undoubtedly, cognitive research has contributed
much to the definition of that goal, of the desired strategies. But cognitive research offers examples of much more powerful methods for controlling the cognitive processes that people employ in a task.

For example, carefully timed, sequenced presentations of information
have been used in cognitive experiments to influence the processing
approach that subjects take. Sternberg's (1977) componential analysis is
an example of this approach, as are the many sentence verification experiments by, for example Clark and Chase (1972) or Carpenter and Just
(1975). When subjects are given partial information, such as the sentence, "Star is above plus," they will tend to carry out the processing
possible with that information, such as constructing an image which the
sentence describes. When all information is presented simultaneously,
subjects show much more variation in strategies. Often, researchers
carefully establish and measure mastery of certain elementary aspects of

a task so that the subject is prepared to perform the more demanding aspects, as was done in Trabasso and Riley's (1975) study of inference processes in children. They ensured that children knew elementary relationships before asking them to make transitive inferences based on those relationships. Many of these techniques could probably be adapted into instructional activities, overcoming some of the evident limitations of verbal instructions as specifiers of cognitive processes.

Verbal instructions presume that the student has enough insight into his or her cognitive processes, and enough mastery of the vocabulary that names them, to understand the instructions. And there is the further presumption that the student can convert the instructions into an internal control mechanism. Obviously, these presumptions are often unjustified, especially when one is considering the students most in need of cognitive assistance in their learning. Similar misgivings have motivated the development of experimental techniques that give better control of processing. However, these techniques are part of the art of doing cognitive research, not part of the body of results and formal theory that appears in summary articles. To extract these potential instructional ideas, one must read the original research reports with a special point of view—or be a practiced master of such experimental techniques, who can generate them anew in order to meet the demands of instruction.

II.D. ENHANCING PRODUCTIVE INTERACTIONS

What lessons can we draw from these chapters about the circumstances that generate productive interaction among these fields? The links between cognitive science and neuroscience are already strong, growing, and have a legitimate claim for further investment of research effort. It is obvious that those interested in describing the functions of neural systems have been heavily dependent upon psychology, if sometimes only naive psychology. The content of standard neurological examinations in use today seems to be drawn from the experimental psychology of the 1920s, 1930s and 1940s, with a heavy influence of Gestalt perceptual psychology. The demonstration that the complete removal of the left cerebral hemisphere does not, as had long been thought, completely spare language development demonstrates the importance of taking advantage of the most sophisticated analyses of performance that cognitive science can provide. Clearly, this finding compels a very different interpretation concerning the plasticity of brain function. Similarly, Squire provided us with an outstanding example of the flexible use of the techniques of cognitive research to demonstrate the validity of clinical impressions of long-term memory loss.

In the very exciting area of neuroscience research on vision, the critical dependence of functional neuroscience upon hypotheses provided by perceptual and cognitive psychology or artificial intelligence is equally evident. Hubel and Wiesel (1962, 1977) have shown that cells of the visual cortex appear to respond to lines, edges, and angles. To trace visual processing beyond that level of complexity requires hypotheses about what subsequent cells in the system might be sensitive to. The generation of such hypotheses is the domain of cognitive science theory. The theory is essential because the single-unit recording situation provides a brief period for exploration and possibilities multiply as one moves to more complex levels of visual processing. The findings in neuroscience, of course, have had profound effects on the cognitive science theories of vision (Marr, 1982).

For cognitive theory, neuroscience can function as an important and powerful source of converging evidence. Frequently in cognitive theory, one tries to show that one's descriptive units are correct by showing that various experimental conditions have differential effects at the boundaries of hypothetical units. Neurological cases, systematic lesion studies, et cetera, can provide an excellent additional source of evidence about what parts of a complex performance are functionally independent. Furthermore, this evidence is often provided without the drastic artificiality that often characterizes experimental situations. (The phenomenon of critical developmental periods for the acquisition of certain skills seems to have similar promise, although their neurological basis remains largely presumptive.) Just as linguistic analysis is providing us with a more-detailed characterization of the impairment in various aphasic patients, the various forms of aphasia provide evidence for important distinctions among the corresponding aspects of language function. Sometimes such cases may suggest a novel hypothesis. For example, Picton's discussion (this volume) of one-sided neglect of objects suggests that the left and right sides of objects might be encoded rather more separately than anyone has suggested in perceptual theories of pattern or object recognition and memory.

The fruitful examples of interaction between these fields illustrate the importance of deep, thorough knowledge of both fields. Kean's work (1980) drew upon rather esoteric linguistic theory, not the knowledge that one is likely to acquire in an introductory survey, even at the graduate level. Similarly, Squire drew upon the resources of cognitive research to design novel experiments to test his hypotheses—an achievement that demands a rather high level of mastery of the field. Reflection on Wittrock's chapter suggested that a similarly thoroughgoing use of cognitive research could also enhance the quality of influence of cognitive research of education.

For those who make policy concerning the support of research and the nature of graduate education, these observations present a formidable challenge: What can one do to create conditions in which deep expertise from several fields is brought to bear upon problems? Too often, the pressures toward early research contributions have led graduate departments to abandon requirements for a broad background even in one's own field, let alone neighboring fields. It may not be easy, or even realistic, for one individual to master several fields to the degree required for successful research. But some mutual knowledge of each other's fields is necessary as a foundation for interdisciplinary collaboration.

Alternatively, new fields of specialization, new research problems that are inherently interdisciplinary in character, can be brought to the attention of researchers early in their careers when they may choose to master the necessary range of theory and technique to be able to contribute to research on these problems. There are a number of general research topics that seem to show promise for future fruitful interaction between neuroscience and cognitive science. Examples follow.

II.D.1. CRITICAL PERIODS

Maturational critical periods and shifts of neural control in domains other than language are possible. Gleitman gave us an account of evidence that argues for the importance of biological maturation in shaping language acquisition. Perhaps there are other areas of knowledge that would yield such evidence if the right questions were asked. Mathematics is an obvious possibility. The youthfulness of many of the persons making important contributions to mathematics is a well-known and striking fact. Their absorption in mathematical exploration has many of the features of the *functionslust*—motivation to exercise emerging capacities—that characterizes the developmental appearance of new capacities. And despite the obvious youthfulness of mathematical contributors, Feldman (1980) has not found an example of a truly young mathematical prodigy in his investigations of child prodigies. Mathematical prodigies are adolescents.

The Swiss developmental psychologist, Piaget, proposed that the formal, hypothetical style of reasoning typified by mathematics emerges at adolescence when children enter what he labeled as the stage of formal operational thinking. Research (Neimark, 1975; Pulos & Linn, 1981) has shown that the style of thinking persons use is not uniformly formal or mature across different substantive domains. Nevertheless, there may be a core of truth in the idea. Perhaps one does not find examples of the kind of formal reasoning that characterizes mathematics prior to adolescence.

Another kind of knowledge worth investigating might be complex spatial skill, the appreciation of complex spatial properties of visual materials, such as characterizes the architect, designer, or artist. Susan Carey's program of research (Carey, 1978; Carey & Diamond, 1977; Carey & Diamond, 1980) investigating the development of the perception and learning of human faces provides one example of the pursuit of maturational hypotheses in the visual domain. Performance in face-encoding tasks improves gradually from ages 6 to 10 years, but declines at about age 12 years, increasing again to the highest levels at age 16 and in adulthood. This pattern appears to reflect a change in the basis or strategy of encoding from a reliance on piecemeal features to a reliance on relational features. There is some evidence to suggest that higher levels of performance are associated with right hemispheric processing. Similar late improvements in performance have been found in studies of children's sensitivity to the structure of visual patterns (Chipman & Mendelson, 1979; Chipman, Mendelson, & Waldner, 1977) and in the Seashore Test of Tonal Memory (Carey & Diamond, 1980). However, as Gleitman pointed out, the connection between these maturational phenomena and presumed maturational phenomena at the neural level remains largely speculative.

II.D.2. SPATIAL COGNITION

Studying the neural substrate of spatial skill may offer more promise for making those connections. The mismatch between the cognitive capacities of human beings, especially those capacities that are educationally interesting, and the cognitive capacities of the research animals used in neuroscience is a serious obstacle to obtaining results with direct and clear educational implications. Given the conditions of their natural life, it seems likely that monkeys might equal or excel human beings in at least some visual–spatial abilities. There is a long history of psychometric investigations of human spatial abilities, which have been found to be diverse and differentiated (Lohman, 1979; McGee, 1979). Furthermore, this is an important topic of modern research into cognitive processes (Kosslyn, 1980). Something, at least, is known about the neural localization of these abilities in human beings, and this knowledge could probably be greatly enhanced by a special investigation. Probably our knowledge of the spatial abilities of monkeys is very limited, and the remedying of that ignorance would be a major research program in itself. Nevertheless, this may be the most promising area in which to explore an animal model of the complex cognitive capacities of human beings.

II.D.3. LOCALIZING BRAIN ACTIVITY

Still, the development of truly noninvasive and precise methods for tracking neural activity must be given high priority if we are to understand the neural basis of complex human cognitive capacities. Many of the linguistic and other higher cognitive functions of interest in humans do not have close animal parallels. Consequently, there are presently severe limitations on what we can expect to learn about the neural foundations of such functions. Current methods for tracking neural activity are either gross in the information they yield or risky because of the chemical and radioactive substances that must be injected, or both. As the technology improves, recordings of the magnetic fields produced by electrical activity in the functioning brain may provide valuable information about ongoing functions without such risk. Evidence from brain damage is unsystematic, subject to uncertainty both about the nature of the damage and about the interpretation that should be given to its effects. There are many ways in which damage might disrupt function; it is not necessarily true that the damaged area normally carries out the disrupted function.

II.D.4. PARAMETRIC STUDIES OF LEARNING

Perhaps attention should be given, once again, to general parameters of learning models that might correspond to something like the efficiency of neural transmission or the rapidity of growth of neural connections. This sort of theoretical goal is somewhat out of fashion in cognitive theory, where attention has been turned to the problems presented by the diversity, specificity, and complexity of what is being learned. But it is important in the pharmaceutical applications of neuroscience to learning. We need a good theoretical framework within which to evaluate the claimed effects of drugs on learning: paired associate learning, typically used as the measure of effects in such research, is no longer considered to be a fully adequate representative case of human learning. That is, the aspects of learning that seem most interesting or important in the current development of cognitive theory may not be quite the same aspects that are important to pursue for these other purposes.

II.D.5.   INDIVIDUAL DIFFERENCES IN COGNITIVE
PROCESSES

There has been a tendency for cognitive researchers to regard individual differences in cognitive processes as a nuisance, something to be eliminated by tighter experimental control. Today, an interest in these individual differences is emerging, but it should probably be encouraged more strongly. It is quite possible that the discovery of such individual differences in processing will provide clues to the functional identity of neural processing elements. Just as we understand quite well what neural circuitry underlies human color vision and its defective forms, it is easy to speculate that many other differences in human capacities might have a similar explanation. The unusual talent of perfect pitch might well have an explanation in the presence of special neural circuitry, whereas tone deafness might result from the absence of neural circuitry that we nearly all possess. Similarly, there may be haphazardly distributed elaborations of visual processing capacity. Most of us claim to have something we call visual imagery, which seems to be a special kind of conscious access to visual processing. But there are others—quite commonly found among researchers in verbal learning—who claim not to know what is meant by visual imagery and who do not seem to be making philosophical quibbles. Most of us seem to be able to mentally represent the rotation of objects, and this may depend upon a special neural hardware just as computers are now being provided with specially designed hardware to perform a similar function. The evolutionary path to human beings can be seen as a story of ever-increasing elaboration on capacities built upon basic perceptual systems. It makes sense to assume that recently occurring elaborations, or functionally rather unimportant ones, would be haphazardly distributed, that each individual would possess some of them and not others. The growing evidence (Goldman-Rakic, this volume) that incredibly specific, detailed neural structures form in early life, primarily under genetic guidance, lends credence to the idea that one will be able to find specific neural mechanisms underlying elemental cognitive processes. Scientifically, this is an exciting prospect. Its premature extrapolation into educational implications may be cause for alarm, however.

III.   EDUCATIONAL IMPLICATIONS(?) OF NEUROSCIENCE

Wittrock, who has given considerable attention to the issue (Pirozollo & Wittrock, 1981; Wittrock, 1980), offers the opinion that, strictly speaking, there are no implications of neuroscience for education. He argues that the three areas—neuroscience, cognitive science, and educational research—represent different levels of explanation that cannot be legitimately reduced to one. Instead, he holds out the prospect of a unified but complex multilevel account of educational phenomena. The conviction that neuroscience is somehow deeply significant for education is widely shared. David Hubel (1979, p. 10) has said, "The entire field of education will be affected if the mechanisms underlying learning and memory are discovered." Yet, in the same article, he made it clear that he envisions very complex research questions that must be answered before such mechanisms can be considered to be understood. Understanding the changes in efficiency of synaptic transmission is not enough: "To get at memory in any real sense it will be necessary to know what goes on when human beings perceive, act, think and experience, in order to know what of all of that is recapitulated when they remember or learn." Thus, it is not neuroscience as we know it today that he expects to have strong implications for education but rather some future unification of neuroscientific and cognitive investigations.

Nevertheless, there are many who are trying to draw implications for education from neuroscience today. As Wittrock points out, these implications are not drawn through a tight chain of reasoning, not via a complete theoretical account that covers the full range of neural, cognitive, and educational phenomena. Instead, neuroscience has a general and analogical influence on thinking about educational problems.

What kinds of implications are being drawn? They fall into several classes. One major group, perhaps the most conspicuous, involves the argument that it has been shown that the two halves of the brain carry out different kinds of thinking and, therefore, the curriculum must be organized to exercise both halves of the brain. Such ideas are extremely popular. In addition to several books that appear to be straightforward popular presentations of research about the brain, a single brochure from a bookseller recently offered all of these titles: *Drawing on the Right Side of the Brain; Two Sides of the Brain; Left Brain, Right Brain; Teaching for the Two-Sided Mind; The Brain User's Guide; The Brain: A User's Manual; The Tao Jones Average: A Guide to Whole-Brained Investment.*

A second group of conclusions involves the attempt to understand learning problems in terms suggested by findings about the effects of brain damage: It is suggested that problem students may be missing essential elements of neural apparatus. A third tendency is to conclude that because synaptic transmission is the most conspicuous and best understood phenomenon in the brain and involves chemical neurotransmitters, a pharmacological cure for learning problems can be found. Currently, for example, there is a fad for something known as the "reading pill."

III.A. "BRAIN-BASED" CURRICULA

Hutson (1982) has provided a useful review of the so-called "brain-based" curricula. It is evident that educators are using appeals to brain research in an attempt to justify recommendations that they believe in for other reasons. One sees many statements like the following: "intuitive right hemispheric functions have an intrinsic value of their own, and attempts to subject them to rational left hemispheric analysis—negative or positive—can be stifling," (Samples, 1976, p. 22). Those who would like to see more curricular attention to the arts, to visual thinking, to creative endeavors, attempt to bolster their case with brain research. Sometimes it seems that these advocates are trying to suggest that half of the brain will rot away inside the head if their recommendations are not followed.

In a popular article, Gardner (1978) effectively criticized the oversimplification of research findings that characterizes these arguments. Of course, the more serious point is that decisions about the kinds of thinking fostered in the school curriculum are largely a matter of cultural values. Claims about the consequences of such educational decisions for later performance should receive empirical investigation in their own domain: It matters little whether the associated brain mechanisms are concentrated in one hemisphere or widely distributed. We have always known that cultures make choices about which aspects of human potential will be fostered.

Another of the widely publicized "brain-based" educational approaches involves extreme extrapolations from somewhat questionable findings about the growth of the brain during development. A possible interpretation of developmental data as showing spurts and plateaus in the growth of the brain (Epstein, 1974a, 1974b) has been elaborated into recommendations that new concepts should not be introduced to students in plateau periods—especially ages 12 to 14 (Epstein, 1974b), that junior high school students should spend their time more profitably in community work than in school (Cramer, 1981), that instruction of adolescents should be sex-segregated (Brain growth . . . , 1980). It has been suggested that girls' brain capacity may atrophy by age 14 years (Toepfer, 1980). These suggestions are certainly not well-founded in brain research. It has not been solidly established that there are growth spurts in individual brain size. While Epstein and Toepfer assume that brain growth is associated with capacity to acquire new concepts, there is no evidence for that. (With equal plausibility, one could propose that growth results in a state of readiness for new learning so that "plateaus" would be the ideal time for the introduction of new concepts.) Their primary argument seems to be that the alleged growth spurts occur at about the same ages typically given for transition between Piagetian stages of cognitive growth, but neither physical nor cognitive growth occurs in a uniform relation to chronological age, and the claims are not based on simultaneous measures in the same individuals. The basis for the assertions about sex differences is unclear. Furthermore, the concept of readiness has a checkered history, as Chall and Peterson discuss elsewhere in this volume.

As an educator, Hutson (1982) is rightly concerned that these unfounded recommendations imply greatly reduced time for the introduction of new concepts—especially for female students—and that these recommendations are being taken seriously by some school systems. Gardner (1978) expressed the corresponding concern that the spurious use of research findings can jeopardize the research enterprise. The prestige of neuroscience is being misused in these arguments about educational philosophy.

III.B. DEFECTS OF CEREBRAL ARCHITECTURE

It is quite possible that individual differences in neurological organization do underlie both unusual learning problems and unusual talents. For example, the finding that a "dyslexic" young man had an abnormal cellular structure in the language area of the brain (Galaburda, 1983; Galaburda & Kemper, 1979) has attracted a great deal of attention. However, there is considerable danger in too simplistic an interpretation of that possibility. Despite the fact that the "language area" of that individual appeared to be abnormal, the report does not suggest that he had difficulty in speaking or in comprehension of spoken language. (Sophisticated testing, of course, might have revealed deficiencies that were not obvious.) The apparent individual differences in the allocation of areas of the brain to particular cognitive functions that were discussed in earlier sections of this chapter make interpretation difficult. Obviously, those individual differences imply great obstacles to attempts to use recordings of brain activity for diagnostic purposes.

One example of research that has attempted to do that is the work by John and his associates (1977). In a publication of the National Science Foundation (1976), these views are attributed to John:

> Mass screening, when perfected, ... could cost as little as $10 per test, and should permit the early identification of youngsters with such brain dysfunction

before serious side effects arise. The costs of developing and applying these new
methods are slight, compared with the present costs to society of about $10,000
per year to keep a child in a special training school. (p. 40)

This seems to suggest that the need for expensive special training would
be eliminated by neurological testing. That is certainly not true. Although less confused classification of learning disabled individuals
would certainly be helpful, the central problem is designing effective
training and education for them. Classification does not make the problem go away. Furthermore, it is not clear that EEG recordings can provide a solution to the problem of classification. If we believe, as we all
do, that the brain is carrying out cognitive functions, it follows that the
brain of a person who does not know how to read will be functioning
differently from the brain of a person who does know how to read,
when both attempt to read. That fact does not prove that the brain of the
person who does not know how to read is in any way defective, nor
does it tell us how that brain would function if the person did learn how
to read. (This point, of course, suggests a research study that would
combine educational and neurological methods to determine how the
measured activity of the brain changes when educational efforts succeed
in improving reading performance.)

There is considerable danger that the belief that reading or other
learning problems arise from brain defects will lead to the abandonment
of efforts to teach culturally important skills. (Indeed, this author once
received a telephone call from a despairing official of a major state university who was being pressured to admit and graduate nonreading
students.) Yet, many such individuals eventually do learn to read. Neither the possibility nor the illusion that brain defects cause these learning problems should be allowed to detract from efforts to understand
how these individuals can be more systematically and effectively helped
to acquire culturally important skills. Perhaps the plasticity of the brain
accounts for eventual success or perhaps a somewhat unusual set of
cognitive processes and strategies can be assembled to give effective
performance. Today it appears that both factors account for the effective
speech developed by persons who lose their left cerebral hemisphere in
infancy.

It is the business of educators to design experiences that shape the
plastic capacities of mind and brain to function effectively in society. A
model that suggests, or can be taken to suggest, that the difficulties
educators encounter are due to immutable characteristics of the student
is dangerous. In the absence of much more thorough understanding
than we can claim to have today, it is important for educators to continue to try.

REFERENCES

Atkinson, R. C., & Shiffrin, R. M. (1968). Human memory: A proposed system and its control processes. In K. W. Spence & J. T. Spence (Eds.), *The psychology of learning and motivation, 2*, 89–195.

Bogen, J. (1980). Discussion comments. In D. Caplan (Ed.), *Biological studies of mental processes* (p. 315). Cambridge, Massachusetts: MIT Press.

Bradley, D. C., Garrett, M. F., & Zurif, E. B. (1980). Syntactic deficits in Broca's aphasia. In D. Caplan (Ed.), *Biological studies of mental processes*. Cambridge, Massachusetts: MIT Press.

Brain growth and the curriculum: Why do some students seem turned-off to learning. *The School Administrator* (1980). *37*(8), 26–28.

Brown, J. W. (1980). Brain structure and language production: A dynamic view. In D. Caplan (Ed.), *Biological studies of mental processes*. Cambridge, MA: MIT Press.

Brown, A. L., & Day, J. D. (1983). Macrorules for summarizing texts: The development of expertise. *Journal of Verbal Learning and Verbal Behavior, 22*, 1–14.

Brown, A. L., & Smiley, S. S. (1978). Rating the importance of structural units of prose passages: A problem of metacognitive development. *Child Development, 48*, 1–8.

Caplan, D. (1980). Changing models of the neuropsychology of language. In D. Caplan (Ed.), *Biological studies of mental processes*. Cambridge, MA: MIT Press.

Carey, S. (1978). A case study: Face recognition. In E. Walker (Ed.), *Explorations in the biology of language*. Montgomery, VT: Bradford Books.

Carey, S., & Diamond, R. (1977). From piecemeal to configurational representation of faces. *Science, 195*, 312–314.

Carey, S., & Diamond, R. (1980). Maturational determination of the developmental course of face encoding. In D. Caplan (Ed.), *Biological studies of mental processes*. Cambridge, MA: MIT Press.

Carpenter, P. A., & Just, M. A. (1975). Sentence comprehension: A psycholinguistic processing model of verification. *Psychological Review, 82*, 45–73.

Chipman, S., & Mendelson, M. (1979). Influence of six types of visual structure on complexity judgments in children and adults. *Journal of Experimental Psychology: Human Perception and Performance, 5*, 365–378.

Chipman, S., Mendelson, M., & Waldner, D. (1977). *The development of sensitivity to visual structure*. Paper presented at the meeting of the Society for Research in Child Development, New Orleans, LA.

Chomsky, N. (1965). *Aspects of the theory of syntax*. Cambridge, MA: MIT Press.

Chomsky, N. (1980). Rules and representations. *The Behavioral and Brain Sciences, 3*, 1–15.

Clark, H. H., & Chase, W. G. (1972). On the process of comparing sentences against pictures. *Cognitive Psychology, 3*, 472–517.

Cramer, J. (1981). The latest research on brain growth might spark more learning in your schools. *American School Board Journal, 168*(8), 17–19.

Dennis, M., & Kohn, B. (1975). Comprehension of syntax in infantile hemiplegics after cerebral hemidecortication: Left hemisphere superiority. *Brain and Language, 2*, 472–482.

Dennis, M., & Whitaker, H. A. (1977). Hemispheric equipotentiality and language acquisition. In S. Segalowitz & F. Gruber (Eds.) *Language development and neurological theory*. New York: Academic Press.

Eimas, P., Siqueland, E. R., Jusczyk, P., & Vigorito, J. (1971). Speech perception in infants. *Science, 171*, 303–306.

Epstein, H. T. (1974). Phrenoblysis: Special brain and mind growth periods. I. Human brain and skull development. *Developmental Psychobiology, 7*(3), 207–216.

Epstein, H. T. (1974). Phrenoblysis: Special brain and mind growth periods. II. Human mental development. *Developmental Psychobiology, 7*(3), 217–224.

Feldman, D. H. (1980). *Beyond universals in cognitive development.* Norwood, NJ: Ablex.

Flavell, J. H. (1963). *The developmental psychology of Jean Piaget.* Princeton, NJ: Van Nostrand.

Fodor, J. A. (1983). *The modularity of mind.* Cambridge, MA: MIT Press.

Galaburda, A. M. (1983). Developmental dyslexia: Current anatomical research. *Annals of Dyslexia, 33,* 41–53.

Galaburda, A. M., & Kemper, T. (1979). Cytoarchitectonic abnormalities in developmental dyslexia: A case study. *Annals of Neurology, 6,* 94.

Gardner, H. (1975). *The shattered mind.* New York: Knopf.

Gardner, H. (1978). What we know (and don't know) about the two halves of the brain. *Harvard Magazine, March–April* 24–27.

Gloning, K. (1977). Handedness and aphasia. *Neuropsychologia, 15,* 355–358.

Gold, P. E., & Zornetzer, S. F. (1983). The mneumon and its juices: neuromodulation of memory processes. *Behavioral and Neural Biology, 38,* 151–189.

Hubel, D. H. (1979). The brain. In *Scientific American* (Ed.) *The brain.* San Francisco: Freeman.

Hubel, D. H., & Weisel, T. N. (1962). Receptive fields, binocular interaction and functional architecture in the cat's visual cortex. *Journal of Physiology, 160,* 106–154.

Hubel, D. H., & Wiesel, T. N. (1965). Receptive fields and functional architecture in two nonstriate visual areas (18 & 19) of the cat. *Journal of Neurophysiology, 28,* 229–289.

Hubel, D. H., & Wiesel, T. N. (1977). Functional architecture of monkey visual cortex. *Proceedings of the Royal Society of London, Series B, 198,* 1–59.

Hutson, B. A. (1982). Brain-based curricula: Salvation or snake oil. *Midwestern Educational Researcher, 3*(1), 1–33.

John, E. R., Karmel, B. Z., Corning, W. C., Easton, P., Brown, D., Ahn, H., John, M., Harmony, T., Prichep, L., Toro, A., Gerson, I., Bartlett, F., Thatcher, R. W., Kaye, H., Valdes, P., & Schwartz, E. (1977). Neurometrics, *Science, 196,* 1393–1410.

Kean, M. L. (1980). Grammatical representations and the description of language processing. In D. Caplan (Ed.), *Biological studies of mental processes.* Cambridge, MA: MIT Press.

Kety, S. S. (1979). Disorders of the human brain. In *Scientific American* (Ed.), *The brain.* San Francisco: Freeman.

Kosslyn, S. M. (1980). *Image and mind.* Cambridge, MA: Harvard University Press.

Lenneberg, E. H. (1967). *Biological foundations of language.* New York: Wiley.

Lewin, R. (1980). Is your brain really necessary? *Science, 210,* 1232–1234.

Lohman, D. F. (1979). *Spatial ability: A review and reanalysis of the correlational literature.* (Tech. Rep. No. 8). Palo Alto: Stanford University, Aptitude Research Project, School of Education.

Luria, A. R. (1969). *The mind of a mneumonist.* London: Cape.

Marr, D. (1982). *Vision.* San Francisco: Freeman.

McGee, M. G. (1979). Human spatial abilities: Psychometric studies and environmental, genetic, hormonal and neurological influences. *Psychological Bulletin, 86,* 889–918.

McGlone, J. (1977). Sex differences in the cerebral organization of verbal functions in patients with unilateral brain leisons. *Brain, 100,* 775–793.

Melton, A. W. (1963). Implications of short-term memory for a general theory of memory. *Journal of Verbal Learning and Verbal Behavior, 2,* 1–21.

Milner, B. (1959). The memory defect in bilateral hippocampal leisons. *Psychiatric Research Reports, 11,* 43–58.

Nadel, L., & Zola-Morgan, S. (1984). Toward the understanding of infant memory: Contributions from animal neuropsychology. In M. Moscovitch (Ed.), *Infant memory: Its relation to normal and pathological memory in humans and other animals.* New York: Plenum.

National Science Foundation. (1976). Sorting out some problems. *Mosaic, 7*(2), 37–41.

Neimark, E. D. (1975). Intellectual development during adolescence. In F. D. Horowitz (Ed.), *Review of child development research* (Vol. 4). Chicago: University of Chicago Press.

Pirozollo, F. J., & Wittrock, M. C. (1981). *The neurophysiological and cognitive processes of reading.* New York: Academic Press.

Postman, L. (1964). Short-term memory and incidental learning. In A. W. Melton (Ed.) *Categories of human learning.* New York: Academic Press.

Pribram, K. H. (1971). *Languages of the brain.* New York: Prentice-Hall.

Pulos, S., & Linn, M. C. (1981). Generality of the controlling variables scheme in early adolescence. *Journal of Early Adolescence, 1*(1), 26–37.

Reder, L. (1980). The role of elaborations in the comprehension and retention of prose: A critical review. *Review of Educational Research, 50,* 5–53.

Ross, D. M., & Ross, S. A. (1976). *Hyperactivity: Research, theory, action.* New York: Wiley.

Ryle, G. (1949). *The concept of mind.* London: Hutchinson.

Samples, R. (1976). Evaluation or acceptance. *Media & Methods,* November 20–22.

Sternberg, R. J. (1977). *Intelligence, information processing, and analogical reasoning: The componential analysis of abilities.* Hillsdale, NJ: Erlbaum.

Toepfer, C. F. (1980, March). *Brain growth periodizations in young adolescents: Some educational implications.* Paper presented to the annual meeting of the American Educational Research Association, Boston, MA.

Trabasso, T. R., & Riley, C. A. (1975). The construction and use of representations involving linear order. In R. L. Solso (Ed.), *Information processing and cognition.* Hillsdale, NJ: Erlbaum.

Winograd, T. (1975). Frame representations and the declarative-procedural controversy. In D. Bobrow & A. Collins (Eds.), *Representation and understanding.* New York: Academic Press.

Wittrock, M. C. (1980). Learning and the brain. In M. C. Wittrock (Ed.), *The brain and psychology.* New York: Academic Press.